STUDIES IN ECONOMICS
Edited by Sir Charles Carter

Policy Studies Institute

19

The Political Economy of the Welfare State

STUDIES IN ECONOMICS

1 EXPECTATION ENTERPRISE AND PROFIT
The Theory of the Firm
by G. L. S. Shackle
2 THE ECONOMICS OF SOCIALISM, 4th Edition
Principles Governing the Operation of the Centrally Planned Economies under the New System
by J. Wilczynski
3 THE ECONOMICS OF AGRICULTURE
by Margaret Capstick
4 THE ECONOMICS OF THE DISTRIBUTIVE TRADES
by Patrick McAnally
5 INDUSTRIAL ORGANISATION, 3rd Edition
Competition, Growth and Structural Change
by Kenneth D. George and Caroline Joll
6 MONETARY MANAGEMENT
Principles and Practice
by A. B. Cramp
7 THE ECONOMICS OF RESEARCH AND TECHNOLOGY
by Keith Norris and John Vaizey
8 THE GROWTH OF THE BRITISH ECONOMY 1919–1968
by G. A. Phillips and R. T. Maddock
9 THE ECONOMICS OF EDUCATION
by John Sheehan
10 ECONOMICS AND DEMOGRAPHY
by Ian Bowen
11 SUPPLY IN A MARKET ECONOMY
by Richard Jones
12 RICH AND POOR COUNTRIES, 3rd Edition
by Hans Singer and Javed Ansari
13 REGIONAL ECONOMIC PROBLEMS
Comparative Experiences of Some Market Economies
by A. J. Brown and E. M. Burrows
14 MACROECONOMIC PLANNING
by Roger A. Bowles and David K. Whynes
15 TRANSPORT ECONOMICS
by P. C. Stubbs, W. J. Tyson and M. Q. Dalvi
16 THE DISTRIBUTION OF THE PRODUCT
by John Craven
17 THE ECONOMICS OF INTERNATIONAL INTEGRATION
by Peter Robson
18 INTERNATIONAL INSTITUTIONS IN TRADE AND FINANCE
by A. I. MacBean and P. N. Snowden

The Political Economy of the Welfare State

THOMAS WILSON
and
DOROTHY J. WILSON

London
GEORGE ALLEN & UNWIN
Boston Sydney

**George Allen & Unwin (Publishers) Ltd,
40 Museum Street, London WC1A 1LU, UK**

George Allen & Unwin (Publishers) Ltd,
Park Lane, Hemel Hempstead, Herts HP2 4TE, UK

Allen & Unwin Inc.,
9 Winchester Terrace, Winchester, Mass 01890, USA

George Allen & Unwin Australia Pty Ltd,
8 Napier Street, North Sydney, NSW 2060, Australia

First published in 1982

British Library Cataloguing in Publication Data

Wilson, Thomas
The political economy of the welfare state.–
(Studies in economics; 19)
1. Public welfare 2. Welfare economics
I. Title II. Wilson, Dorothy J.
III. Series
338.4′7′361 HB99.3
ISBN 0–04–336077–7
ISBN 0–04–336078–5 Pbk

Library of Congress Cataloging in Publication Data

Wilson, Thomas, 1916–
The political economy of the welfare state.
(Studies in economics; 19)
Bibliography: p.
Includes index.
1. Welfare economics. 2. Welfare state. I. Wilson, Dorothy. II. Title.
III. Series: Studies in economics (London, England); 19.
HB846.W53 330.15′5 82–4007
ISBN 0–04–336077–7 AACR2
ISBN 0–04–336078–5 (pbk.)

Set in 10 on 11 point Times by Photobooks (Bristol) Limited ,
and printed in Great Britain
by Biddles Ltd, Guildford, Surrey

CONTENTS

FOREWORD

For a quarter of a century after the end of the Second World War economic growth throughout the world was, by historical standards, both rapid and steady. Over these years of rising affluence the range and scale of social benefits, both in cash and in kind, was greatly extended. There was no question of the welfare state's withering away in a climate of prosperity. On the contrary, public expenditure under this general heading was to grow more rapidly than gross national product and to absorb a high proportion of national expenditure.

The welfare state was, however, subjected to increasing criticism from two extreme points of view. At one extreme were those who held that the expenditure incurred so intensified inflationary pressure and that the benefits so undermined self-reliance and self-respect that its scope should be greatly curtailed; at the other extreme were critics who complained that little or nothing had yet been done to achieve even the basic objective of removing the evil of poverty. Although such extreme views may be rejected, there is an undeniable need to look closely and critically at the objectives of the welfare state and to assess the effectiveness of the means used for their achievement. That need, already present, has been sharpened by the severe recession of the late 1970s and early 1980s, and it will remain even after recovery begins, especially if the trend rate of growth of national output is lower than in the past and if high levels of employment are not to be regained for many years. This book, written by an economist and a specialist in social administration, is intended to be a contribution to this task of critical evaluation. Although we have worked closely together in writing this book, there has been some division of labour. Thus Chapters 1, 2, 4 and 5 were written mainly, but not entirely, by T. W. and Chapters 3, 6 and 7 mainly by D. J. W. The last chapter, in which some conclusions are drawn together, was naturally a joint effort.

We are much indebted for comments and suggestions to Sir Charles Carter, Professor C. V. Brown, Professor David Donnison, Professor George Teeling-Smith, Mr F. G. Hay and Mr R. G. Milne. They are not, of course, to be held responsible for any errors of fact or judgement that remain. We must also express a particular debt of gratitude to Miss Christina MacSwan, without whose unflagging and infinitely patient assistance the book could not have been typed and prepared for publication.

University of Glasgow T.W.
December 1981 D.J.W.

The Political Economy of the Welfare State

CHAPTER 1

The Welfare State: Its Meaning and its Development

THE IMPORTANCE OF THE WELFARE STATE

The title of this book – *The Political Economy of the Welfare State* – requires at the outset some explanation and comment. The familiar expression 'welfare state' came into general colloquial use about half a century ago. Although its boundaries have not been firmly and clearly delineated and are drawn rather more widely by some commentators than by others, there is no doubt or disagreement about its central territories. These include, first, the various social security transfer payments: retirement pensions, widows pensions, invalidity pensions, unemployment pay, sickness benefit, child benefits and so on. Secondly, there are the benefits in kind from the health service and the personal social services. The third category is state-financed education. Fourthly, some of the subsidies provided by government are usually included, such as the subsidization of school meals or of the rents of public housing. There are various other subsidies that would not normally be included, such as those given to agriculture or other particular industries, but the boundary becomes hard to discern. Some people would wish to include, for example, subsidies for industrial development in the less prosperous areas; others would not. The subsidization of public transport is another debatable case. The uncertainty increases when we turn to the fifth category: special tax allowances or 'tax-expenditures', as they are now, somewhat misleadingly, called. Such allowances may be substitutes for cash grants, although the effects will not usually be identical. Thus families may be helped by means of child benefits or by means of tax allowances for children. Or, to take another example, it will not do to confine attention to rent subsidies to the neglect of allowances against the mortgages of owner-occupiers. With tax allowances, as with subsidies, there are borderline cases. To quote from two authors who have devoted detailed attention to the subject: 'The choice of the term "tax expenditure" indicates that, because they are not inherent in the structure of the tax, these reliefs are equivalent in terms of revenue foregone to direct government expenditure and should be judged by the same criterion.'[1] What, however, is meant by 'inherent in the structure'? Who determines what is 'inherent'?

It would, however, betray a lack of proportion, to become too closely preoccupied at this stage with borderline problems. Even if attention is confined to what we have described as the central areas, the massive quantitative importance of the welfare state is apparent. That this is so can be seen by directing attention in the first instance to personal incomes before tax and the sources from which these incomes are derived. In all developed countries much the most important source is employment, which usually accounts for 70–75 per cent. Social security transfer payments contribute a substantial proportion, ranging from over a tenth in the USA to almost a fifth in some European countries. For Britain the figure in 1979 was 12·5 per cent. It is of some interest to observe that these benefits represented a larger proportion of personal income than did income from property (which is here taken to include the imputed rental value of owner-occupied houses). For the USA the social transfers were roughly equal to property incomes, a fact which may not be widely known. In some Continental European countries total welfare benefits were quite substantially larger than property incomes. Dividend payments – which in Marxist terminology may be described as 'distributed surplus value' – were only one part of income from property and were very much smaller than social transfers. Indeed, social transfers were about four times the amount of dividend payments in both the UK and the USA in the late 1970s and early 1980s. The distribution of dividends is still rather unequal even after allowing for pension funds, whereas everyone, or virtually everyone, will be able to claim social benefits at one time or another in the course of his life. Nevertheless, these comparisons illustrate the need to exercise care in applying the term 'capitalist'. In particular, the use of such expressions as 'social security in the capitalist economy' can be misleading and had better be avoided.

The figures given above are for cash transfers only. If public expenditure on the health services and on education is added to the transfer payments and the total expressed as a fraction of gross national product, it comes to about a quarter for the UK. For a number of Continental European countries the fraction is substantially larger. For the USA it is about a fifth.

Figures such as these for income and expenditure convey some impression of the importance of the welfare state in modern Western societies – without, it must be said, conveying any suggestion that these proportions are, by some as yet undisclosed measure, either too high or too low. But there should be no further need, for the moment, to labour the point that the purposes of these large programmes and the manner of their implementation warrant close attention from social scientists.

These topics are, of course, of central interest to students of social administration, a subject that, by its very nature, needs to draw upon a number of disciplines, of which economics is one, though obviously not the only one. There may be some justification for suspecting that the contribution of economics has received too little attention from those whose special field is social administration, though there are notable exceptions. It is necessary to add that in so far as this is the case, part of the explanation must be sought in the comparative neglect of the welfare state by economists themselves. Of course, the neglect has been far from complete, and again there have been outstanding exceptions. Nevertheless, it is undeniable that the welfare state has been accorded a somewhat peripheral position in the work of the profession as a whole. Fortunately, the situation has been changing and improving over the past decade or so, with a gradually swelling stream of books and articles in Britain and a much more substantial flow in the USA. Indeed, this is now a growth area in economics. The needed shift of emphasis has begun, and we can expect the balance to be gradually redressed. Even so, a perusal of textbooks and syllabuses would suggest that the welfare state is still widely regarded as a specialised topic within the special field of public finance, too near the edge of the subject to require close attention from most students of economics.

There are, no doubt, various reasons for the limited attention that has been devoted to the welfare state by economists, but it can scarcely be doubted that one reason has been a reluctance to become entangled in the moral issues and the matters of public controversy with which this subject abounds. Do not welfare services involve some redistribution of income? And is it not the case that the problems thus raised entail moral issues of a kind that scientists, in their professional role, should be most careful to avoid? Now, it is indeed important that expressions of opinion on political and moral issues should not be disguised as the firm conclusions of scientific inquiry. It does not follow, however, that the *positive* study of the welfare state need, for this reason, be neglected, and this in itself is an expansive and difficult area of investigation. Moreover, it is not really sensible to assert that *normative* policy recommendations should be resolutely ignored by scientific investigators on the ground that such recommendations embody basic moral value judgements that are not, by their nature, susceptible to scientific treatment. For the value judgements, though present, are almost always to be found in a setting of assertion and assumption about the facts of a particular situation. Let us, at this stage, define a difference of opinion reflecting *different basic value judgements* as one that would emerge if two people who held precisely the same opinions about the facts of some particular situation nevertheless put forward different recommendations as to what should be done. Differences of opinion and conflicting recommendations about policy may, however, reflect not any such difference in basic value judgements, but rather different views about the facts themselves. It is of the utmost importance to determine the extent to which this is so. For a conflict of basic values means that it is 'thy blood or mine'[2] – and that is a position that should not be reached prematurely and perhaps unnecessarily! Admittedly, the facts, including the factual consequences of some recommended policy, are often exceedingly hard to assess, and differences in basic value judgements may then be reflected in different interpretations given to the uncertain facts. To be warned is to some extent to be forearmed. At all events, the welfare state should not be neglected by social scientists simply because moral issues are involved. For if they do not use their specialised knowledge to disentangle the factual propositions from the moral judgements and to pronounce professionally upon the former, it must be asked how this task of elucidation can ever be properly carried out.

Economists who turn their attention to recommendations relating to the welfare state are thus obliged to sort out the basic value judgements and to treat them with proper circumspection. In doing so, they have to study the facts relating to this particular field of social activity, including the political processes by which objectives are determined and the administrative means used for their achievement. It is in order to suggest considerations such as these that we have chosen to use the older term 'political economy' rather than 'economics' in the title of this book.

Let us now attempt to identify the common characteristics of those public services that are usually grouped together as constituting the welfare state. These services can be described as providing *benefits in cash or in kind to identifiable individuals which can not be regarded as payments for current contributions to national output*. This is only a provisional definition, which must now be teased out.

It should be observed that the benefits are said to be received by *particular individuals* and are different in this respect from such *public goods* as the preservation of law and order or from defence against foreign aggressors. A *public good*, as strictly defined, has two characteristics: first, it is impossible to exclude a person from the benefits conferred on the ground that he has not paid specifically for these benefits as one pays for food or clothing on the market; secondly, the receipt of benefits does not entail rivalry between different beneficiaries, for the benefits received by some people are not reduced when others also receive them. National defence is perhaps the most important example. A lighthouse is another: there is no way of excluding ships in the area from seeing the light, and the fact that one ship sees it does not prevent another from doing so. As Dorfman has put it: 'There are certain goods that have the peculiarity that once they are available no one can be precluded from enjoying them.'[3] As these are goods for which a charge cannot be made through the market, they must be financed from the compulsory levies of the tax collector. Obviously, such public goods are intended to contribute to welfare but, as defined in this sense, cannot properly be included as part of the welfare state, for the definition of the welfare state given above makes common usage explicit by referring to benefits accruing to 'identifiable individuals'.

The term 'public goods' may, however, be used more loosely to include goods that are publicly provided to individuals free of charge at the time of use, *as though* these goods were public goods in the narrow sense. Government-financed health services and educational services are familiar examples. These goods can be, and often have been, supplied through the market and sold like any other marketed commodity. In order to distinguish them from public goods, as strictly defined, Musgrave designated them *merit goods*,[4] perhaps a confusing and somewhat emotive label which has now acquired wide currency. Unfortunately, it is not easy to hit upon a satisfactory alternative. *Optional public goods* might convey rather better the meaning that is intended, although this expression has already been adopted for another purpose that does not immediately concern us.[5] We shall have to make do with *quasi-public goods* as a substitute for *merit goods*.

According to our definition, welfare benefits are not provided in return for any *current* contribution to production. This does not mean, of course, that no such contribution has been made in the past or that none will be made in the future. Indeed, it was a basic objective of the national insurance plan put forward in 1942 by the Beveridge Report, *Social Insurance and Allied Services*, that in the course of time people should, where possible, pay at least in part for what they received. But there are periods in the lives of most people when support is required beyond what they are currently receiving from production. Thus in childhood, in frail old age, in sickness and so on, it is not possible to earn by working, and income from property, if any, may be quite insufficient. In all societies provision for such support is made – in primitive tribal societies as well as in developed industrialised societies, in communist economies as well as in capitalist economies.

The source of these benefits varies and need not, of course, be the state itself. In less developed societies assistance is provided by the family, usually one that extends well beyond the nuclear family of parents and children. State welfare services now exist in many less developed countries but only on a restricted scale. Even in developed societies the role of the family is still, of course, crucially important in providing for children, although responsibility for the old has been shifted away from their families to a substantial extent. The part played by charities must also be kept in mind. It is a larger role than may be generally appreciated. Thus in 1975 registered charities in Britain had an income of over 4 per cent of GNP.[6] It is true that part of this income was used for purposes other than the support of individuals, but it would seem reasonable to suppose that about 2 per cent of GNP was expended by charities for purposes similar to those associated in common usage with the welfare state – equivalent to about a sixth of the sum supplied as social security cash benefits. These private sources of assistance are not, therefore, to be neglected. It is, however, to benefits supplied by the state that our definition must, rather obviously, be confined.

The full range of receipts that could be covered by our provisional definition is clearly too wide to correspond to what is understood by the welfare state. Interest on the national debt is the most important of the cash transfers that must now be excluded. Moreover, although certain subsidies and tax allowances can be held to fall within its purview, others must be left out, as we have noted above. Some additional criteria are required to explain these inclusions and exclusions, and to these we must now turn.

One criterion that suggests itself immediately is that the benefits provided by the welfare state are designed to provide protection against poverty. That this is indeed a large part of the answer is undeniable, but it would be an oversimplification to leave it at that. For the welfare state, as it has evolved, goes far beyond what would be required to help those who, by any acceptable standard, would otherwise live in poverty. Many who receive welfare benefits in cash and kind could not possibly be described as people who would be poor in the absence of such benefits. This fact helps to explain why the disbursements under the welfare state are now so large. The reasons for this development can best be understood by tracing the main features of the history of the welfare state, which reveals how a number of different influences have been at work and are now reflected in its modern structure.

THE EVOLUTION OF THE WELFARE STATE

The purpose of the earliest forms of state provision was to afford some protection against complete destitution. The Tudor poor law laid the responsibility for providing such relief on local justices of the peace, who interpreted these responsibilities in various ways and with differing degrees of generosity. It need scarcely be said that even at best this assistance was exceedingly meagre, although it is necessary to recall that the standard of living of the active population was also extremely low by modern standards. The new poor law of 1834 was designed to abolish outdoor relief, and assistance was subsequently to be confined to that provided by the parish workhouses. These grim institutions were regarded with fear, and the shame of being 'on the parish' strengthened the distaste for public charity that was to persist to modern times.

Relief of poverty, although on less demeaning terms, was still the objective when the Liberal Government introduced Britain's first old-age pension scheme in 1908. This pension was financed from general taxation and was given in cash, subject to a means test. The acceptance of direct responsibility by the *central* government was itself an innovation for Britain. Indeed, the centralisation of responsibility was to be extended in Britain and carried much further between the wars and after the Second World War. In most other countries, although the role of *local* means-tested assistance – or social aid, as it is often termed – has been greatly reduced by the vast growth of social insurance schemes, some with means-tested minima built in, assistance from local sources continues to be provided in order to meet a variety of residual needs.

To return to Britain, in the early years of the twentieth century important developments in the private sector had already taken place that were to affect indirectly the subsequent development of the public sector. Thus the eighteenth century had seen the formation of a large number of friendly societies which provided their members with sickness benefits, funeral grants, help for widows and orphans and so on. Their members belonged, however, not to the really poor but to the rather better paid groups of the working population that could afford the contributions. The nineteenth century witnessed a great expansion of these societies and of other forms of mutual aid with the growth of a variety of institutions which helped with the accumulation and investment of small savings. Occupational pensions were also provided, although only on a limited scale and almost exclusively to salaried workers. In a number of industries employers began to pay compensation for injury at work, and the state entered the field in 1897 by making such compensation compulsory.

At a slightly earlier date Germany had embarked upon a somewhat different course, when Bismarck introduced, during the 1880s, a series of government schemes to provide earnings-related insurance against sickness, industrial accidents, old age and invalidity. These were important innovations. The new German official schemes were obviously analogous to the private occupational pensions and to many of the more ambitious friendly society schemes, in that the benefits were not on a uniform flat-rate basis, calculated to maintain a minimum standard, but instead reflected differences in previous earnings. These benefits provided protection against poverty, but the graduation showed that this was not their sole purpose, for these schemes could also be regarded as official ways of arranging for the partial deferment of pay until this could be claimed as a benefit. Graduation was to be a feature of most of the subsequent European schemes. It was also a feature of the US social security legislation of 1935.

In 1911 the British government entered the field of social insurance by establishing a new scheme which provided cover in sickness for the majority of workers and in periods of unemployment for workers in occupations particularly subject to instability. Britain was, in fact, the first country to introduce a national unemployment scheme. In 1925 the social insurance principle was extended to include old-age pensions, widows' pensions and benefits for orphans. These schemes were compulsory and covered all manual workers, but not the better paid salaried employees. Moreover, the benefits were flat-rate. For the emphasis, in Britain, was still on the prevention of poverty rather than the replacement of a proportion of previous earnings, as in the graduated German model. Thus the notion of national insurance was adopted but not the graduation of benefits, which is a natural feature of private insurance when people pay voluntarily at different rates for different scales of benefits. There was the further feature that the state in Britain met part of the cost from general revenue. This contrast in national attitudes persisted until modern times, with Britain, the Scandinavian countries and the Netherlands in one group and Germany, France, Belgium and the USA in the other. This is, of course, only a rough grouping of countries, which requires some reservations and qualifications.[7]

So far attention has been confined to benefits in cash. In 1911 free medical treatment by 'panel' doctors and free medicine were provided to insured persons, although not to their dependants. Nor was hospital treatment provided, even to the insured workers. Such treatment continued to be supplied by the voluntary hospitals, sometimes free of charge, sometimes according to what the patient could pay, increasingly through hospital savings funds which gave free treatment when needed in return for weekly contributions.

An important stage in the development of the British welfare state was the publication in 1942 of the Beveridge Report.[8] Its recommendations were to be largely, though not completely, embodied in the legislation of the late 1940s, which has been the foundation stone of the postwar welfare services. Although much has happened since its publication, some familiarity with the main features of the Beveridge Report is still necessary for an understanding of the welfare state as it has emerged in modern Britain, and also for an understanding of some of the criticism directed against it, in which frequent appeals are made to Beveridge's recommendations. Moreover, this report was to receive attention and to exert some influence on views about policy in other countries as well, although, naturally, its proposals were not followed as closely elsewhere as in Britain.

Beveridge was not the founder of the British welfare state, as appears sometimes to be supposed. He did not have to start building from ground level for, as we have seen, there was already an extensive range of cash benefits in existence when he started work on his report. Indeed, one of his main contributions was to propose ways in which the variety of existing benefits could be rationalised and simplified. This is not, of course, to deny that his proposals for the extension of the range of cash benefits and for a new, free health service were of great importance. What was also important was the explicit way in which Beveridge stated the principles on which his proposed reforms were based. These principles can now be briefly reviewed.

The basic objective was still to afford protection against poverty. For this objective to be made operational, it was necessary to determine where the poverty line should be drawn. That is not something that can be done on a strictly scientific basis; judgement must be exercised and controversy must be anticipated. We shall return to this issue in Chapter 4, and it will suffice for the moment to record that Beveridge presented an estimate of what would be required for subsistence. This was to be the minimum, and for this the state was to accept responsibility. It was a modest enough minimum, but it is important to record that Beveridge never suggested that official benefits should be the sole source of income on which people could be expected to rely. Thus he said: 'The State in organising security should not stifle incentive and responsibility; in establishing a national minimum it should leave room and encouragement for voluntary action by each individual to provide more than the minimum for himself and his family'.[9] In modern times commentators have sometimes fallen into the habit of assuming that state provision is the only possible kind of provision, but Beveridge did not do so. The next point to observe is that, with protection against poverty as the objective, it followed that a uniform benefit should be paid to all families of any given size. Thus there would be no difference, when the scheme was mature, between benefits paid to the elderly, the sick, the unemployed and so on. He firmly rejected the case for officially provided graduated benefits related to previous income, which, as we have observed, were introduced initially in Germany and subsequently adopted in a number of other countries, including the USA, in 1935. Benefits should be flat-rate and would be received, as of right, by insured persons on the basis of the contributions, also flat-rate, that had been made by them or made on their behalf. Means-tested benefits for retired people were to have a continuing and important role to play during the first twenty years of the proposed new scheme, while the right to full pensions was still being earned; but thereafter benefits provided on this basis would be required only in order to deal with a limited number of special cases. Apart from cases of this kind, the payment of benefits would be selective only in the sense that the beneficiaries had to belong to the specified categories – the retired, the unemployed, the sick and so on – but selection would not be made through an assessment of the individual needs of every family. Everyone within these specified categories would be covered. There was to be no question of restricting the cover to sub-categories, as had been the case in the past, when, for example, pensions and unemployment insurance were not available to all members of the population.

Although Beveridge placed so much stress on the case for benefits obtained as of right through social insurance, his scheme was not really an insurance scheme. There were a number of reasons for this. First, some of the causes of loss of income – notably unemployment – were not really actuarial risks, as inter-war experience had already demonstrated clearly enough. Secondly, benefits were not to be related strictly to contributions, for they were to differ according to size of family. Thirdly, potential beneficiaries were to be required to contribute only a third of the cost of the scheme, with another third coming from an earmarked tax on employers, which would have an uncertain final incidence, and a final third from the general revenues of the state. Fourthly, the contributions were not to be paid into an accumulating fund but would be passed on to beneficiaries (the pay-as-you-go method discussed in Chapter 5).

These proposals were designed to provide protection against poverty for the non-employed adult population but would not have helped the working poor. It was working families with children that were most likely to have incomes below the poverty level, and Beveridge recommended that assistance be provided in the form of cash allowances for all children after the first. (The exclusion of the first child was based not so much on grounds of economy as on the desire to encourage larger families and thus to counter the threat of a declining population that was forecast when Beveridge was preparing his Report.)

In estimating the cash income needed to keep families out of poverty, account must obviously be taken of any benefits in kind that may also be provided without a direct charge to the recipients. Health services had already been available between the wars that were free in this sense, but the service was limited and geographically very uneven. Beveridge therefore proposed that there should be a universal, free health service. He was not invited to report on education, but the free educational service, already substantial, was to be extended notably by the legislation of 1944. All these provisions must, of course, be placed in the general context of economic affairs as influenced by other economic policies. Of these others, measures to maintain a high level of employment were, of course, accorded central attention, not only by Beveridge but by all economists. What was proposed and recommended was, therefore, a whole package of interrelated measures which would together bring about a great social advance. Those were days of hope.

Enough has been said to indicate that the welfare state itself was assuming a much larger role than would have been required if the aim had been restricted to the provision of assistance to those whose need for it, if poverty was to be avoided, had been established. For the traditional way of establishing need had been by means tests, and these were widely unpopular, partly as a consequence of the harsh way in which means tests had often been applied between the wars. Beveridge, for his part, was a firm opponent of selectivity by means tests and an advocate of universality in the provision of benefits. The social insurance scheme would cover the whole population and would provide benefits for all, both rich and poor. Family allowances were also to be provided with no test of means, as was access to the exceedingly important health service.

This approach, which was to be followed fairly closely by the legislation introduced just after the war, had the inevitable effect of increasing greatly the scale on which finance was required and expenditure incurred. The scheme which thus emerged could not then be described as essentially one that provided for redistribution in favour of the poor. The principle of universality had transformed its character. This transformation occurred notwithstanding the fact that (as is explained in Chapters 3 and 4) means-tested benefits continued to be used on a much larger scale than Beveridge had envisaged. When account is taken of the postwar extension of free education, with a test of means applied only at the university level and then with an exemption income well above the poverty level, it becomes apparent that the welfare state has turned out to be very much more than a poverty programme. Nor is this all. For a departure was to be made in the 1960s, and pursued further in the 1970s, from Beveridge's principle of flat-rate benefits. What may be described as the Continental principle of graduation was introduced by stages, and thus the welfare state has been extended still further beyond the provision of protection against poverty.

It would be altogether premature to imply at this stage that these developments should be either endorsed or deplored. Our purpose so far has been simply to record. Before any attempt can be made to assess the outcome, a much closer look must be taken at the various arrangements currently in force and at the possible course of their future development and the possible changes that might be made. In attempting to do this, it will be necessary to limit our scope. Free or subsidised education can be deemed to be an important part of the welfare state, but we shall not try to subject that immensely complicated topic to detailed examination. Attention will in the main be confined to the cash benefits that fall under the heading of 'social insurance', to the means-tested benefits, to the other non-contributory cash benefits paid without means tests and to the benefits in kind provided by the health and personal social services. In seeking to review and to assess the various policies proposed. we shall be concerned primarily with the UK, but not exclusively so.

Where appropriate, comparisons will be drawn with the social security and welfare services in the USA and some European countries. Within its limited compass, the review will therefore be comparative. The inclusion of such comparative references should not, however, be interpreted as a futile desire to be geographically comprehensive. The point is rather that policies may assume different forms, and various proposals for change have been made from time to time in Britain and elsewhere. When it is possible to refer to a country that has already had experience of measures corresponding to this recommendation or that, the task of assessment is naturally less abstract and hypothetical.

Chapter 2 is mainly theoretical. It seeks to explain the relevance of economic analysis to the study of the welfare state and goes on to examine the problems presented by interpersonal comparisons of utility and by the need to ensure that basic moral value judgements are not confused with the conclusions that may emerge from empirical scientific analysis. Chapter 3 is devoted to cash transfers for income maintenance. It begins with an account of the modern British welfare state and draws attention to the similarities and differences to be found in some other European countries and in the USA. A number of controversial issues then emerge, and these are taken up in turn in Chapters 4 and 5. Chapters 6 and 7 deal with benefits in kind rather than in cash – first with the health services and the problems there encountered and then with the personal social services. In the final chapter the various issues are drawn together. The evidence concerning the degree of redistribution achieved by the welfare state is examined, and objectives other than redistribution are further discussed. Some arguments for and against the reform of the welfare state are presented in a final summary, and some tentative conclusions are drawn about appropriate courses for further development under economic conditions which may, for a time at least, be less propitious than those experienced over the years between the end of the Second World War and the oil crises of the 1970s.

NOTES

1 J. R. M. Willis and P. J. W. Hardwick, *Tax Expenditure in the United Kingdom* (London: Institute for Fiscal Studies, 1978), p. 1.
2 L. C. Robbins, *The Nature and Significance of Economic Science* (London: Macmillan, 1932).
3 R. Dorfman, 'General equilibrium with public goods', in J. Margolis and H. Guitton (eds), *An Analysis of Public Production and Consumption and their Relations to the Private Sector* (New York: Macmillan, 1969).
4 R. M. Musgrave, *The Theory of Public Finance* (New York: McGraw-Hill, 1959).

5 A. Weisbrod, 'Collective-consumption services of individual-consumption goods', *Quarterly Journal of Economics*, vol. 78 (August 1964), pp. 471–7.
6 M. Austin and J. Posnett, 'The charity sector in England and Wales – characteristics and public accountability', *National Westminster Bank Quarterly*, no. 281 (August 1979).
7 *Public Expenditure on Income Maintenance Programmes* (Paris: OECD, 1976), p. 13.
8 *Social Insurance and Allied Services*, Cmd 6404 (London: HMSO, 1942).
9 ibid., p. 7.

CHAPTER 2

Welfare Economics, Political Economy and the Welfare State

At the beginning of Chapter 1 stress was laid on the importance of the welfare state as a topic for economic investigation and analysis. In directing attention to this topic, it is clearly necessary to identify the nature of the contribution that economics can be expected to make and also to recognise the limitations of any analysis that claims to be scientific. The scope of economics and its limitations are, moreover, of analytical interest and practical importance not only to economists themselves but also to students and practitioners of social administration. For the economic contribution can be, and often is, misconceived. That there are important and relevant empirical issues on which economists have no special competence to pronounce is obvious enough, for these reflect the degree of specialisation in the social sciences. But there are also problems of a different kind that apply to *all* branches of the social sciences, in particular the handling of basic value judgements. The purpose of the present chapter will be to attempt to disentangle some of the difficult issues.

ECONOMIC OR SOCIAL OBJECTIVES?

The first step, at least, is a fairly easy one, but important nevertheless. It is to rebut the view that economics is concerned with only 'economic' objectives and can therefore have at most a restricted relevance to the welfare state because the latter is designed to achieve 'social' objectives. The word 'social' is clearly the cause of much misunderstanding. It must be said at once that economics is a *social* study. Admittedly, some of the important problems of choice in the use of scarce resources can be illustrated by envisaging the position of an isolated individual – the Robinson Crusoe of some of the older texts. But this is only an expositional device. Economics is concerned essentially with human behaviour in society, especially in situations in which the extensive division of functions raises problems of communication and control. So much may indeed be conceded, but a second objection may then be raised. This is that economists are obsessively preoccupied with market mechanisms, and the blinkers they thus assume conceal from their vision a whole range of social objectives. Indeed, the phrase 'economic criteria', as it is often used, would appear to be identified with market criteria, which would presumably lead to the extreme conclusion that any issues not settled by the market must lie outside the scope of economics. In the literature on social administration further confusion may have been caused by the particular use of terms introduced by Richard Titmuss,[1] who distinguished between the 'economic market', where buyers and sellers both hope to gain from exchange, and the 'social market', where people give unilaterally without receiving any reward in exchange. It need scarcely be said that the distinction between these two types of transaction is important; but it must also be heavily stressed that the market itself is a *social* mechanism, and a very important one, that has, unfortunately, often been misunderstood and underrated. It is particularly important when the 'economic market' is viewed, as it was by Titmuss, in a strongly unfavourable moral light, as this is to confuse different functions that have to be performed in society. It is inconceivable that the enormously complex network of economic activity could be organised on the basis of unilateral exchanges. It is true that the voluntary charity sector is quantitatively more important than is often recognised but it could not possibly provide a full substitute for what he describes as the 'economic market'. In any case, there is no reason why people who are able to produce should not offer this output in exchange for what others have produced. Self-respect is a virtue as well as charity, and it is interesting to observe the difference of emphasis in this context between Beveridge and Titmuss.

The *only* alternative to the so-called economic market is the official planning of production and the allocation of output, apart from public goods, by means of rations and controls. In some circumstances (as in a war economy) much use must be made of this alternative, and in all circumstances some measure of official intervention is necessary, to a limited extent in this form and to a greater extent in the form of measures designed to complement and to modify the working of the market without replacing it. But it is seriously misleading to use the term 'social market' and 'economic market', as Titmuss has done.

There is another and more common error. That is to say that if some particular project cannot be financed by payments received through the market, it is 'non-economic'. For this statement is valid only if there are no other considerations that can, with propriety, be taken into account. It has, however, long been recognised in economic literature that there may well be additional considerations which the market cannot take into account and which may warrant the payment of a subsidy that will make a project economic in the sense that costs *can* then be covered. There may also be cases in which a project that does pay its way on the market involves costs not reflected in the books of the producers that should be taken into account; in these cases the operation of the market needs to be modified. The standard example is the cost of industrial pollution, clearly recognised and properly stressed in Pigou's *Economics of Welfare*.[2] The possibility of there being *external* economies or diseconomies – *external* in the sense that persons engaged in market transactions may not automatically take them into account – is one of the central topics of welfare economics. It is still necessary, however, to ensure that an alleged externality is a genuine one and not just a disguise for a sectional interest, and it is also necessary to determine both the nature and the scale of the correction required. Then there are the *public goods* mentioned in Chapter 1, which are of such a kind that the beneficiaries cannot be individually identified and excluded from the benefit thus conferred if they have not made a payment. As was also observed in that chapter, a number of other goods – the so-called *merit goods*, or *quasi-public goods*, as we have termed them – may also be supplied by the public authorities as though they were private goods, notwithstanding the fact that these goods can be, and in the past usually have been, supplied through the market. In all these cases of public goods and merit goods choices are made by the public authorities, and the preferences thus reflected in supply may or may not correspond fairly closely with those held by the electorate. The problems associated with public choice will be discussed in the last section of this chapter. Meanwhile, it is in place to observe that in the more highly planned communist countries the state controls the production of the great bulk of the goods for private use, as well as that of goods for public use, but these goods are in the main distributed through markets in exchange for money, not doled out as rations in exchange for coupons or other permits.

The extent to which control is exerted by the state or by the market is a matter of great importance. In all cases, however, a basic economic problem is that of making the best use of resources given the preference pattern that is to be followed, however that pattern is determined. For it is always obviously desirable to relate the satisfaction of preferences to the costs entailed in doing so, where by 'costs' is meant sacrificed alternatives – say, more or less geriatric care in place of less or more heart surgery. This last example has been chosen because it illustrates the fact that economic decisions are required in all branches of activity, not merely in the factory or on the Stock Exchange. In particular, it may be worth emphasising that students and practioners of social administration are constantly asserting or rebutting what are essentially *economic* propositions, although many of them would be inclined to reject, perhaps with distaste, any suggestion that they had the slightest interest in economics!

One of the basic contributions of economics theory is to provide protection against falling into the trap of supposing that because some commodity or service is important, an unassailable claim can be made for the use of more resources in its production. Thus from time to time it is said that the health services must be accorded 'first priority' because these services save lives and reduce suffering. But it is also held from time to time that education must have 'first priority' because the future development of the nation depends upon having an educated population. Such reasoning can, of course, be extended indefinitely. Food could also be said to deserve 'first priority' because, without food, we should die; agriculture is therefore the most 'basic' of all industries. And so on. The fallacy in such reasoning is to think in terms of the total utility derived from using resources in some particular way and thus to argue in terms of all or nothing. The real choices to be made are, of course, of a different kind. These are the choices between a bit more or a bit less, and it is a prudent rule to avoid altogether that insidious and misleading expression 'first priority'.

Economics is concerned with the allocation of scarce resources, capable of being used in different ways in the service of different competing objectives. When this is understood, it becomes clear that economics is not confined to a compartment of life but is rather an aspect of all human activity. It is wrong to suppose that economics relates only to 'material welfare' – whatever that may mean.[3] There is an economic aspect to the affairs of churches and orchestras and art galleries as well as to the affairs of manufacturing industry. When those responsible for what is broadly described as social administration make decisions about health services, or education, or urban renewal, they are necessarily involved in economic issues – a rather obvious point, but one that may have been obscured by specialisation within the social sciences.

That this point is indeed obscured is shown clearly enough by the way in which 'economic objectives' are often contrasted with 'social objectives' by some politicians and journalists, who appear to imply that economic objectives relate solely to such matters as a high and rising level of output. There is, however, only one strict sense in which the term 'economic objective' may be used: this is to mean that resources should be employed as effectively as possible in the satisfaction of competing wants, whatever these wants may be and however determined. In short, the economic objective is simply to economise – not in the sense of cheese-paring but in the sense of avoiding the waste and misuse of resources. Economic science does not provide a guide or a set of criteria for choosing between different wants. The use of the word 'wants' rather than 'needs' is, in itself, deliberate and significant, for it means that no claim is being made to some right to select between wants. Cigarette smoking is a contemporary example. Many people have a 'want' for cigarettes, which they can satisfy through the market. An economist may well feel that this is a want that people should not have; he may therefore support a campaign against the use of the advertising media to strengthen and extend this want. In doing so, however, he is behaving as any private citizen may properly behave; his support for the campaign is not based on his economic analysis, which does not purport to assess different wants or to place them in some ordered scale.

Although it is assumed that people try to satisfy their wants, it is not assumed that the satisfaction of wants can be identified with the pursuit of happiness. Modern welfare theory does not rest on any assumption that the basic objective of activity is the maximisation of happiness or that some felicific calculation can be employed in order to determine the desirability of particular courses of action.

It may appear at first sight that this approach to economics, however proper, is severely stultifying. In reality, the scope for economic inquiry remains very wide indeed, for it is still necessary to investigate how wants are determined, how they are expressed and how satisfactorily production responds in order to meet them. A very large part of the subject matter of economics is indeed concerned with the manner in which such issues are resolved when the market is the social mechanism that is being used. When, however, the wants are determined and expressed by the political authorities, economists are drawn into a study of the working of the political machine. With the vast increase in public expenditure from about a tenth of GNP at the beginning of the century to over two-fifths in the 1980s, they have naturally devoted increasing attention to this field. Within this field lie the various services that are taken to comprise the welfare state.

So much must be accepted, but it is still necessary to consider the nature of the contribution that economic science can be expected to make. Even if, on the positive side, economic inquiry proves to be valuable and enlightening the range of legitimate, *normative* propositions is a different matter. The still dominant modern school of welfare economics, which bears the title 'Paretian', has laid much stress on the difficulties involved in making *scientific* recommendations about income distribution which involve interpersonal comparisons of utility that cannot readily be subjected to any objective test and which require value judgements. How, then, could welfare economics make any significant contribution to the assessment of the functions performed by the welfare state in so far as these involve, and are meant to involve, some redistribution of income?

There is another reason for scepticism about the usefulness of economic science, although it turns out to be less fundamental. If one may judge from what some economists have said, economic analysis appears to rest on a particular assumption about moral psychology: the assumption that human behaviour is relentlessly egoistical. Everyone is assumed to be seeking in a rational and determined way to maximise his satisfaction. Admittedly, this postulated aim is not so crudely over-simplified as to mean nothing more than the maximisation of wages or salaries or profits. Account will naturally be taken of differences in the conditions of work, differences in its arduousness and differences in security of income; full weight will be given to the enjoyment of leisure, freedom from stress and so on. The assumption that satisfaction is being maximised does not, in short, entail any assumption about participating in the rat race. What it does entail – or seems at first sight to entail – is the pursuit of selfish objectives. If this is so, how can such an analysis be of much help in understanding and assessing the welfare state, the objectives of which would appear to be less individualistic and less selfish?

It is scarcely surprising if students of social administration are sometimes inclined to the view that economics is the 'science of egoism' and that economists can therefore have little to contribute to the understanding of the welfare state. Thus a barrier would appear to be erected between these two branches of social inquiry. But this is not all. For it is not merely that doubt is cast on the relevance of economics. What also follows is that the market is viewed with suspicion and distaste and, as a consequence, the recommendations made about the welfare state may be biased against the use of the market mechanism. There is a confusion here that results from identifying, on the one hand, the individualism expressed in the exchange of goods and services on the market with egoism and, on the other hand, collective activities with altruism. To quote Pinker: 'Outside the confines of academic and political debate one rarely encounters a confrontation between egoism and altruism, in their uncompromising forms. In any case we shall discover more by looking at the various forms of qualified egoism or altruism which set the tenor of everyday welfare services.'[4]

ALTRUISM, EGOISM AND DISTRIBUTION

The first step in considering this last point is to inquire whether it is really the case that altruism is the foundation of the welfare state. It is true that transfers are made through the various welfare services, but this is also true of private insurance. Most people insure their houses against fire, but only a small number make calls on the insurance industry and, when they do, they get back far more than they contributed, at the expense, apparently, of those whose houses have not been burned down. But insurance is simply a scheme for mutal coverage against risks, and the transfers made do not imply an assumption about altruism. As was observed in Chapter 1, a large part of the official arrangements for cash transfers has been described as social insurance. This description is, of course, inaccurate from an actuarial point of view, but the fact remains that many people would voluntarily wish to belong to such schemes in view of the protection thus provided. In short, the welfare state could be simply a government-designed device for the more efficient pursuit of selfish objectives. For this to be so, however, membership would have to be *voluntary*. Anyone who preferred to do so should be allowed to opt out, with no obligation to contribute to its cost and no claim to receive its benefits. If, as a consequence, he found himself hungry and destitute, this would be of no concern to other egoists, or would be so only to the extent that they might be afraid of being harmed should the destitute become violent.

The fact that membership of the welfare state is compulsory, offering only limited scope to opt out of certain benefits, could be explained by arguing that those who expect to be net beneficiaries want to extract contributions from other citizens (presumably the better-off citizens) who might choose to opt out if they were allowed to do so. Thus the power of the ballot box is being used in order to achieve some redistribution of income through the welfare state, or that at least may be the intention. Selfishness is, in fact, one of the basic assumptions of much of the best-known work on the theory of public choice. As Mueller has put it: 'The basic behavioural postulate of public choice (theory) is that man is an egoistic, rational, utility maximiser.'[5] The welfare state should then be regarded as a particular area of activity in which this broad objective is pursued through political means, with voters exerting their influence to this end, with politicians seeking to win their votes and with officials eagerly building the bureaucratic empires required to implement such policies and thus to advance their own careers. It is indeed a strong and entirely reasonable presumption that the welfare state would not have emerged on anything like the same scale if the franchise had not been made universal but had been restricted to a prosperous minority of citizens.

There can be no doubt that this explanation contains a large element of truth. The welfare state does rest in part on a foundation of egoism. What is open to question is whether this is the whole truth. Common observation would suggest that people normally act from mixed motives, both selfish and altruistic. Indeed, it would be rather inconsistent to avoid, in the most punctilious manner, any interpersonal comparisons of utility on the ground that such comparisons cannot be tested or any basic value judgements which are by their nature untestable, and then to come down in favour of one particular and controversial theory about human motivation. It is, of course, entirely proper to adopt as a hypothesis the view that all action is self-seeking and then to examine the consequences. It emerges that there may be a great deal of mutual benefit – as Adam Smith showed in the *Wealth of Nations*. Public policy should therefore be based in part upon the acceptance of this fact and should be so designed as to ensure, as far as possible, that self-interest is pursued along lines that are likely to have this beneficial outcome. This old truth is clearly recognised in a recent monograph by Schultze with the title *The Public Use of Private Interest*.[6] It is a different matter to assert as a fact that philanthropy is only a pleasing myth. Economists who do so have moved well outside their proper sphere.

The point is of importance in understanding the welfare state. In developed societies there appears to be a consensus in support of the view that no one must be allowed to starve or to die from exposure, and that no one who is desperately ill must be denied medical attention if this cannot be paid for. Assistance must be provided even in those cases in which desperate need is the consequence of laziness or improvidence; but an organised system with compulsory contributions makes it more difficult for anyone to get a free ride. If people were quite indifferent to misery and disaster, except in so far as it touched them personally, the improvident and the unlucky might simply be allowed to sink when they could not swim.

The fact remains that a large part of economic analysis seems to ignore this sense of community obligation and to accord little attention to caring. As Vickrey has put it: 'In the more extreme form of this approach, the world is represented as a model in which each person is apparently assumed to exist in a cell connected with the rest of the world only through the exchange of goods and services.'[7] With this basic approach there would seem to be little chance of understanding either voluntary altruism on the part of private people or the sense of social obligation that has undeniably been *one* of the driving forces behind the establishment and extension of the welfare state – although there have been other forces at work as well.

The explanation is to be found in a great muddle. When people are exchanging goods and services they can be expected to behave in a way that appears to be egoistical but need not be so. The housewife buying vegetables at the greengrocer's naturally wants good fresh vegetables and naturally looks at the price. It would be absurd to suggest that if she is a philanthropic person, she will be ready to accept a bad bargain because her loss is the shopkeeper's gain. The same reasoning applies to a person who is considering accepting a particular job: he is not required by altruism to be content with a wage below one that he could get elsewhere simply in order to benefit his employer. In these transactions people do not – exceptional circumstances apart – feel under any moral obligation to make sacrifices in order to benefit the person with whom they are trading. Nor is it, in general, desirable that they should do so. For such misplaced philanthropy would simply result in preferences being imperfectly transmitted and in resources being inefficiently used in the meeting of wants. The point can be made by saying that people have, and should only try to pursue, the limited objectives that are their particular responsibility. This is true of planned economies as well as of market economies. Thus the manager of a state factory is not required by the socialist ethic to be indifferent if he receives less than his allocation of some raw material because some other manager will have been fortunate enough to get more. On the contrary, he must protest. He has his own plan to fulfil, and this is the objective he must pursue. Each person has his job to do, and only confusion will result if he tries to take all kinds of other considerations into account. Misconceived 'philanthropy' would lead to the inefficient implementation of the plan or, in a market economy, would reduce the market to impotence. It is in this sense that people can be assumed to live 'in isolated cells'.

But this does not imply that everyone is an egoistic utility maximiser. In seeking to be paid for what his labour is worth, a man may be thinking of the welfare of his family or of what he is going to give to charity – or any number of other things. He need not be concerned with his own welfare alone; he may have other beneficiaries in mind. What he is not required to do, and should not do, is to allow himself to lose out simply in order to benefit the person with whom he is trading. It is *that* person's gain he should *not* consider. This is what Philip Wickstead called 'non-tuism':[8] it is not *you* whom I must consider, where you are the person from whom I am buying or to whom I am selling. But ultimate objectives are likely to be mixed. Objectives of a more philanthropic kind may then find expression in maintaining a family, in giving to a charity or in lending political support to the welfare state even if one does not expect to be a net beneficiary. Thus the false identification of 'non-tuism' with egoism helps to explain the hypothesis that economic analysis rests on the assumption of universal selfishness – an assumption about human nature which many would regard as false and one which it would, in any case, be *ultra vires* for economists to make.

It is true that some qualifications must be made. In pursuing one's own objectives without feeling any particular obligation for the welfare of the person with whom one is trading, it would be generally agreed that one must not cheat. More generally, common sense suggests that 'non-tuism' needs to be softened a little at the edges in order to avoid excessive impersonal harshness when the trading partner is in a position of great difficulty. There is a another point of obvious relevance to the study of the welfare state which is illustrated by the relationship between doctor and patient. The patient may feel that he wants medical attention, but he is unable to express this want in the same way that he can express his desire for a nice dinner, or a new car, or a record player. It is true that many of his other wants will be influenced, and sometimes even created, by the promotional activity of the suppliers; but the situation is even then obviously different in degree from the ignorance with which he confronts his doctor. The latter is the supplier and also, to a large extent, the person who assesses the nature of the want. The impersonal approach of 'non-tuism' cannot really be adopted in this case.

There is a further very important complication. It is one thing to say that individuals on the market ought quite properly to restrict the objectives that they are seeking to pursue; it is a different matter when people are organised in clubs, corporations or government departments. It is still true that the pursuit of limited objectives is necessary and certainly true that this is what will happen, but the consequences may clearly be harmful when large groups relentlessly pursue their respective interests. The labour market is a familiar example. Trade union leaders may be highly responsible people, fully aware of the evils of inflation and of the further evils, in the form of lost output and unemployment, that will follow if inflationary wage demands can be contained only by the restriction of national expenditure. Yet it may be hard for any one union to moderate its demands if others are not doing so. A rather similar situation arises when government departments are competing with one another for limited financial resources. Every department will press its own case as strongly as it can without feeling obliged to be more modest in its demands for the sake of the wider national interest – which is not a departmental responsibility. Of course, it is useless to say that the wider objectives should always be given more weight by every department than its own particular objectives. For all departments have their own special obligations, and it is their prime responsibility to meet these obligations. What is so difficult, then, is for the Cabinet (or whatever the top-level authority may be) to impose a rational allocation of resources, notwithstanding its limited knowledge of many relevant facts, that will be reasonably satisfactory from the national point of view. One suspects that the pursuit of group loyalty – whether in a market where there are large firms and large unions or within the government machine itself – may do as much harm as the pursuit of personal selfishness by separate individuals.

INTERPERSONAL COMPARISONS AND VALUE JUDGEMENTS

It has been necessary to clear the ground in this way by removing some misapprehensions about welfare economics. But nothing that has been said so far provides an adequate scientific basis for recommendations about compulsory measures designed to change the distribution of income or to modify the timing of personal expenditure from any given life-time income.

At an earlier stage in the history of economic thought economists such as Edgeworth and Pigou were prepared to make recommendations about redistribution that did involve interpersonal comparisons of utility and moral value judgements. The reasoning then ran roughly as follows. The utility a person gets from a commodity declines as he gets more of it; from this it was assumed that the utility of his total income declines as his income rises. An interpersonal comparison was then brought into play, for it was inferred that a pound would be worth more to a poor man than to a rich one. Income should therefore be transferred from the rich to the poor, given that the aim is to maximise total utility. These transfers should not, however, be carried to the point of achieving complete equality. Some inequality is needed to provide incentives to work and to save, so that if redistribution were carried too far, all would be worse off. It was – and is – an extremely difficult empirical task to assess how production would be affected by any given reduction in inequality, but, subject to this important reservation, redistribution was deemed socially desirable. In other words, the onus of proof was placed on the defenders of inequality.

Subsequently, this approach was abandoned. The objective of maximising total utility not only implied a value judgement which could be questioned but also was so poorly defined and vague that it was open to devastating criticism. Moreover, it came to be generally accepted that interpersonal comparisons of utility should be avoided. It is true that such comparisons are constantly made in everyday life, but different people reach different answers and there is no way of applying a scientific check. Admittedly, there would be general acceptance of the proposition that a small transfer from a millionaire to a starving man would enhance the utility of the latter more than it would reduce the utility of the former. But such extreme cases are too simple. The quantitatively important transfers are not between the very rich and the very poor, and views will differ about their effect. Thus welfare economics, in its Paretian guise, has avoided comparisons of this kind and has shied away from questions of distribution. Welfare analysis provides useful guidance about how resources could best be used to satisfy wants *with any given distribution of income* but cannot prescribe a social optimum, because there is an indefinite number of distributional patterns between which economists could not choose without straying beyond their professional limits. Welfare could be said to have increased between situation 1 and 2 only if at least one person is better off in situation 2 and no one is worse off – only, in short, if there is at least one gainer and no losers.

The expression 'interdependent utility functions' is a polysyllabic way of making what is, after all, a familiar point about human behaviour. In the eighteenth century the word 'sympathy' was used to mean putting one's self in another person's shoes. Both David Hume and Adam Smith had a good deal to say about 'sympathy'. The capacity to share in the joys and sorrows of others was a clearly observable feature of human nature. 'Sympathy', in this sense, could inspire compassion and lead to charitable behaviour. Adam Smith, commonly regarded as the apostle of self-interest, had the highest praise for unselfishness. Thus he said:

> to feel much for others, and little for ourselves . . . to restrain our selfish, and to indulge our benevolent affections, constitutes the perfection of human nature: and can alone produce among mankind that harmony of sentiments and passions in which consists their whole grace and propriety.[9]

That was a normative statement. His empirical observation, which led him to recognise that people often behaved in this way, also led him to recognise that people were often selfish. Moreover, the range of sympathy was limited, and compassion was likely to be restricted, with its force declining as the range was extended beyond those for whom a potential donor felt direct personal responsibility. His empirical observation then led him further, and, as was observed above, one of his most important contributions was his demonstration that even the pursuit of self-interest often brought benefit to others, even if the conferring of the benefit was not conscious and deliberate. It was this last observation that received so much prominence in *The Wealth of Nations*, and it is this that was to be further illuminated and significantly modified by Wickstead's theory of 'non-tuism'.

Whether one uses the term 'sympathy' or whether one prefers to talk of 'interpersonal utility functions', a somewhat critical eye must be turned on what was described above as a fundamental proposition of modern welfare economics: welfare has increased if at least one person is better and no one is worse off. If being better off or worse off depends solely upon every person's own supply of goods and services, then this proposition is open to challenge. A gets more, while B and C get no less; but it is not to be inferred that welfare has increased unless every person is indifferent to what others receive. When it is recognised that people are not indifferent, it follows that the unchanged incomes of B and C may seem to them to have been depreciated in terms of the utility afforded if, when A gets more, this leaves them with a feeling of unfair deprivation. A, for his part, may feel a little guilty about his relative good fortune. If, then, the validity of this basic welfare proposition is to be restored, the terms 'better off' and 'worse off' must be given so broad an interpretation as to embrace any feelings of deprivation on the one side and guilt on the other that may be engendered by the change that has taken place.

It was the sense of guilt – the so-called 'middle-class conscience' – that Hochman and Rogers were concerned with when, in a well-known article,[10] they investigated the manner in which the interdependence of utility functions could establish an acceptable basis in welfare theory for the compulsory net transfer payments of the modern state. ('Net' means the difference between contributions and receipts and may be negative.) Their analysis may be briefly summarised.

Economic efficiency is concerned with the satisfaction of wants, but the wants to be met must be so interpreted as to recognise the fact that many people are concerned not only with their own wants but also with what they regard as the wants of other people who are worse off than themselves. If no transfers to the less fortunate are made, then not only will those with lower incomes be left unaided but also those with higher incomes will also feel themselves to be worse off. With utility functions thus interdependent, transfers are required if resources are to be used *efficiently*. This is the gist of the argument, and it would not be surprising if those who are unfamiliar with economic theory were to feel that a very simple point were being expressed in a cumbersome and pedantic way. It is important, however, for non-economists, including students of social administration, to recognise that the making of interpersonal comparisons of utility undeniably presents a real difficulty. It is not that such comparisons are impossible but rather that it is impossible to arbitrate between conflicting comparisons made by different people. In the Hochman–Rogers analysis, as presented so far, every potential net contributor is making his or her *own* assessment. An external measuring rod is not, apparently, required. No one's preferences are being overridden, at least not among the relatively better-off group. On the contrary, the net transfers that take place reflect those preferences. So far so good. Their theory provides a formal basis for voluntary giving. Compulsory transfers made by fiscal authority are, however, a different matter. For such transfers imply the adoption of a generally applied, uniform scheme, which cannot be expected to correspond to the transfers that would be preferred by all those now compelled to surrender part of their incomes, as there is bound to be a diversity of preferences about transfers. Nevertheless, a compulsory scheme, even if it overrides these preferences, may be voluntarily accepted in order to prevent some people from behaving as free-riders. For some may indeed want to see chronic invalids properly cared for but may be quite content to allow others to provide the caring. A compulsory scheme will prevent this from happening. It should be observed, however, that in justifying compulsion on the ground that it is needed to prevent free-riding, an additional consideration is introduced. This is a regard for 'fairness' which lies behind the desire to prevent free-riding, and, as we shall see, there are far-reaching implications when this consideration is taken into account.

Two lines of inquiry may then be followed. First, it may be asked whether total satisfaction is likely to be increased – the utilitarian approach. It must, however, be recognised at once that no answer can be given without making interpersonal comparisons of utility which must be controversial. Thus we are faced with the difficulties already mentioned. Various simulations can then be attempted that attach assumed weights to the utility of different persons, and these exercises may illustrate the choices that have to be made without, however, providing a firm answer. Maximising the social welfare function is, to say the least, a highly speculative exercise, and this approach also embodies the value judgement that the maximisation of satisfaction should be accepted as the social objective.

The second approach is to ask questions about justice. What would be a fair distribution whether or not satisfaction is deemed to be maximised? Let us now turn to this second approach.

A JUST DISTRIBUTION?

If public policy with regard to income distribution is really to reflect interpersonal utility functions, as prescribed by Hochman and Rogers, then only those who are to be net contributors to the welfare of others should be allowed to vote on this particular issue. Not only is it difficult to see how this could be done in practice, but it may also be objected, on grounds of principle, that the redistribution thus accomplished might well differ from 'what justice would demand' because it will simply reflect the sensitivity of the donors to the needs of others and the weighting that they give to their assessment of these needs. Moreover, to quote Wicksell: 'Justice from above to below always smacks of condescension or contempt.' He adds: 'Justice from below to above has only too often been synonymous with revenge.'[11] There is the further important point that the final distribution will reflect the initial distribution before these transfers were made. That distribution may be thought by some people to be markedly unjust, but the modifications made will be determined only by the views of those who happened to be in a favourable position in the initial stages. Students of public finance will recognise the Hochman-Rogers thesis as an application of the 'benefit' approach to taxation. Wicksell himself laid much stress on the desirability of relating benefit to sacrifice and thus on the impropriety of imposing taxes which have not unanimous, or close to unanimous, support. But in doing so he made quite explicit the crucial assumption that the initial distribution was deemed to be just. If this assumption does not hold, a different approach is needed.

What, then, is meant by a 'just distribution'? In the nature of the case, this question cannot be answered by economic science, including economic welfare theory, which is held to have strictly scientific foundations. Hence the avoidance in this modern welfare theory of recommendations about distribution. Moreover, the preference for the term 'political economy' in the title of this book must not for a moment be taken to imply that political economy can somehow resolve the difficulties of welfare economics and provide clear-cut answers, untroubled by such matters as the differences that will emerge in the making of interpersonal comparisons or by conflicts between basic value judgements. A change of title in itself works no magic. The term 'political economy' has been used, rather, to imply an extension of interest, where appropriate, to other fields and in the present context the relevant field is social ethics. It is noteworthy that economists have shown an increasing readiness in recent years to extend their interests thus. Admittedly, this statement may be misinterpreted to mean that political economy must be practised by polymaths who can cope satisfactorily with a range of other subjects in addition to economic science. The point is, rather, that some of the main propositions of moral philosophers can be taken up and their implications explored from an economist's point of view. There is an analogy here with sensitivity analysis in forecasting. In the latter case different assumptions about this variable or that can be used in turn, and the effects that follow from thus changing the assumptions can be assessed. In a similar fashion, different assumptions about social ethics can be made and the implications explored of what could be termed, perhaps a little fancifully, ethical sensitivity analysis. It would be particularly helpful, then, if it were possible to discover some propositions about justice that commanded a consensus. Even a near-consensus would be helpful, although it would then be wrong to exclude consideration of other views, for this would, of course, stifle intellectual exploration.

If anything is to be said about a just distribution, this must obviously be done from a position of impartiality. On this point at least there can be a full consensus. Various myths and metaphors have been used to illustrate what is required for this purpose. Thus Rawls[12] assumes that everyone steps behind a 'veil of ignorance' which conceals his or her own future position in the income scale and then, with objectivity thus ensured, enters into a social contract that will establish a just society. Ackerman[13] proceeds by way of imaginary conversations between those concerned – conversations that are constrained by a proper regard for neutrality and rationality. Some of the moral philosophers of the eighteenth century, notably Hume and Smith, employed the image of an

Impartial Spectator to whom appeals could be addressed. This Impartial Spectator was, in fact, a metaphor for conscience, and appeals were therefore being made *continually*, a point that can be obscured by the suggestion of a once-for-all act in theories of a social contract.

Given the assumption of impartiality, what conclusions are likely to be reached about a just ordering of society? Is it reasonable to suppose that at this second stage the conclusions drawn will be unanimously endorsed or, at the very least, will rest on the support of an almost complete consensus? Rawls believed that something close to unanimity would emerge. Everyone would be ignorant about the position in which he would in fact find himself but would be sharply conscious of the danger of his being, in the event, one of the worst off. Although prepared to step behind the 'veil of ignorance', every person, having done so, would relentlessly pursue his own interest and would interpret this to mean insuring himself against the risk of being relatively badly placed. Inequality would therefore be regarded as fair only to the extent that this inequality, by providing incentives, raised the level of output and, in doing so, improved the standard of living of the worst off in the community. This 'difference principle' – the difference made to the poorest – would have to be satisfied in order to justify any particular pattern and degree of inequality. The 'difference principle' is clearly a special case of the wider qualifications that Edgeworth and Pigou felt obliged to make when, in presenting the utilitarian case for equality, they said that the effect on total output must be taken into account (see above p. 24).

What must now be observed is that the maxi-min theory of justice, as put forward by Rawls, was by no means generally accepted, even by his fellow philosophers. On the contrary, it was met by a flood of criticism.[14] To take up one central point, there was no general support among the commentators for his assumption that people behind the 'veil of ignorance' would behave as very cautious, prudential egoists. A different view had been expressed by Harsanyi,[15] who held that since everyone has the same chance of being in any position in the distributional scale, everyone ought to support a constitution that would foster the maximisation of average incomes. This whole question of choosing a distributional pattern under conditions of uncertainty has, of course, been examined, with various objectives in mind, by a number of other contributions.[16] For our immediate purposes, the first point to stress is the absence of a consensus as to what would constitute 'fairness'. There is not, therefore, a dominant conclusion that could be taken up as a basis for an exploration of the economic implications. The most that can be said is that there would be a good deal of support for the view that the onus of proof rests with the defenders of inequality. Here, unfortunately, we come to an empirical problem of great technical difficulty, to which reference has already been made above. This is the problem of assessing the probable effect on the output level of different degrees of inequality. As Brown has shown,[17] simple generalisations about incentives will not do. The Rawls 'difference principle' is, to say the least, hard to quantify!

The conclusions so far must be regarded as somewhat discouraging. This is so, at all events, with regard to income distribution in general. We venture to suggest, however, that there would be much more agreement about the proposition that everyone should be protected from poverty. This assertion, if true, is highly relevant to the subject of this book, the welfare state. In so far as the purpose of the welfare state is to provide a minimum, there may be quite a strong consensus to support it. Naturally, this implies some degree of redistribution but does not involve commitment to measures that would determine distribution over the whole range of incomes. It is still necessary, however, to decide how the minimum, or poverty level, is to be determined - and determined not just in principle but in practical, quantitative terms (see Chapter 4 below). Distributional changes that go beyond the establishment of a minimum (however assessed) clearly raise more controversial issues. This is not, of course, to imply that such questions should therefore be avoided in the study of political economy. An excessive regard for consensus would paralyse intellectual speculation and would inhibit legitimate political activity. It is nevertheless important to observe how far consensus appears to extend and where it appears to stop.

The emphasis that has just been placed on there being a broad consensus in favour of protection against poverty may be held to reflect an insular interpretation of the welfare state - the one dominant in Britain until recent times. For, as was observed in Chapter 1, the cash benefits in many other countries - including, it should be added, the USSR - have been on a graduated basis. It is true that there is normally a minimum level of benefit which implies some scope for redistribution in favour of the poor, and there is always a maximum. Between these limits, however, graduated benefits reflect forward into retirement the inequality of working life. This is quite a different matter from achieving consensus about the 'right' distribution of income. It is, in effect, an acceptance of what is there. An attempt to justify graduation might be made along the following lines - unconvincingly, in our view. It might be argued that what is regarded as a poor standard of living is always relative. What would be a tolerable minimum to those not previously well off would be grinding hardship for the rich. The aim, therefore, should be to provide a minimum level of satisfaction rather than just a minimum level of goods and services. If different people require different amounts of goods and services in order to achieve the same degree of satisfaction, should this fact not be recognised by the provision of graduated benefits? This line of argument must be rejected, however. Admittedly, it may be thought right that someone who is physically handicapped should be treated more generously than someone who is not, in order to allow him to achieve the same level of satisfaction.[18] It would be an entirely different matter to apply this argument generally and to insist that because person A has had a higher income than B in the past, A must be assured by the state of a higher income in the future when both are retired. Such reasoning sets on its head the old utilitarian case for greater equality, which rested on the assertion that a pound is worth less to a rich man than to a poor man. For it could then be inferred that the rich man must have more pounds – and that the state must ensure that he has more – because more are necessary if he is to achieve equality of satisfaction. Of course, those who are relatively well off when at work will want to ensure that they are also relatively well off when no longer at work. But this is a matter for personal decisions about life-time expenditure. It is hard to find any satisfactory argument in social ethics which would require the state to accept an obligation to assist in this matter. Reasons for graduation can indeed be found and will be investigated in Chapter 4, but these are of a different nature.

BENEFITS IN KIND

The problems discussed in the preceding sections arise whether benefits are in cash or in kind, but benefits in kind raise further issues of great difficulty.

Why should it be thought to be right to treat certain benefits – in particular, health services and education – as though they were public goods rather than to have them supplied, as used to be the general practice and is still to some extent the case, through the market? It can be pointed out that it is better to use the market for the allocation of a very wide range of goods consumed by individuals – food, clothing, entertainment and so on – if it is indeed accepted as a social objective that individuals should get more satisfaction rather than less from the resources at their disposal. This is so basically because tastes differ. The whole range of consumer goods could theoretically be supplied in the form of rations, which would imply that the political authorities were attempting to decide what each person's wants should be. For them to do so would be to assume a degree of uniformity in preferences that can be demonstrated empirically to be unrealistic. Experience shows that when this degree of control is attempted, people will set out to frustrate it by exchanging goods among themselves. Why, then, are merit goods – which constitute a large part of the expenditure of the welfare state –

assumed to be different? It will not do simply to say that such goods are required in order to redistribute income in favour of the less well off, for this objective could be achieved by cash transfers. Nor is it enough to say that the health services and education are important. Food and clothing are also important and necessary for survival but are not supplied as quasi-public goods. One answer is that in the latter case there are external considerations which the private consumer, preoccupied with his own affairs, cannot be expected to take into account – externalities that affect other people and must therefore be the concern of the public authorities. Thus it may be held that some people would not spend enough, if left free to choose, on what would be required to prevent contagious diseases from which others might suffer. This, however, is an old example of a danger that can largely be met by such public goods as a proper sewerage system, by various regulations applied to the food industry and by some restricted official health services that might be supplied without charge to those in need. A universal free health service, available to all for all forms of illness, is not required to cope with this particular externality. If it were, Britain might have been afflicted with plagues before 1948, and the USA would be in danger of being so afflicted today. Another possible external consideration – probably a rather modest one – that might seem to warrant a universal service is that if such a service were indeed to improve public health, then absenteeism for health reasons might be reduced, and this would ease the problems of industrial management and thus raise output. The externality argument is, however, stronger in the case of education, for the training given to the younger generation will ultimately affect a nation's capacity to produce and thus the volume of scarce resources available to meet competing wants.

In a well-known article Tobin observed that, in his view, people in America were prepared to accept a good deal of inequality in income and wealth. He went on to add, however, that this attitude was 'tempered by a persistent and durable strain of what I shall call *specific egalitarianism*. This is the view that certain specific scarce commodities should be distributed less unequally than the ability to pay for them.'[19] It is undoubtedly the case that most people would want to see more equality in the distribution of, say, food intake, as measured by calories, protein or vitamins, than in the distribution of money income. But it may be pointed out that this is what does in fact emerge, even without rationing or the subsidization of food, except in such special circumstances as those of wartime, when supply falls and is inelastic. It is still not clear that benefits in kind can be held to be necessary in the case of such requirements as medical services or education. Further reasons can, however, be adduced, though these too may not be regarded as fully decisive.

If the welfare state were to extend only to the distribution of cash incomes some might not choose, when thus left free, to spend 'enough' on such goods as health services and education. This is, of course, a paternalistic argument: some people, perhaps many people, do not know what is good for them and must be restrained and guided accordingly – if given cash, they might spend 'too much' on drink and 'too little' on medical care. It must be said at once that 'paternalism' should not always be interpreted in a pejorative sense. Obviously, some degree of paternalism is needed in the case of children and of other people mentally incapable of looking after themselves. The defenders of paternalism might then extend their case in order to include interference with the freedom of normal adults on the ground that there will be a general tendency to spend too much money in the wrong ways. Indeed, the case can be put still more strongly by saying that some people would actually welcome paternalistic restraint, for they are conscious of the fact that they do not always use their incomes in ways which *they themselves* believe would be to their best advantage. They often do what they feel they should not do. In the words of St Paul: 'The good that I would, that I do not. The evil that I would not, that I do.' Orthodox economic theory ignores St Paul. People are assumed to have certain wants which they seek to satisfy in a consistent and strong-willed manner. It is not assumed, except in special static models, that they have perfect knowledge of the benefits to be derived from all the commodities they buy; it is assumed, however, that they usually know better than any outside authority which would impose a pattern on expenditure and would override diverse preferences. They may indeed make mistakes; but inconsistency and weakness of will are outside the usual economic models but should not, for this reason, be ignored.

It would therefore be wrong to reject out of hand the case for paternalism, but an incautious acceptance of this case can lead one into dangerous channels. In sacrificing their freedom to choose, even if they do so voluntarily, people are accepting the tutelage of outside authority, and the mental attitudes thus fostered, if allowed to grow and to extend too far, can become the basis for totalitarianism. Even if the extension of control stops well short of that disaster, it may be held that the personalities of those who submit will be weakened. Underlying traditional economic analysis is a value judgement – rarely made explicit in today's mathematical texts – that people ought to be treated as responsible adults, and that failure to treat them thus will not merely lead to less satisfaction (because the diversity of preferences will be disregarded); they will also, in a sense, be demeaned, for the exercise of free choice is necessary for the development of personality. It is a question of the emphasis to be given to personal responsibility and self-respect – that is to say, to deontological rather than utilitarian considerations. It is certainly inconsistent to denounce the use of means tests in the provision of benefits as destructive of self-respect and at the same time to advocate the indefinite extension of benefits in kind provided by a paternalistic government. Yet this inconsistency is to be found in some of the literature on social administration. Who is to determine what is the appropriate distribution of expenditure in meeting personal needs? By what right can such an opinion be imposed on to other people? Ackerman has put the case against paternalism succinctly, as follows: 'A power structure is illegitimate if it can be justified only through a conversation in which some person (or group) must assert that he is (or they are) the privileged moral authority.' He goes on to propound his *principle of neutrality*: 'No reason is a good reason if it requires the power holder to assert: (a) that his conception of the good is better than that asserted by his fellow citizens, *or* (b) that regardless of his conception of the good, he is intrinsically superior to one or more of his fellow citizens.'[20]

On what grounds, then, can a reasonable case be advanced for the provision of benefits in kind, as in the British health service? As is explained in Chapter 6, there are a number of difficult and complicating problems involved in this case. It may suffice to anticipate what is said below by mentioning two of them at this stage. First, medical attention is not, for most people, a want that occurs regularly and can thus be satisfied by following a regular routine of expenditure. The uncertainty about what will be needed and when is a crucial feature of the situation, as Arrow has stressed.[21] Secondly, the cost involved may be very large, sometimes beyond what could be met out of the current income or the accumulated savings of even the most prudent of individuals. Now, insurance is designed to meet situations of this kind, but the cost of private insurance on an individual basis will be high if the coverage is to be comprehensive – too high for many people. In any case, it cannot even be assumed that everyone who could afford to do so would bother to insure himself if there were no compulsion. The next step is to recognise that most people are not prepared to allow others to die or to suffer severe pain when remedial services can be supplied. If the cost cannot be met by the sufferers, it must be met in some other way. The reasoning is similar to that which leads to the acceptance of social arrangements designed to ensure a minimum total income and thus provide protection from poverty. This does not, however, dispose of the matter. For it is necessary to ask whether this reasoning properly applies to all forms of the health services or only to those required in acute cases. It is also necessary to consider whether the provision of a minimum entitlement to health services need also entail the imposition of a maximum determined by the amount that can be obtained from taxpayers through the budget. That is to say, if some people are prepared to pay for health services on a scale above what is officially provided, are there good reasons for preventing them from doing so? In some circumstances there may well be, but these circumstances need to be carefully specified.

We have said that the onus of proof should be seen to rest on those who recommend paternalistic measures that interfere with an individual's freedom of choice. As always, there are value judgements involved, but it must be recognised that there are important instances in which the proof would seem convincing to many people, sometimes to all. It is also usually the case that such issues cannot be settled on the high plane of generality. As is only natural, the special features of each case need to be explored and assessed before a confident conclusion can be reached.

PUBLIC CHOICE

When one is frustrated by the difficulty of formulating a social welfare function based on the preferences of those who comprise society or perplexed by conflicting assertions about what a regard for justice would seem to require, it is tempting to opt out by saying 'This is a political matter' or 'This is an issue which must be left to society to decide.' This temptation has not always been resisted successfully in discussions of general economic policy or of the problems of the welfare state in particular. To take one example, the minimum provided as Supplementary Benefit in Britain has been quite often described in such terms as 'the poverty level determined by society'. This use of the term 'society' may be helpful as rhetoric, but it can clearly be misleading. For what is 'society' in this context? How is it envisaged as reaching conclusions of this kind? The politicians and bureaucrats who determine the level of Supplementary Benefit, however well informed, have no key by which they can solve the problems discussed in preceding paragraphs; nor has the electorate as a body. To say that society has made its decision is to suggest a degree of conscious deliberation and choice and, furthermore, a degree of consensus, that is unrealistic.

At the beginning of this section it may then be in place to make explicit two anti-metaphysical assertions. First, the welfare of society is simply the welfare of the persons who comprise it or will do so in the future. There is no mystical entity apart from them. Secondly, there is no decision-making body that can be legitimately described as 'society'. Decisions are made by people, acting as voters, politicians and officials, who are organised in various ways. It is obviously important to investigate their behaviour in these roles, to observe the extent to which they agree and differ and to examine how their decisions are finally reached. But inquiries of this kind may be discouraged and criticism muted by the personification of 'society' as the body that takes the decisions.

In a good deal of economic literature, especially before and just after the war, there was a tendency to bring in the state as *deus ex machina* to cope with the problems of 'market failure'. That action by the state may indeed be highly desirable is not in doubt, both in order to do what markets cannot do and to correct certain distortions in market behaviour. But the state itself is liable to err even when its policies are framed in the most impartial way. In practice the political authorities are always under pressure from different quarters and cannot be assumed to act always in a fair and unbiased manner. Such reservations are obvious – boringly obvious. It is necessary, however, to make these points explicitly in order to reduce the risk that, as has often happened, they will be neglected.

The Marxists, for their part, have never regarded the state in 'capitalist bourgeois societies' as a detached and fair adjudicator. On the contrary, the state has been for them an instrument in the class war. Even a parliamentary system is no more than a device which, as Lenin put it, allows the exploited and oppressed to choose, every few years, the particular group that will exploit and oppress them. The welfare state itself may be viewed in this light. When benefits are provided, these can be seen as mere sops designed to divert attention from the far more important facts of exploitation. It must be admitted at once that there is an important element of truth in this disillusioned explanation of the emergence of the welfare state, although welfare benefits are now far too large in relation to profits to be described plausibly as a sop (see p. 2 above). The Marxist approach is thus a corrective to the assumption that the welfare state is essentially an expression of the social conscience. Unfortunately, the Marxists carry their scepticism too far and have long underrated the gains that may be extracted through the parliamentary process by those who are neither capitalists nor rich. Moreover, their cynicism in this context has been matched by the naive optimism of their assumption that after the revolution the new single-party government will be fair, benign, altruistic and egalitarian. Rawls was fully justified in laying prior emphasis on basic political and civil liberty. This emphasis is not to be regarded as simply the expression of a value judgement. It has a sound, empirical foundation. In the light of experience, it is folly to recommend that liberty, in this basic sense, should be sacrificed for the sake of equality. In the event, equality, in so far as it has been initially achieved, has not survived for long in the Marxist totalitarian regimes. Indeed, the welfare state itself may be used as an instrument of political discrimination, as it is in the USSR, where dissidents are deprived of the right to social benefits. By way of contrast, it may be observed that the dissidents in Northern Ireland – who have not confined themselves to verbal criticism – have received an uninterrupted flow of social benefits, even in the 'no-go' areas which at one time the security forces did not enter.

A critical view of the role of the state has also been adopted by some modern economists who are, as it happens, very far from being Marxist.[22] Their models of public choice, like so many models of market behaviour, are based on the assumption that people behave in all their different spheres of activity as rational utility maximisers. Politicians and public servants will pursue this objective in their own particular fashions, but the objective itself is basically the same as that of the merchant or the worker. Thus the basic hypothesis, as applied to parties under a system of representative government, was sharply expressed by Downs as follows: 'parties formulate policies in order to win elections rather than win elections in order to formulate policies.'[23]

Like the Marxists, this school pursues its arguments too far. The above quotation from Downs is obviously only partly true. Parties do have convictions and do try to win elections in order to implement them, not just to win power. Nevertheless, light has been thrown on political processes by analysing the implications of hypotheses which, if not fully realistic, contain an important element of truth that had previously been too often neglected.

No attempt can be made to summarise the large and growing volume of literature on the theories of public choice. It must suffice in what follows to put forward a number of points relevant to the study of the welfare state which reflect in part this work on public choice.

(a) Although people usually act from mixed motives, the importance of egoism must not be overlooked in political activity any more than in market behaviour. Moreover, even when their actions are not designed exclusively to advance their personal interests, people must set themselves limited objectives. Within the government machine there must be some devolution of responsibility, and everyone must seek to advance the particular objectives that are his concern. 'Non-tuism' is present inside the huge official administrative machine as well as on the market, and its effects clearly need to be assessed. Anyone who has ever worked in government must have experienced the immense pressure of departmental loyalty. If one is in the Department of Education, one must press its interests as strongly as possible, and it is not part of one's duty to moderate the claims made for education because one is also aware that a different ministry, say the Department of Health and Social Security, is also pursuing worthy objectives. Even within a department those in particular branches must press the interests of their own branches. If there is no tight control over public expenditure, the outcome will be a gradual rise in the total. Or, given such control, the allocation of resources between different claimants will depend partly upon the skill, persistence and force of character of different ministers and officials, and the outcome will be affected by log-rolling and inter-departmental alliances of one kind or another. In short, there is bound to be a good deal of empire-building, both because this will advance the personal careers of those concerned and also because, apart from such selfish considerations, departmental loyalties are paramount. There is, then, a danger not only that the allocation of resources may differ from one that an Impartial Spectator might endorse but also that given objectives could be achieved more economically. It is, of course, the duty of the Cabinet and its committees and, in a more detailed way, of the Treasury, to prevent this from happening, but it is important not to underestimate the difficulty of obtaining, assimilating and assessing the relevant information, of making well balanced decisions and of enforcing them.

These pressures, as they affect spending for the purposes of the welfare state as distinct from other purposes, may swell the total beyond what could reasonably be regarded as essential. There is a further point that may be easily overlooked. This is that empire-building may lead to unnecessary complexity in the arrangements as different groups within government fight to acquire and retain places in the sun. Such complexity is only too evident in the welfare services.

(b) When a good is sold on the market, people must be prepared to buy it voluntarily if the decision to produce is to be vindicated. The link between the producers of government services and their consumers is through the polling booth. There are circumstances in which this may be the only link that could be devised (for example, in the case of public goods), but the fact remains that the link is not usually a firm one. Suppose, however, that a particular programme has received the conscious support of a majority of the electorate and can, in this sense, be held to be democratic. This does not obviate the fact that the minority who oppose it will be coerced. The market operates differently, for it is not restricted to satisfying the demands of a majority. A whole range of different preferences will be met, provided people are willing and able to pay, otherwise there would be little classical music or high-brow literature. It is not, of course, to be inferred that the market should, for this reason, always be preferred. What does follow is that good grounds must be advanced in order to justify a resort to methods of supply that, by their nature, take less account of the diversity of personal preferences.

(c) A great deal of work has been done in recent years on voting systems, and it has been shown that it may be impossible to ascertain what the majority would prefer, even if votes were cast, not for a package of policies, but separately for each particular policy. The point is an old one, which goes back to the work of Condorcet, but its importance has come to be more widely appreciated.[24] In fact, people rarely vote on single issues of national policy but are rather presented with a choice between packages. Suppose a party were to acquire an absolute majority under a system of proportional representation primarily because of its attitude to nuclear policies and membership of the European Community. Those who voted for it might hold a variety of different opinions about a variety of other issues. It is true that they would then be voluntarily subordinating their views on these issues in pursuit of those that they regarded as more important. But it could not then be claimed that, in following whatever policies it decided to pursue on these other issues, the new government would be implementing even majority opinion. The position is still more complicated when there is no proportional representation or when representation on this basis does not produce a majority vote for any one party.

Perhaps more use could be made of referenda on particular national issues, so organised as to inform the voters about the cost in taxation of particular measures.[25] To organise referenda at all frequently would, however, be an expensive business. Moreover, Members of Parliament would to this extent be turned into delegates rather than representatives. Sample inquiries to test opinion would be much less costly than referenda and would also be seen to provide guidance rather than to impose obligations on government, but they could scarcely be used extensively.

(d) Representative government reflects the view that there is a need for a division of labour. The electorate cannot make rational decisions about a whole range of complicated issues. This must be done by the government and the bureaucracy without too much continuous interference even from its own supporters in Parliament, for this would reduce the speed of executive action. This does not mean that the government will exercise dictatorial power, as in a fascist or communist state, for it can be thrown out of office at the next election by peaceful means, if people do not like the package it has provided. But it does mean that the control exercised by the electorate cannot be detailed and precise.

(e) In the study of voting attention has properly been directed to identifying that group along the spectrum of opinion that may exercise decisive power. Consider a situation in which votes are being cast on some policy of which the basic issue is its effect on the distribution of income. Those who are very poorly off will want to vote for greater equality but cannot hope to win a majority if they push their case hard and alienate those who are rather better off, though still below the average. A similar argument applies to the very rich. In short, those at either extreme must woo those in the centre. From this has emerged the conclusion that the median voter can usually determine the outcome.

At first glance, this theory would appear to be a feature – or what is alleged to be a feature – of the welfare state, for it has been held that the middle class gains more from the benefits provided than does the working class. The theory of the median voter would seem to afford an explanation. Even if it were true that the middle class benefits more, however, it would be quite wrong to identify the 'middle class' in the sense in which the term is used in such statements with those at or near the median in the income distribution. The middle class really includes everyone with an income *above* some specified point or, more vaguely, everyone who is not a member of the proletariat. In short the middle class does not really consist of those in the middle. It is also worth recalling that the average gross earnings of manual workers are close to the median income.

An interesting variant of the theory of voting pressure has been introduced by Browning.[26] In his view, this pressure is likely to be biased in favour of the retired population and would be so even if all taxpayers were fully aware of the extra burden imposed by higher pensions. He points out that the middle-aged will be serving their own interests if they ally themselves with those already retired, for they will have to pay the heavier contributions over only a limited period before they themselves become pensioners. This alliance will naturally be particularly strong in a population in which the older age groups are gaining relatively in numbers. Whether this *a priori* analysis is important in practice is, of course, a matter for empirical inquiry.

This chapter may conclude with a recognition of the danger of assuming too much knowledge and too much rationality in the expression of opinions through political channels and in the implementation of the policies adopted. It is an error that runs through a good deal of the economics of the market, and it is also present in much of what has been written on theories of public choice. In fact, people are often poorly informed even about welfare benefits that may affect them in a direct and personal way. Moreover, people are by no means always consistent; they may be inclined to support welfare programmes as voters but reluctant to accept the consequences as taxpayers. Market behaviour may also be ill-informed and inconsistent, although the limited amount of money in people's pockets may prevent inconsistency from being carried too far. There are also some services, notably the health services, which present special difficulties, as will be seen below. Therefore when in subsequent chapters we examine more closely the empirical evidence about welfare schemes, in order to make some assessments and to proffer some suggestions, it will be important to bear in mind the fact that people are often poorly informed about the facts and inconsistent in responding to them.

NOTES

1 R. M. Titmuss, *Commitment to Welfare*, 2nd edn (London: Allen & Unwin, 1976), p. 22.
2 A. C. Pigou, *Economics of Welfare* (London: Macmillan, 1920).
3 L. C. Robbins, *The Nature and Significance of Economic Science* (London: Macmillan, 1932).
4 R. Pinker, *The Idea of Welfare* (London: Heinemann, 1979), pp. 6–7.
5 D. C. Mueller, *Public Choice* (Cambridge: Cambridge University Press, 1979), p. 1.
6 C. L. Schultze, *The Public Use of Private Interest* (Washington, DC: Brookings Institution, 1977).
7 W. S. Vickrey, 'An exchange of questions between economics and philosophy', in A. D. Ward (ed.), *The Goals of Economic Life* (London: Harper, 1953); reprinted in E. S. Phelps (ed.), *Economic Justice* (Harmondsworth: Penguin, 1973).
8 P. Wickstead, *The Common Sense of Political Economy*, ed. L. C. Robbins (London: Routledge, 1933), p. 174. See also Roland N. McKean, 'Economics of trust altruism and corporate responsibility', in Edmund S. Phelps (ed.), *Altruism, Morality and Economic Theory* (New York: Russell Sage Foundation, 1975); Pinker, *The Idea of Welfare*; T. Wilson, 'The market and the state', in T. Wilson and A. Skinner (eds), *The Market and the State: Essays in Honour of Adam Smith* (Oxford: Oxford University Press), pp. 81–2.
9 Adam Smith, *The Theory of Moral Sentiments*, eds D. D. Raphael and A. L. Macfie (Oxford: Oxford University Press, 1976) 1.i.5.5
10 H. Hochman and J. D. Rogers, 'Pareto optimal distribution', *American Economic Review*, vol. 59 (1969).
11 K. Wicksell, 'A new principle of just taxation', reprinted in R. A. Musgrave and A. T. Peacock (eds), *Classics in the Theory of Public Finance* (London: Macmillan, 1967), p. 74.
12 J. Rawls, *A Theory of Justice* (Oxford: Oxford University Press, 1972).
13 B. A. Ackerman, *Social Justice in the Liberal State* (New Haven, Conn.: Yale University Press, 1980).
14 See, for example, N. Daniels (ed.), *Reading Rawls* (Oxford: Blackwell, 1975).
15 J. C. Harsanyi, 'Cardinal welfare individualistic ethics and interpersonal comparisons of utility', *Journal of Political Economy* (August 1955); reprinted in Edmund S. Phelps (ed.), *Economic Justice* (Harmondsworth: Penguin, 1973).
16 For example, A. J. Culyer, *The Political Economy of Social Policy* (Oxford: Martin Robertson, 1980), pp. 88–95; A. Lerner, *The Economics of Control* (London: Macmillan, 1944); A. Sen, *On Economic Inequality* (Oxford: Oxford University Press, 1973).

17 C. V. Brown, *Taxation and the Incentive to Work* (Oxford: Oxford University Press, 1980).
18 A. Sen, *On Economic Inequality* (Oxford: Oxford University Press, 1973).
19 J. Tobin, 'On limiting the domain of inequality', *Journal of Law and Economics*, Vol. 13 (1970). See also Edmund S. Phelps (ed.), *Economic Justice* (Harmondsworth: Penguin, 1973), p. 448; A. J. Culyer, *The Political Economy of Social Policy* (Oxford: Martin Robertson, 1980), pp. 64–5.
20 Ackerman, *Social Justice in the Liberal State*, pp. 10–11.
21 K. J. Arrow, *Social Choice and Individual Values* (New York: Wiley, 1951).
22 See, for example, A. Breton, *The Economic Theory of Representative Government* (Chicago: Aldine, 1974); J. M. Buchanan and G. Tulloch, *The Calculus of Consent* (Ann Arbor: University of Michigan Press, 1962); A. Downs, *An Economic Theory of Democracy* (New York: Harper & Row, 1957); Mueller, *Public Choice*.
23 Downs, *An Economic Theory of Democracy*, p. 28.
24 See, for example, Arrow, *Social Choice and Individual Values*.
25 Mueller, *Public Choice*, pp. 72–4.
26 E. K. Browning, 'Why the social insurance budget is too large in a democracy' *Economic Inquiry*, vol. 13 (September 1975); also subsequent exchange of views with K. V. Greene, *Economic Inquiry*, vol. 15 (July 1977) and with B. Bridges, *Economic Inquiry*, vol. 16 (January 1978).

CHAPTER 3

The Cash Transfers: An Account of the Schemes

The first part of this chapter presents some statistics which illustrate more fully what was said in Chapter 1 about the importance of expenditure on the welfare state. It begins with aggregate expenditure on both goods and services and on transfer payments. The allocation of this expenditure between various functions in a number of countries is then analysed. This is followed by an examination of the benefit systems in the UK, and some comparisons are made with other countries in order to provide a preview of the way in which the schemes operate in practice. With the main facts thus set in perspective, the chapter goes on to review the various policies for the provision of cash benefits in Britain and to indicate some of the main features of policies in force in the USA, Sweden and some selected EC countries. Although a detailed comparative study cannot be attempted, it is illuminating to consider in this way some similarities and contrasts. A number of important and controversial issues are thus suggested, and these are then taken up in Chapter 4.

STATISTICAL REVIEW

Expenditure on the welfare state has been growing in all Western countries relative to gross national product since the beginning of the century. In the UK social expenditure, including education, accounted for only 2·6 per cent of GNP in 1900. By 1979, as can be seen in Table 3.1, which presents the statistics for the EC countries, expenditure on cash benefits, health and various other services exceeded a fifth of GNP in the UK and a quarter of GNP in France and West Germany, and came to approximately a third in the Netherlands. In Sweden too such expenditure amounted to about a third of GNP, and even in the USA, often regarded as a country where the welfare state is on a modest scale, expenditure accounted for about a sixth. Table 3.1 also shows how, as might be expected, expenditure under the different headings varied from country to country, partly as a reflection of differences in the emphasis placed on various services. Thus the relatively large proportion devoted to the family in France and Belgium reflects a particularly strong and long-standing concern about the birth rate and family living standards.

Table 3.1 *Government social expenditure by function in EC countries, 1979 (percentages)*

	West Germany	*France*	*Italy*	*Nether-lands*	*Belgium*	*Luxem-bourg*	*UK*	*Denmark*	*Ireland*
AS % OF GDP AT MARKET PRICES	26·6	25·2	22·9	31·2	27·1	25·4	20·4	26·9	18·7
Sickness	30·7	26·8	23·0	28·7	23·3	23·2	24·7	27·7	37·0
Invalidity and disability	7·7	5·7	19·6	19·8	7·7	9·4	8·8	9·7	6·9
Old age	27·7	35·4	34·6	27·9	38·0	36·2	42·0	34·1	34·0
Survivors	15·1	6·4	9·7	5·0	—[2]	14·5	2·3	0·6	—[2]
Occupational accidents and disease	3·5	3·7	2·5	—[1]	3·5	5·4	0·8	0·7	0·5
Maternity	0·7	1·9	0·8	0·4	0·5	1·1	1·5	0·9	2·2
Family	9·1	12·7	7·0	9·2	12·2	7·8	12·4	9·7	9·7
Unemployment	2·0	5·6	2·3	6·9	9·9	2·0	4·8	11·6	7·7
Placement, vocational guidance, etc.	1·0	0·4	0·1	—	2·2	—	0·4	0·6	—
Miscellaneous	2·3	1·5	0·4	2·2	2·7	—	2·3	4·4	2·0

[1] Included in validity/disability.
[2] Included in old age.
Source: Eurostat, *Social Protection*, 1–1981.

In all countries the elderly and other pensioners claim the highest proportion of expenditure. It is scarcely surprising that this should be so when social insurance benefits, occupational pensions and means-tested benefits are available to elderly people, who constitute a high and growing proportion of the population. There is, of course, a considerable amount of overlap between the categories in this table. For example, the elderly, in addition to their cash incomes, make extensive use of the health services, although this is not apparent from the table. Total expenditure on the health service in many of these countries will be higher than appears in the table, as the figures do not include private expenditure. The extent to which public expenditure is thus boosted can be inferred, in general terms, from the character of the schemes (see pp. 128–34 below).

By comparison with the elderly, the number of unemployed was a good deal lower even in the late 1970s and early 1980s, which were scarcely years of high prosperity, and this largely accounts for the very much smaller share of expenditure assigned to cash benefits for the unemployed and to job creation and placement services. With the

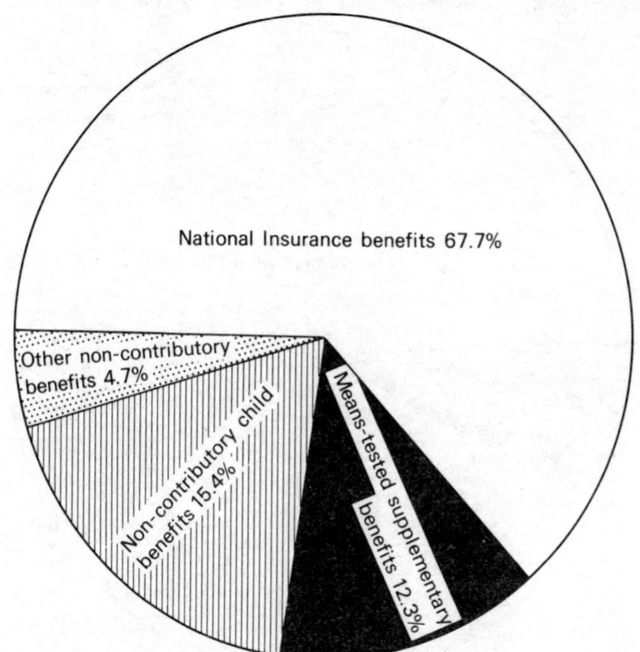

Figure 3.1 *Cash transfers by manner of provision, UK 1979 (percentage composition)*
Source: National Income and Expenditure (London: HMSO, 1980).

deepening recession, expenditure on the unemployed has subsequently risen drastically. Nevertheless, this particular item will remain substantially less than expenditure on the elderly. For even with 3 million out of work in the UK, for example, the number of elderly people is nearly three times as high, and the benefits they receive per head are somewhat larger.

It was observed in Chapter 1 that cash transfers are the second biggest source of personal incomes in the UK. In Figure 3.1 these transfers are analysed according to the manner of their provision in 1979. (a) National insurance benefits, received as of right, accounted for about two-thirds of the total. (b) Benefits which were both non-contributory and not means-tested came to a fifth. It should be recalled that benefits of the latter kind had been recommended by Beveridge, in addition to national insurance benefits, mainly in order to provide assistance with the cost of children. Expenditure under this general heading has, however, been swollen for two main reasons. First, the child benefit scheme introduced in 1979 extended provision to cover the first child, previously excluded, and also raised the scale on which provision was made. There was, however, a partially offsetting change (not shown in

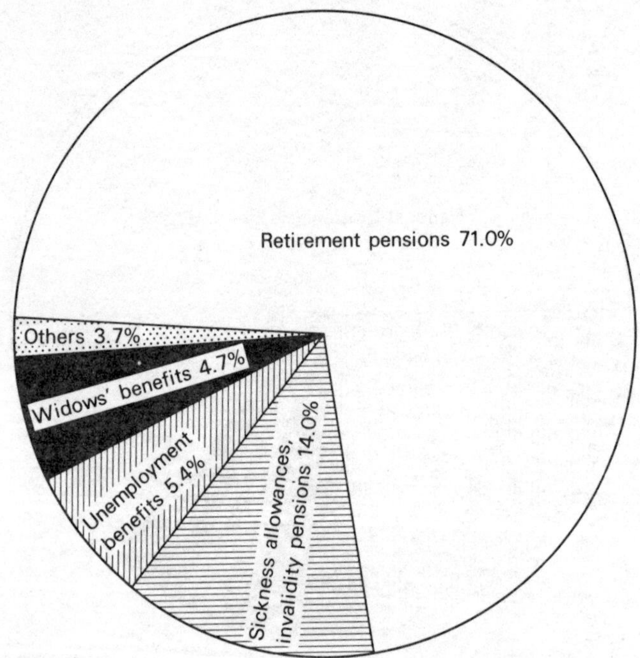

Figure 3.2 *National insurance benefits by recipients, UK 1979*
Source: National Income and Expenditure (London: HMSO, 1980).

this figure), in that tax allowances for children were also abolished in 1979. Secondly, some of the newer non-contributory benefits - attendance, mobility and invalid care allowances – have constituted an increasing addition to this category. (c) Means-tested benefits – mainly supplementary benefits (SB) – came to over 12 per cent in 1979. These benefits were therefore a fairly small proportion of total expenditure, although more than a modest residuum, the role assigned them by Beveridge. The controversial issues raised by selectivity according to means are taken up in Chapter 4. Meanwhile, it should be recorded that the proportion of all *beneficiaries* receiving this form of means-tested assistance was very much larger than the proportion of *expenditure* which these benefits represented. The explanation lies in the fact that some four-fifths or more of those receiving means-tested benefits were receiving them as a topping-up of national insurance benefits.

In Figure 3.2 the national insurance benefits are further broken down to show the proportions of expenditure received by various groups of beneficiaries. Retirement pensions made up over 70 per cent of total expenditure. Short-term sickness and long-term invalidity benefits accounted for a seventh; invalidity pensions in the UK, as in many other countries, have been one of the fastest growing areas of cash transfers and may in some cases be providing an early retirement pension for older workers. The figure shows the relatively small amounts spent on unemployment insurance benefits even by 1979, when unemployment was already high by postwar standards, although to this would have to be added the very substantial means-tested SB payments made to the unemployed. Table 3.2 indicates the extent to which provision for the different groups of beneficiaries are means-tested, and the importance of such benefits in the incomes of the unemployed – 51 per cent of the

Table 3.2 *Cash benefits by category of beneficiaries, 1980–81*

	Total of national insurance and means-tested benefits	*Percentage of benefits on means tests in each category*
Elderly	52·7	9·0
Disabled and long-term sick	11·3	8·9
Short-term sick	3·4	2·3
Unemployed	10·9	51·2
Widows and orphans	4·0	1·3
Family	17·7	17·8
	100·0	14·6

Source: Based on Table 2.12.1 in *The Government's Expenditure Plans 1981–82 to 1983–84*, Cmnd 8175 (London: HMSO, 1981).

total – is at once apparent. Families with children too relied on means-tested benefits, although to a much lesser extent, but the largest part of their cash benefits came in the form of the universal non-conditional child benefits. For the elderly and the disabled, means-tested benefits, although important, made up only a relatively small proportion of their cash benefits (about 8 per cent). The national insurance retirement and invalidity pensions were their main source of support. For the disabled, non-means-tested special payments such as mobility and attendance allowances were also important. (Assistance with housing costs is not included in these figures, which relate to cash benefits only.)

Table 3.3 *Replacement ratios: benefits as percentage of average earnings at November 1980 uprating*

	All adult male earnings		*Adult male manual earnings*	
	Gross	*Net*	*Gross*	*Net*
Retirement pension				
Single person	19·8	28·6	23·7	33·8
Married couple	31·6	43·8	38·0	51·2
Standard rate sickness/unemployment benefit				
Single person	15·0	21·8	18·0	25·7
Married couple	24·3	33·6	29·2	39·4
Man, wife + 2 children	30·9	41·7	36·6	48·1
Man, wife + 4 children	36·7	48·5	43·0	55·3
Supplementary benefit scale rate plus rent addition				
Single person	22·1	32·0	26·6	37·8
Married couple	32·4	44·9	38·9	52·6
Man, wife + 2 children[1]	42·4	57·3	50·3	66·1
Man, wife + 4 children[2]	48·9	64·7	57·3	73·7

[1]Two children under 5.
[2]Two children under 5; two aged 5–10.
Source: Department of Health and Social Security.

In Table 3.3 the principal cash transfers are expressed as percentages of gross and net earnings rather than in terms of cash, for money values change rapidly and are, in any case, of little significance unless related to appropriate bench-marks. These figures may be said to provide a preliminary summary of the effects of the various schemes to be discussed in some detail below. It will be seen that in 1980 the retirement pension in Britain for a single man would have replaced 19.8 per cent of the gross average earnings of all male workers or 23.7 per cent of the average for all male *manual* workers. A pensioner with no source of income other than his pension would have had only a very small liability for tax because the pension barely exceeded the income tax threshold and, of course, no national insurance contributions would have been paid. The gross pension may therefore be compared with net average earnings after tax, and for a single man the ratio then rises to 28.6 per cent of the average for all workers and to 33.8 per cent of that for male manual workers. For a pensioner married couple the corresponding proportions were 43.8 and 51.2 per cent respectively. The replacement ratios were naturally higher for those who had previously earned less than average earnings, as can be seen from Table 3.4. It is fair to add, however, that those who were formerly low-paid workers would be less likely

Table 3.4 *Replacement ratios of British retirement pension at different levels of gross average male manual earnings, 1980*

	Single man	*Married couple*
As percentage of gross average earnings	24	38
As percentage of 75% of gross average earnings	36	57
As percentage of 50% of gross average earnings	48	76

Source: Based on Department of Health and Social Security and Department of Employment statistics.

to have had additions to their pensions in the form of income on capital, and occupational pensions would usually make a smaller contribution.

In comparing the financial position of different households allowance must naturally be made for the number of persons. It is not appropriate, however, to give equal weighting to all individuals, and the official equivalence scale is designed to provide suitable weights. Thus, for example, a single person counts as 1·0 and a dependent spouse as 0·61. The choice of any set of ratios is bound to involve difficult statistical analysis and also the exercise of judgement.[1] The allowances for dependent wives and children, of course, give a married man a higher rate of return on contributions paid than a single man – one of the several departures from the insurance principle in 'social insurance'.

The standard pension is not the minimum benefit a pensioner may obtain, for the pension may be augmented on a means-tested basis by SB in particular in order to meet housing costs, which means in practice that the pensioner will have his housing costs met in whole or in part depending on whether he has any sources of income other than the state pension. The minimum income for a pensioner would then be equivalent to some 46 per cent and 63 per cent of average net manual earnings for single and married persons respectively – significant figures again, as these are, in fact, the operational poverty level. At half average earnings, this minimum income might give a married pensioner an income higher than his wage at work.

These replacement ratios raise the question of how much of his previous earnings the pensioner needs to receive in retirement. The British pension was originally paid at the same rate to all, irrespective of previous income, but as time has gone by the emphasis has shifted to the maintenance of previously attained living standards. Even if the objective were to allow the pensioner to maintain his former standards of living, the full replacement of earnings would not be necessary, of course; income tax liabilities would be less, partly because of the age allowance; national insurance contributions would not be payable; travel and other work expenses would no longer have to be met. Research into this question in Finland and the USA suggests that 70 per cent of previous earnings would be sufficient to maintain the living standards of the average earner, with rather more in the case of lower paid workers.[2] The British retirement pension does not approach the 70 per cent level, although SB raises the replacement ratio and is not subject to tax. About one in two pensioners also have occupational pensions, although in many cases these are small, and they are rarely adequately protected against inflation. Income from work makes up an estimated quarter of the total incomes of the elderly and income from savings and investment another 10 per cent. Short-term insurance benefits are lower than those for the long-term, as Table 3.3 shows, although again many beneficiaries have additional sources of income. Four-fifths of the workforce have rights to occupational sickness benefits, and in some cases wages are made up in full. Some of the newly unemployed have redundancy payments and also refunds of Pay As You Earn (PAYE) income tax. Large numbers of unemployed, however, have only the national insurance benefit, or partial benefit because of incomplete contribution records, or have exhausted their entitlement or have never earned insurance rights. The effective income for the unemployed, of course, is the cash SB scale rate, which is virtually the same as the insurance benefit, *plus* the housing allowance and some other minor means-tested benefits. Initially, long- and short-term insurance rates were the same, but from 1973 to 1981 the long-term rates were adjusted in line with rising earnings and the short-term with rising prices, which allowed the long-term rates to rise by 22 per cent in real terms, while the real value of the short-term benefit fell slightly. The short-term benefit gave a single manual worker about a quarter of average *net* earnings in 1981. An average manual worker with a wife and four children received the equivalent of over half of his former *net* earnings. Most of the unemployed have, however, been earning less than average earnings in the past or can expect to do so in the future. It is not necessarily to be inferred that the benefit level is 'too high' in the latter cases, for attention needs also to be directed to the problems posed by low incomes at work.

It is instructive to compare the replacement ratios of the British benefits with those of benefits provided in other countries. The welfare state in the UK has come in for criticism in certain quarters on the grounds that the rising cost of the social services has contributed to low rates of economic growth and that welfare benefits have had disincentive effects on the individual worker. Other countries, whose growth records are more impressive than those of the UK, also spend higher proportions of their larger GDPs on their welfare systems than the UK, as Table 3.1 shows. The benefits provided by these other countries also give higher rates of protection to the old, the unemployed and the sick, as comparisons of the replacement ratios of some of these benefits show. In Sweden in 1978, for example, the minimum flat-rate citizen's pension, which may include a means-tested housing allowance, was equivalent to 36 per cent of gross average earnings for a single pensioner and 62 per cent for a married couple. But the majority of pensioners have a second graduated state pension, and many have additional occupational pensions. The three pensions together would have given replacement ratios in 1978 of about 70 per cent and 85 per cent of average gross earnings for a single pensioner and married couple respectively.[3] These pensions were, in fact, considerably higher than the targets initially aimed at, largely because of frequent and full price indexation at a time of rising inflation, when real earnings were beginning to fall. A change has subsequently been made in the method of price indexation, which now excludes changes in the price of energy.

The Netherlands, like Sweden and the UK, has a flat-rate pension, but the state does not provide any earnings-related component. This is left to private occupational pensions. The overall targets for these two pensions combined are high, at 85 per cent replacement of the minimum guaranteed industrial wage as the minimum and 70 per cent of previous gross income for the average wage-earner, with biannual adjustments of pensions in payment in line with rising wages.

In West Germany there is a minimum pension, but above this pensions are wholly earnings-related. The target aimed at is 60 per cent of average earnings, but this has not yet been reached, and the average replacement ratio is nearer 50 per cent. Full indexation of pensions in payment, in relation to a lagged three year moving average of earnings, was the previous practice, although this was not a statutory commitment. This practice was changed during the recession, and the discretionary adjustments have become smaller.

In the USA, as in Sweden, pensions reached higher limits than originally intended, in this case because of over-compensation for inflation, which was, however, rectified over a transitional period between 1979 and 1982. Pensions are earnings-related, but with a pension formula kinked in favour of the low-paid, the replacement ratios vary widely according to previous levels of earnings. For three levels of earnings, the ratios in 1981 were as shown in Table 3.5. The replacement ratio of 89 per cent for a married couple, in cases in which the breadwinner's lifetime earnings have been near the federal minimum, looks very high. In practice, however, because of the low earnings to which it applies, the pension itself falls below the official poverty line, and large numbers of pensioners are eligible for federal means-tested supplementary security, a situation comparable with that in the UK.

Table 3.5 *Estimated US social security replacement ratios for single persons and married couples, the insured person reaching 65 in 1981*

	Level of earnings (pension as percentage of earnings)		
	Low income[1]	*Average income*	*Maximum income*
Single person	59	48	29
Married couple	89	72	44

[1] 'Low income' in these estimates is defined as lifetime earnings near the federal minimum; 'average income' is lifetime earnings at the average annual wage level; 'maximum income' is lifetime maximum taxable earnings for social security purposes.

Source: Social Security Administration, US Department of Health of Human Services.

Where *short-term benefits* are concerned, there are much wider differences between countries in administrative and financial practice and in the levels of benefit, with the arrangements often left to sub-central levels of government or even to the employers or trade unions. In Britain flat-rate benefits are uniform throughout the country and, as shown above, give low replacement ratios by international standards, although they may be supplemented on a means-tested basis. In West Germany wages are paid in full by the employer for the first six weeks of sickness absence. After that the sickness insurance funds, to which all workers must belong, pay 80 per cent of previous gross earnings, normally for an unlimited period. National unemployment benefits also provide high replacement ratios. Benefit at the rate of 68 per cent of previous *net* earnings up to a ceiling is paid for a period varying between thirteen and fifty-two weeks, according to the worker's employment record, after which unemployment assistance at the rate of 58 per cent of *net* wages is payable for an unlimited period.

In Sweden the national insurance sickness benefits provide 90 per cent replacement of gross earnings between certain limits, equivalent to 25 and 175 per cent of average industrial wages. Benefits may be paid at half-rates to any worker who returns to work on a part-time basis. Unemployment benefits have some interesting features. These have traditionally been the responsibility of the trade unions, although for many years with government subsidisation, and have been used as an inducement to trade union membership, which is very high in Sweden. Trade union members are entitled to benefits at the rate of 90 per cent of previous earnings up to a ceiling. Only in the mid-1970s did the government intervene to provide national unemployment benefits for non-union members, but at very low rates. The sickness and unemployment benefits are taxed to ensure that incomes when people are not in work cannot exceed incomes derived from working.

In the Netherlands too replacement ratios are high – 80 per cent of earnings up to a maximum – for both sickness and unemployment.

The US arrangements are complex. Unemployed benefits, which are a state not a federal responsibility, range between states from 25 per cent to 45 per cent of earnings and are normally payable only for twenty-six weeks. Means-tested assistance for the unemployed not in receipt of insurance benefits is at the discretion of the individual states and is paid at much lower rates. Only some 60 per cent of the working population have sickness insurance coverage, and benefits replace between 50 and 60 per cent of previous earnings.

Replacement ratios, once determined, will not subsequently be maintained unless benefits are adjusted in line with some index of earnings. This is taken care of automatically if benefits are expressed as a proportion of previous earnings, as is the normal custom in many countries. If benefits are flat-rate, as in The UK, and adjusted only for changes in prices (the practice since 1978), then although their real value will be restored when an adjustment is made, the replacement ratios will obviously decline when real wages are rising, as was the case for so many years after the war that such growth came to be taken for granted. The frequency and regularity with which benefits are adjusted can have important consequences. Annual adjustments are made in a number of countries, including Britain. In some cases, however, the changes are biannual. Such changes were indeed proposed as a permanent arrangement for Britain by Sir Keith Joseph in 1972. After the Conservative defeat in 1974, the new Labour Government did, in fact, make a second increase in that year, but subsequently both Labour and Conservative Governments have reverted to annual changes. What must be stressed in the present context is that the replacement ratios are those calculated just *after* a change in benefits has been made. Between reviews the real value of benefits must fall when prices are rising as can be seen from the saw-edges of Figures 3.3 and 3.4. These figures show the changes in the real value of the retirement pension and the supplementary scale rate for single persons between July 1948 and

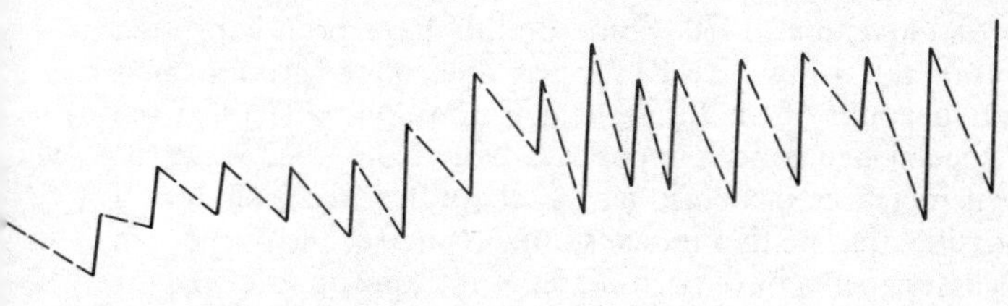

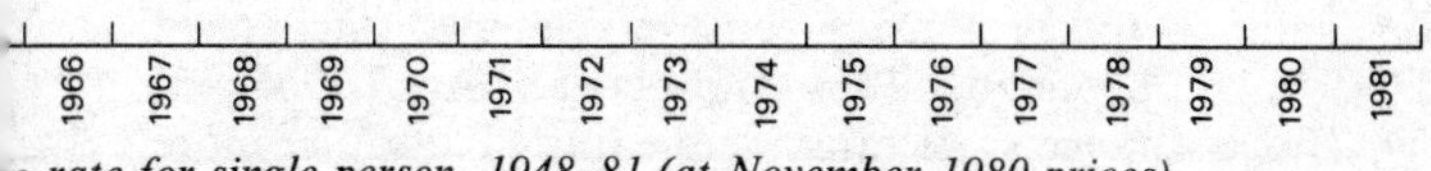

e rate for single person, 1948–81 (at November 1980 prices)

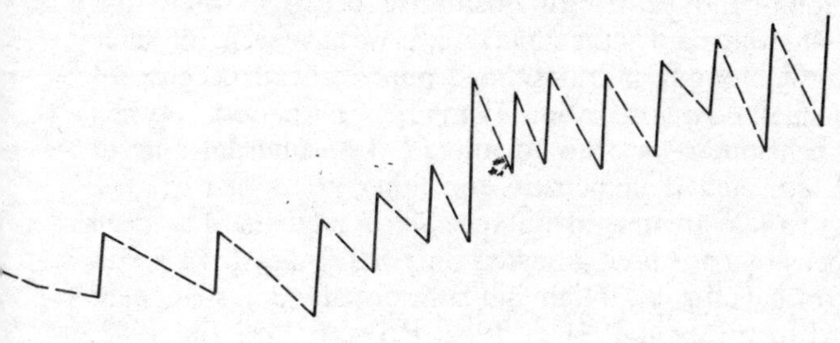

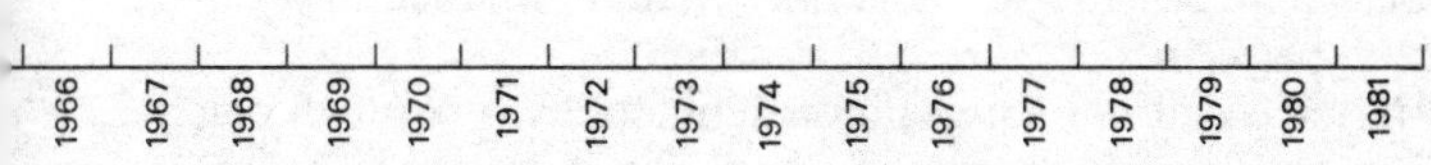

ɔle, 1948–81 (at November 1980 prices)

November 1980. The benefits have been deflated by the Retail Price Index (RPI) for November 1980. Some doubts have been expressed about the suitability of using the RPI for pensions, on the grounds that it does not take account of the different consumption patterns of the elderly.[4] The special pensioner's index available from 1962 onwards gives lower real increases in pensions, but the difference is slight. Of course, it is possible that neither index is satisfactory for the purpose in hand. Various assessments have been made of the appropriate weights for an index to be applied to low incomes, and official investigation of the case for the construction and the regular publication of a new low-income price index appears to be warranted. While this is so, it is also reasonable to assume that the use of the RPI will give a reasonably good indication of the order of magnitude of the changes in real benefits over the trend.

Figures 3.3 and 3.4 demonstrate how the real value of both the retirement pension and the assistance scale rate have risen over time. There were, however, long periods in the 1950s and 1960s when the real value of benefits fell between the infrequent ratings, as the dotted lines indicate. For example, the retirement pension remained unchanged between July 1948 and September 1951, and between April 1955 and January 1959. The assistance scale rates were adjusted at rather more frequent intervals; there were twenty-seven upratings between 1948 and the end of 1980, as compared with twenty in the case of pensions. Some correlation can be traced between upratings and impending general elections. The long- and short-term insurance benefits, when first introduced in 1948, were paid at the same rate, as we have seen, but since the early 1970s the long-term rates have pulled ahead because of differences in the method of indexation. For part of this period, between 1978 and 1980 pensioners had the advantage of an unusual type of indexing, which adjusted their benefits for either prices or earnings, whichever was to their greater advantage. Since 1980 this has been dropped, and pensions are now adjusted only for forecasted rises in prices. Short-term benefits, although still substantially adjusted, were not fully indexed to prices in 1981 or 1982. Between 1973 and 1982, therefore, the difference between long- and short-term benefits increased substantially from 5 to 30 per cent. A special long-term *assistance rate*, designed primarily to help the pensioner, had been introduced as early as 1967, and subsequently, due to differences in indexation, the difference between the long- and short-term assistance rates has increased to 25 per cent.

The long-term record of changes in benefits looks very much better than might be supposed from repeated complaints about the 'erosion' of benefits by inflation. Between July 1948 and November 1981 the purchasing power of the retirement pension and of the long-term assistance rate increased by some 136 per cent and the short-term insurance benefits and assistance scale rates by some 100 per cent. The pension, in fact, more or less kept pace with rising earnings.

A REVIEW OF THE SYSTEMS OF CASH BENEFITS

As was observed in Chapter 1, Beveridge set out to simplify and standardise the complex arrangements that had been gradually evolved over the years before his Report appeared in 1942. Subsequently the legislation of the late 1940s did, in fact, establish a system much less complicated than the one it superseded. For a variety of reasons, however, new variants were to be added between the late 1940s and the early 1980s, and the system now in force is far from simple. It is scarcely surprising, therefore, that proposals have been made from time to time for a fresh attempt at rationalisation. Moreover, dissatisfaction with existing systems is not confined to Britain but has been expressed as well in other countries whose systems have also become increasingly complex. In particular, it has frequently been suggested that the benefit system and the tax system could be integrated into a more straightforward and coherent whole, with negative income taxes taking the place of cash benefits, a question which is taken up again in Chapter 8. That there is force in these complaints is not in doubt. It is necessary, then, in attempting any assessment of the scope for reform, to ask whether some aspects of existing systems can be regarded as little more than rococo embellishments while other special provisions can be justified as meeting special needs.

NATIONAL INSURANCE BENEFITS

Traditionally, the British social security system provided, in return for flat-rate contributions, the same flat-rate benefits for all that were designed to provide a minimum income in old age, sickness and unemployment. Various earnings-related benefits have since been grafted on to the original scheme, most notably the earnings-related pension that was established by the legislation of 1975. Contributions are now graduated, but some of the benefits are flat-rate and some earnings-related. These contributions are levied on all earnings between a minimum that is equivalent to the basic retirement pension for a single person and a maximum of about seven and a half times that amount. (Thus accountable earnings range from roughly a quarter to rather more than one and a half times average earnings.) The exchequer provides a contribution out of general tax revenues, normally equivalent to about 18 per cent of contribution income, and investment income on the small fund accumulated adds about another 3.5 per cent. In April 1977 a surcharge was imposed which raised the employer's contributions by 2 per cent, and this was increased to 3.5 per cent in October 1978. The proceeds of this surcharge are not paid to the account of the national insurance funds, however, but go to the general exchequer, which continues to subsidise the social insurance account – a Grand Old Duke of York performance!

The single contribution covers not only the social insurance benefits mentioned but also industrial injury and health benefits, and the Department of Health and Social Security (DHSS) has overall administrative responsibility. The British system differs in many respects from practice in other countries, where there are generally separate administrative and financial arrangements for pensions, short-term benefits, industrial injuries and health services. In most countries too the different schemes are generally self-financing, and exchequer contributions are the exception. This greater financial autonomy is strongly defended on the grounds that any substantial reliance on annual budgetary allocations would mean increased political risk.

THE LONG-TERM BENEFITS: RETIREMENT, WIDOWHOOD AND INVALIDITY

As we have recorded, the most important of these is the standard flat-rate retirement pension to which every man on reaching the age of 65 and every woman on reaching 60 is entitled, providing contributions have been paid for nine-tenths of his or her working life. The married man receives a supplement to his pension of 60 per cent for a dependent wife who is also of pension age. The pension is reduced if it is drawn before the official retirement age, and increases may be earned at the rate of 7·5 per cent for each year worked between age 65 and 70. Although it is a retirement not an old-age pension, full retirement is not required. If the pensioner chooses to draw his pension and continue in part-time work, he loses £1 in pension for every £2 earned up to a certain limit, corresponding to about two-fifths of average male manual earnings, and any earnings above a somewhat higher limit are fully offset by reductions in pension. At the age of 70 the pension becomes an old-age pension and is paid in full irrespective of earnings. The Conservative Government which came into office in 1979 had undertaken to phase out the earnings rule, but this promise was subsequently deferred until economic circumstances should become more propitious (see Chapter 4, pp. 98–9). Pensions are liable for tax, but no tax will be paid unless the pensioner has, in addition to his basic pension, sources of income that bring his income above the income tax threshold.

Under the new pension arrangements which came into operation in

1978 a second-tier, earnings-related pension has been added to the flat-rate pension. A contribution period of twenty years is required for full entitlement to this second pension. Meanwhile, persons retiring between 1978 and 1998 will be eligible for proportionate pensions. The second pension is assessed on the basis of earnings in the 'best' twenty years of working life, with every year's earnings grossed up to reflect the rise that had occurred in the level of earnings by the date of retirement. Each year of contributions entitles the pensioner to 1·25 per cent of relevant earnings, giving a full graduated pension equal to 25 per cent of such earnings after twenty years' contributions. The official objective with respect to the flat-rate and earnings-related pensions combined was that together they should produce an income that would replace about 50–55 per cent of the pre-retirement earnings of the average married worker. These figures, it is now clear, underestimate the effect of the scheme.

Alternatively, employers may contract employees out of the state earnings-related pension scheme and may pay reduced contributions, on condition that they satisfy the Pensions Board that their occupational schemes provide a minimum pension corresponding to the state earnings-related pension and that adequate provision is made to protect preserved pensions against the effects of inflation. There has been an enormous increase in the membership of occupational schemes since 1945, and by 1979 just over half of the employed population were members – over 6 million in the private sector and over 5 million in the public. In the same year an estimated 3·7 million people were actually drawing occupational pensions, and these were adding in many cases large supplements to the basic state pension. On average, the pensions of public-sector ex-employees more than doubled the state pension and average private-sector pensions added an increment of about 70 per cent, as well as the lump sum which some pensioners, usually in the private sector, would have received on retirement. There was, however, a wide dispersion around these averages, reflecting the differences between the former earnings of pensioners, the length of time they had been members of pension schemes and the 'quality' of the schemes.

Occupational schemes have undoubted attractions. First, unlike contributions to the state scheme, contributions are deductible from gross income when the income on which tax is to be levied is assessed. Secondly, the Government has undertaken to adjust for price rises that part of occupational pensions in payment which lies below the ceiling for state earnings-related pensions. Thirdly, national insurance contributions are reduced by 7 per cent if employees are contracted out, although this rate of abatement may not be maintained in the second quinquennium starting in 1983, as the Government Actuary warned in his survey of occupational pension schemes published in 1978.[5]

To return to the state insurance arrangements. These provide for *widows* a range of flat-rate benefits, apart from the entitlements to the new earnings-related pensions, based on their late husbands' contributions. A distinctive feature of the British arrangements is the *widow's allowance* which most widows under 60 years of age receive. This is paid for six months at a rate which is about one and a third times that of the standard widow's pension, in order to give a woman time to adjust to her change in status. After six months the receipt of a widow's benefit, its type and its amount will depend on age and dependent children. If the widow is over 50 years of age, she will receive a *widow's pension* at the same rate as the retirement pension. If she is over 40 but under 50 when left a widow, the latter benefit will be proportionately reduced. If under 40 and childless, she receives nothing after the first six months. If she has dependent children, she will be entitled to a *widowed mother's allowance*, again at the same rate as the retirement pension, together with supplements for her children. Further, the widow, if over 50, inherits her late husband's entitlements to earnings-related pension in full and will receive a proportionate amount if over 40 but under 50. This is in addition to any earnings-related pension she may have earned on her own work record. Contracted-out occupational schemes are also required to pay widow's pensions at a rate of at least 50 per cent of the guaranteed minimum pension to which the husband would have been entitled at the time of his death, and this is made up to the full minimum by the state scheme.

After the retirement pension, the most important of the long-term benefits in terms of number of recipients are the *invalidity pensions*, introduced in 1971. These are paid to insured persons who are unable to return to work at the end of six months, when their entitlement to short-term sickness benefit comes to an end. The benefit is payable at a higher rate (about 25 per cent above the short-term sickness benefit) in recognition of the increasing costs of long-term absence from work. Supplements for dependent wives and children are paid at the same higher rate as those for the dependants of widows and the industrially disabled. *Invalidity allowances*, which are paid as additions to the pension in the majority of cases, introduce another concept. These allowances, varying with the age of the onset of invalidity, are designed to give some small compensation for the loss of earning power and are similar in principle, if not in size, to some of the additional benefits paid to the victims of industrial accidents or disease (see below, p. 63).

The *status of women* under these arrangements requires comment. Traditionally, for social security purposes the married woman was treated as the dependant of her husband. If she did not work, she nevertheless received benefits on the strength of her husband's contributions, without paying any contributions herself, and was likely, because of the lower pension age and the longer life expectancy of women, to draw the most important of these, the retirement pension, for a lengthy period.[6] This meant, of course, that her husband received a higher rate of return on his contributions than did the single man or woman. Before 1978 the married woman who was in paid employment gained little by choosing to pay full contributions, and few did so. Since 1978 gainfully employed married women have been required to contribute on the same basis as men or single women. In return they receive the same rates of benefit, with the added advantage that years spent out of the labour force caring for children or invalids count towards 'home responsibility credits'. The married woman is thus entitled to a full pension if she has contributed for twenty years between the ages of 16 and 60 instead of the more normal forty years. This may appear a very real advantage at first glance, but if during those twenty years her earnings have been part-time or low for some other reason, then she may find that the pension she has earned in her own right is less than the one to which she is entitled as her husband's dependant. She has the choice of opting for the latter, but the contributions she has paid will earn her no additional pension entitlement and, in that sense, are 'wasted'. If widowed, the gainfully employed wife will, however, have the advantage of her years of contribution. Then, subject to the age qualifications mentioned above (p. 60), she will not only inherit her husband's earnings-related pension rights but she will also keep any pension rights she has earned on her own contributions.

Similar anomalies occur in the social security arrangements of other countries and have received particular attention in the USA.[7] Various proposals have been made there to safeguard the position of the working wife: that she should receive any benefits she has earned on her own contributions in addition to the dependant's allowance; that the dependant's allowance should be abolished or at least reduced now that over half of all women work outside the home; that there should be some system of aggregating and sharing the contributions and benefits of husband and wife.

SHORT-TERM CONTRIBUTORY BENEFITS: SICKNESS, MATERNITY AND UNEMPLOYMENT

Short-term benefits in the UK, as we have seen, are covered by the same administrative arrangements as are long-term benefits and are financed out of the same inclusive national insurance contribution. A sick person who is off work for more than four days becomes entitled, provided his contribution record is satisfactory, to the *standard flat-rate sickness benefit*, with supplements for a dependent wife and children which, like the benefit itself, are lower than the supplements to the long-term pension. Special benefits are payable for *maternity*. These include a lump-sum maternity grant for virtually all mothers and maternity allowance and paid maternity leave for working mothers. Until 1982 earnings-related supplements were paid in addition to all the short-term flat-rate benefits for a period of six months. These were calculated as a proportion of earnings between a certain minimum and maximum, with the proviso that total benefits should not exceed 85 per cent of normal earnings.

The whole future of sickness and maternity benefit is under review at the time of writing. In 1980 the Government proposed in a Green Paper, *Income during Initial Sickness: A New Strategy*, that the responsibility for the first eight weeks sickness payments should be transferred from the DHSS to employers. The reasoning behind this proposal was that 80 per cent of full-time employees were covered by occupational sick-pay schemes, which in some cases made up their incomes in full. The DHSS still had to deal with 10 million claims for state sickness benefit every year, the great majority of them short-term. There would be obvious administrative economies if employers were to assume full responsibility for sickness benefit, with compensatory reductions in their national insurance contributions. These controversial proposals, similar to those which have operated in West Germany for a number of years, were embodied in a government Bill in November 1981.

More stringent conditions apply to the payment of *unemployment benefit*, as in other countries, as a protection against possible abuse. As well as a satisfactory contributions record, the unemployed claimant must be registered for work, may not refuse 'suitable' employment, will not receive benefit if directly involved in a trade dispute and can be disqualified from benefit for six weeks if he has given up his work voluntarily or has been dismissed for bad conduct. The standard unemployment benefit, at the same rate as sickness benefit, is payable for twelve months. After twelve months the allowance stops, and the insured person must work for thirteen weeks before he becomes eligible for another period of benefit. With rising unemployment in the early 1980s and longer periods out of work, about half of the unemployed have had no insurance rights. In such cases SB is the only source of social security income. In many other cases this is making up insurance benefits to the SB level, which includes an allowance for housing.

Some of the unemployed also receive lump-sum *redundancy payments*, made to workers who have been with an employer for at least two years. These payments were originally designed to encourage labour mobility by easing the transition from one job to another and to reduce opposition to structural change which might entail a spell of unemployment. The lump sum payable depends on the number of years worked, the age of the worker and the level of his earnings; there is a ceiling on reckonable earnings (at about average male earnings), and the maximum payment is thirty weeks' pay. Central government refunds some 40 per cent of the payments made by employers from an ear-marked element in the employers' national insurance contribution; while these payments reduce the hardships of structural adjustments, they also impose a penalty on the employer. The unemployed may also receive refunds of PAYE income tax.

INDUSTRIAL INJURY INSURANCE

In the UK the contributions for these benefits, which cover injury at work and certain prescribed industrial diseases, are paid as part of the inclusive earnings-related contribution, but the benefits are administered by a separate section of the DHSS and, more important, both the range and the level of benefits are more generous than the comparable provision for non-industrial beneficiaries. For the first six months *industrial injury benefit* is payable at a slightly higher rate (112 per cent) than sickness benefit but with the same allowances for wife and children. At the end of six months, or earlier if permanent disability has been established, the claimant becomes entitled to *industrial disablement benefit*, which is calculated on the degree of loss of faculty not loss of earnings. This is an important distinction; it means that the benefit may be paid in addition to earnings from work or other insurance benefits if the claimant is unable to work. For 100 per cent permanent disablement the benefit is twice as high as the sickness benefit. There are other supplements to this long-term benefit to compensate for loss of earnings power, for unemployability or for the constant attendance which may be required. In cases of severe handicap it is possible to draw a combination of pension and supplements which would equal about three-quarters of average male earnings and would be payable in addition to any earnings from work or to sickness or invalidity benefit.[8] A White Paper issued in November 1981[9] proposed substantial changes in these arrangements, with the aim of concentrating more resources on benefits for the more severely permanently disabled, to be paid for out of savings on benefits for the less severely disabled.

The industrial benefits in other countries exhibit much greater diversity. In some instances the employer may be left to insure the risk privately; in other cases there are national progammes run independently of other insurance schemes. Medical benefits may be provided through national health schemes or through special arrangements. Almost invariably, however, the medical benefits are more extensive and the cash compensation more generous than the provision made for non-industrial injury and sickness. The Netherlands is alone in providing the same income for the disabled irrespective of the cause of disability.

MEANS-TESTED CASH AND OTHER BENEFITS

The British system of means-tested maintenance, SB, is not to be confused with social aid as provided in many other countries. Supplementary benefit is a national scheme, operated by local offices of the DHSS and, providing the same sets of benefits and applying the same tests of means throughout the country. It has come to play a very important part in the overall social security arrangements, either as the sole source of support for people without any other income or as a secondary source of income for social insurance beneficiaries whose benefits do not reach the SB level. In the great majority of countries *social aid* is the responsibility of local units of government which have considerable autonomy in determining levels of benefit and the means tests to be used for determining eligibility. In such cases, however, social aid plays a residual role, and the numbers of beneficiaries and the level of expenditure in no way compare with the British. The USA is the exception here. It too has a national federal system of means-tested income maintenance for certain categories of the needy population, such as the old, the blind, poor families with dependent children. National means tests and national benefit levels apply, although the states administer the Supplemental Security Income scheme (SSI) on behalf of the Federal Government and, again, as in the UK, large numbers of federal pensioners have their pensions supplemented by SSI. Apart from this, the states may, at their own discretion and without federal financial support, provide so-called general assistance to other sections of the 'less-deserving' poor, such as the unemployed.

Although social aid may play a minor role in some countries, means tests may be used in other important ways. In France the minimum pension in the general insurance scheme is itself means-tested. In Sweden a means-tested housing allowance is built into the pension legislation and is, in fact, received by about half the pensioners. About two-fifths of families with dependent children also receive housing assistance. These facts call for some emphasis. They mean that *a higher proportion* are on means tests than in the UK, but means tests are not, as in Britain, a target for criticism and attacks. Apart from these instances, many countries employ means tests to determine eligibility for a variety of other benefits, mainly provided by local authorities.

To return to SB in Britain. The claimants are generally people aged 16 and over who are not in full-time employment. Entitlement is determined by comparing an applicant's resources with what would be needed to cover living costs as laid down by Parliament and reviewed annually. The payment, if any, is the amount required to raise cash income to the official minimum scale rate, together with the actual costs of rent and rates, or mortgage interest payments and rates in the case of an owner-occupier. An important distinction is that between the short-term and long-term rates, the long-term rates being between 25 and 30 per cent higher than the short-term rates so as to cover the renewal of clothing, footwear, household equipment and so on. Pensioners are entitled to the long-term rate from their first application; other claimants must have drawn SB for a year before they transfer to the higher rate. Unemployed applicants did not qualify for the higher rate until 1981.

In working out a claimant's entitlement to SB, income from earnings (including those of a wife), from national insurance benefits, child benefits, occupational and war pensions is taken into account. Certain amounts of earnings and of some benefits are disregarded, so that it is possible for the claimant's final income to be higher than the SB scale rate plus the housing addition. The claimant may also have capital up to the value of £2,000 without his claim being affected; above that sum he has no claim at all to SB. The value of an owner-occupied house (which will, of course, be a much larger sum) is completely disregarded; nor is any account taken of the addition to income which the imputed rent of the house represents, and there is no requirement to turn the capital represented by the house into income by means of a mortgage. On the contrary, assistance with existing mortgage interest charges, if these have not been completed, may be provided, as may assistance with some of the other costs of the owner-occupier.

The scale rates are designed to cover 'ordinary' living expenses – food, heat, light, the replacement of clothing, normal household costs and something for extras, such as a TV licence, newspapers and so on. It is possible to claim regular additions to benefits to meet special needs. Until the introduction of changes in November 1980, these additions were made at the discretion of individual SB officers, which occasioned much controversy. Regulations have since been laid down to replace discretion, and now any claimant who satisfies the requirements for additions to his benefit receives them as of right and at pre-determined rates. Regular *additional requirement* payments (ARs) are automatically made to cover heating costs on the grounds of age, health or the exceptional costliness of heating a particular type of house. Other additions may be made for a variety of needs, such as special diet or domestic help. Lump-sum *single payments* (SPs) may be made to meet exceptional needs (for example, essential furniture, funeral expenses or exceptional clothing needs). If the claimant has capital of over £300, the SP will be reduced, but even if the claimant does not satisfy the required conditions, an SP may still be made if it is 'the only means by which serious damage or serious risk to the health or safety of any member of the assessment unit may be prevented'.[10] This safety net leaves *some* discretion at least to the SB officer which might be used, for example, when an old person or a family with a young child is in danger of having fuel supplies disconnected if bills have not been paid.

ASSISTANCE WITH HOUSING COSTS

Many of the refinements – or complexities – introduced into the income maintenance system in the 1970s were designed to provide means-tested assistance with specific needs, as distinct from the general assistance given by SB that we have just discussed.

It is often contended that specific assistance of this kind is more acceptable to the recipients than general assistance, particularly if it is attached to a common and 'respectable' need. This would help to account for the popularity of assistance with housing costs, one of the most widely used of the specific means-tested benefits. Such assistance may be provided by SB or by the local authority. When it is provided by the latter it is available to anyone, whether employed or drawing national insurance benefits, who has difficulty in meeting housing costs from normal income. *Rent rebates* provide assistance to council housing tenants, *rent allowances* to the tenants of privately rented accommodation, furnished or unfurnished. *Rate rebates* may be claimed by both council and private tenants and by owner-occupiers. The amounts paid in all cases depend upon three factors: the amount of income, the size of the family and the *actual* rent or rates payable. It is possible for a large family with a very low income to pay no rent at all, while at the other extreme some help is available to smaller families with incomes up to about average male earnings or to childless couples, single people or pensioners with modest work or transfer income. Rent and rate rebates are not payable to anyone in receipt of SB, and it is often extremely difficult for, say, a retirement pensioner to calculate whether it is to his advantage to apply for a local authority rent or rate rebate or to claim assistance with housing costs from SB. A strong case can be made, in the interests of the recipients of the service and on grounds of administrative efficiency, for the amalgamation of these two systems, as was proposed in the discussion document *Assistance with Housing*, published in the spring of 1981 and, later in the year, put forward in the Social Security and Housing Benefits Bill. Other countries too provide assistance with housing. The arrangements in Sweden stand out: the means tests and benefits are generous, and the administration is relatively simple. As a result, two-fifths of families with dependent children and about 5 per cent of single people and childless couples are receiving assistance with their housing costs, and the greater part of these costs may be met in the case of large, low-income families. This is in addition to the large number of pensioners receiving housing allowances as part of their pensions. In West Germany and France, on the other hand, take-up of housing allowances has been low because of the complexity of the schemes and the failure to adjust the means tests or the benefits themselves to take account of wage and rent inflation.[11]

SUPPORT FOR FAMILIES WITH DEPENDENT CHILDREN

There are a number of objectives here: to protect children from poverty, to share out the burden of child-rearing among all sections of the population, to raise the standard of living of all children irrespective of parental income. The means used to meet these objectives are complex. Assistance may be provided in cash or in kind, and both cash and in-kind benefits may be available on a universal basis or on a test of means.

In money terms, universal free education and heath care provide the largest subsidies to most families with children. *Child benefit* is the most important form of direct cash assistance. This took the place of family allowances in the late 1970s, when child income tax allowances were phased out. It is a non-means-tested, tax-financed demogrant payable in respect of every child under the age of 16, or 19 if the child is still at school full-time: in 1981 it added nearly 4 per cent for each child to the earnings of an average male manual worker. Obviously, the importance of the subsidy varies with the size of family and of income and the regularity with which the benefit is adjusted for rising prices.

Other benefits for the family are means-tested, although in some cases – notably housing and university grants – the means tests are such that families with quite substantial incomes are eligible. A specifically British benefit is *family income supplement* (FIS), a form of cash assistance for *working* families with low incomes introduced in 1970 as a less costly alternative to a general increase in family allowance. The amount of supplement depends on the relationship between the family's gross earnings from work, the number of children and the prescribed amounts laid down annually by Parliament as necessary for the maintenance of families of different size. If the family's income is below the prescribed amount, a supplement is payable, but this is only 50 per cent of the difference, in order to pre-empt any possible disincentive effects on work. Receipt of the supplement automatically entitles the family to a range of other benefits – free school meals and milk, free prescriptions, dental treatment and glasses, grants for school uniform and so on, which may in some cases be worth more than the FIS itself.

These additional selective benefits are available not only to families receiving FIS or SB but also to other families with incomes not much above these levels; in these cases they have to undergo separate means tests for each benefit. In the case of local authority benefits, the authority exercises considerable discretion as to whether or not to provide benefits, the means tests to be used to decide eligibility and the size of the benefits. The result is a bewildering array of means tests which vary from area to area and from benefit to benefit, which may deter the family with an income not much above the S B level from making full use of its entitlements. Take-up is consequently very much lower among families that have to face these multiple means tests than among families on F.I S or S B, which have automatic entitlement. The further problem arises that entitlement to one benefit may raise a family's resources and make it ineligible for another – the so called 'poverty trap' which is discussed in Chapter 4. A strong case can be made for simplifying the complex maze of benefits and means tests. One national means test might be used by all local authorities to determine eligibility for all benefits. The more important of the benefits might be made mandatory obligations and the level of benefits made national, as was once suggested for the school maintenance allowance which is paid in some areas to children staying on at school after the official leaving age. A more radical – and more costly – solution would be to raise the child benefit and scrap the local authority benefits.

With the exception of the United States, income support for families with dependent children, in the form of direct cash allowances, is provided in all developed countries, in addition in most cases to free or heavily subsidised education and health services and a variety of tax concessions and welfare services, which do not permit of summary treatment. Family allowances vary in many respects as between countries. In some cases, such as Sweden, West Germany, and the United Kingdom, such cash allowances are straightforward subsidies to the family, financed out of general taxation; in other cases, like France and Belgium, they have developed as part of the contract of employment and are paid for, in large part, out of an employers' payroll tax, together with a state subsidy.

The allowance may be paid at the same rate to all children, as in Sweden and the United Kingdom. Alternatively, allowances may vary with the age of the child in order to take account of the increasing costs of maintaining older children, or with the place of the child in the family, in recognition of the increasing burden imposed on the family by each additional child it has to maintain. The latter is the case in West Germany and the Netherlands, while in Belgium and France the rate of allowance takes account of both age and place in the family. More recently, special family allowances have been used by some countries such as Denmark, France and the United Kingdom to help meet the special needs of single-parent families. In Sweden and Norway there are special guaranteed maintenance payments, in addition to the normal family allowances, for children in one-parent families, which may be reclaimed from the defaulting parent. Family allowances in the majority of countries are paid up to the age of 20, 25 or even 27 if the young person is an apprentice or in full-time education. Sweden and the United Kingdom make special financial provision for students in higher education. The British student is the more favourably placed as a university grant, although varying with his parents' income, is not repayable; in Sweden the comparable allowance is one sixth grant, five-sixths repayable loan – and repayable in real terms. A loan scheme has long been proposed for the UK but not adopted.

Family allowances in many countries have suffered from infrequent adjustments for inflation or growth. Belgium, Denmark and the Netherlands are the exceptions in this respect. In Belgium allowances are adjusted throughout the year for price rises and once a year for changes in the general standard of living. Denmark adjusts the allowances twice a year if prices have risen by so many percentage points; the Netherlands twice a year in line with changes in the wage index. In other countries, the UK included, adjustments require legislation, and there is no guarantee of regular indexation. It is time that the child benefit in Britain was brought into line with other benefits and reviewed on an annual basis, with some commitment to price indexation. This would be costly, but there seems to be no overwhelming argument against recouping the cost from the better-to-do families through the fiscal system.

BENEFITS FOR THE DISABLED

The insurance incomes received by the long-term disabled vary, as we saw above, according to the cause of disablement. For people who had been disabled from birth and had never been able to work there was only means-tested assistance until the reforms of the early 1970s. These reforms were intended, first, to remove some at least of these disparities of treatment and, secondly, to relate the assistance provided to the special expenses that disability may entail. The non-contributory invalidity pension (NCIP) for the first time gave an income, as of right, to disabled people with no insurance record. It is paid, however, at a lower rate than the contributory benefits, which may seem to accord with the Beveridge principle that the insured person should see some return for the contributions he has paid. In practice, it means that the majority of recipients of NCIP are having these pensions increased on a means-tested basis by supplementary benefit.

The other special benefits introduced in the early 1970s were designed to meet the additional expenses of disability and are therefore paid whether or not the disabled person is able to work and without any test of financial need. *Attendance allowance* is payable at two different rates, according to whether attendance is required by day only or by day and night. *Mobility allowance* provides a weekly payment towards the cost of transport for the disabled person who is unable, or virtually unable, to walk. *Invalid care allowance* is paid to men or single women (but not to wives) who have to give up paid employment to care for a severely disabled person. The mobility and attendance allowances may add considerably to the income of a disabled person; if the recipient of NCIP, for example, receives both allowances, his benefits will be more than trebled. In many ways Britain provides, by international standards, a wide range of benefits specifically related to the needs of disabled people, although the basic incomes for the handicapped are, in general, low.

Although there have been difficulties with medical assessment and with publicising these benefits, they have on the whole proved popular, and take-up rates are high. Another solution to the income needs of the disabled, and one favoured by pressure groups such as the Disablement Income Alliance, would be one income for the handicapped irrespective of the cause of disability. This would be costly and in many ways less sensitive to the particular needs of individual disabled people; a better use might be made of scarce resources by retaining, and improving, the present benefit system.

Throughout this chapter various recommendations have been made for reform, in many cases proposals for getting rid of, or at least trimming, the embellishments or barnacles, which have from time to time been added to our welfare edifice. Such a process might be regarded as a return to Beveridge, who placed much emphasis on simplicity. In considering these suggestions, and the more far-reaching proposals which will be made in subsequent chapters, especially those for the reform of the pension system, we may have much to learn from the experience of other countries, of which a little has been said in this chapter.

NOTES

1 L. D. McClements, *The Economics of Social Security* (London: Heinemann, 1978).
2 P. Henle, 'Recent trends in retirement benefits related to earnings', *Monthly Labour Review* (June 1972); P. Kuusi, *Social Policy for the 1960s* (Helsinki: Finnish Social Policy Association, 1964).
3 D. Wilson, *The Welfare State in Sweden* (London: Heinemann, 1979).
4 National Consumer Council, in evidence to the Royal Commission on the Distribution of Income and Wealth, Report No. 5, *Third Report on the Standing Reference*, Cmnd 5999 (London: HMSO, 1976), Appendix B.
5 *Occupational Pension Schemes 1975*, Fifth Survey by the Government Actuary (London: HMSO, 1978).
6 R. Cuvillier, 'The housewife: an unjustified financial burden on the community', *Journal of Social Policy*, vol. 8, no. 1 (1979).
7 M. Flowers, *Women and Social Security: An Institutional Dilemma* (Washington, DC: American Enterprise Institute, 1977).

8 T. Lynes, 'Industrial injuries scheme at the cross-roads', *New Society*, 13 November 1980.

9 *The Reform of the Industrial Injuries Scheme*, Cmnd 8402 (London: HMSO, 1981).

10 T. Lynes, *The Penguin Guide to Supplementary Benefits*, 4th edn. (London: Penguin, 1981), p. 131.

11 R. Lawson and C. Stevens, 'Housing allowances in West Germany and France', *Journal of Social Policy*, vol. 3, no. 3 (1974).

CHAPTER 4

Poverty and Selectivity

POVERTY: ABSOLUTE, RELATIVE AND STATIC

In all countries one of the central objectives of the social services, in the widest sense of that term, has been to provide protection against poverty. In Britain this objective has been of central importance in the past and even today, when certain other objectives are also being increasingly served, protection against poverty would still, one suspects, be accorded a position of central importance by the greater part of the nation. It is therefore appropriate, in moving from an examination of the schemes for income maintenance to an appraisal of their effectiveness, to begin by asking whether poverty has, in fact, been eliminated or at least greatly reduced in its severity and scale. The answer on which any verdict on the welfare state must greatly depend would appear at first glance to be deeply discouraging. Whatever sense of achievement may have been felt in the postwar years was shaken in the 1960s by the 'rediscovery of poverty',[1] and its persistence has been a matter of concern ever since. It seems puzzling that this should be so. For a very elaborate and extensive set of institutions has been established which were described in the last chapter, and expenditure has risen substantially in real terms. If, nevertheless, large numbers are still in poverty, something would seem to be terribly wrong with the policies adopted or with their implementation. Indeed, grave doubt would seem to be cast on the basic assumption that state action can be at all effective in coping with the problem of poverty. There would appear to have been little success so far.[2] Why, then, should anyone suppose that more of the same will be more successful in the future? Should the whole enterprise not be abandoned? This is not exclusively a British problem. In some other countries with highly developed social services poverty has persisted, as was shown, for example, by a comparative study organised by the OECD and published in 1976.[3]

That there may indeed be scope for the radical reform of the welfare arrangements is a possibility that must be explored. There are, however, other explanations of the apparent failure to cure poverty to which attention must be directed first. These are the ambiguity of the term and the elasticity of the measuring rod by which its magnitude is often assessed. The first step, then, is to distinguish between 'absolute' and 'relative' poverty.

ABSOLUTE POVERTY

One of the pioneers in the study of poverty in Britain, B. S. Rowntree, defined poverty as a condition in which the income of a family was 'insufficient to obtain the minimum necessaries for the maintenance of merely physical efficiency'.[4] He then set himself the task of estimating what would be required to achieve this bare-minimum standard. Experts on nutrition were able to give some guidance about the required expenditure on food, but the rest was more difficult, and he was driven to use estimates of the actual expenditure of poor families together with some arbitrary allowances for minor items. The minimum income thus assessed was therefore a combination of the normative (for food) and, mainly, the actual for other items. This hybrid characteristic remained in Rowntree's later estimates and in that made by Beveridge for his Report in 1942. When a poverty level was estimated for the USA in 1962 the starting-point, again, was the sum held to be necessary for food in the case of farm and non-farm families respectively, and these amounts were roughly trebled in order to reflect the empirical observation that food accounts for about a third of the expenditure of poor families.[6] It must therefore be recognised at once that even when calculations refer to one time and one place, there is no unique and unequivocal poverty line, based solely on objective scientific inquiry. Even the estimates for food requirements are bound to be somewhat uncertain and open to debate.

There is a further complication. If a family's income is so low that, however prudently it is spent, it will not suffice for the minimum that has been specified, the family is described by convention as being in 'primary poverty'. If the income is sufficient but is not allocated between different items in the way assumed in composing the minimum budget, whether from ignorance or preference, the family is deemed to be in 'secondary poverty'. A question that must then be posed is whether the aim of policy should be the prevention of primary or of secondary poverty. A realistic view of human behaviour would seem to suggest the latter, but this conclusion could lead to indefinite assistance in the form of transfers that would be 'misspent' by the standards decreed by the investigators. Clearly, the term 'misspent' is question-begging. If some families prefer to spend their incomes in ways of which the social investigators disapprove, should they not have the freedom to do so? Is paternalism not creeping in through the back door? Lack of information is, however, a different matter. If the poverty line is drawn strictly, the avoidance of malnutrition, to take the obvious and perhaps most important example, may call for the application of scientific skill to a degree that cannot reasonably be anticipated from most poor families – or, indeed, rich ones. A certain margin for so-called secondary poverty would seem to be appropriate, although the additional allowance thus made is bound to be somewhat arbitrary.

'Absolute' poverty standards of the kind just described have fallen out of favour in Britain over the past quarter of a century or so, for it has become generally accepted that no assessment of what corresponds to poverty can be made without taking account of the general contemporary standard of living in the particular country and in the particular period under consideration. It is true that at very low levels of income the meaning of poverty is clear and sharp. There is nothing ambiguous and equivocal about the poverty manifested by dead bodies in the streets of Calcutta. In the face of such want, any analysis of the meaning of poverty must appear to be mere academic trifling. The fact remains, however, that there are degrees of poverty above the level of total destitution even in the less developed world; and in the developed world as 'poverty' becomes less savage, its definition becomes more elusive. For example, the dole in Britain in the early 1930s provided a miserable standard of living by the standards of the 1980s, but it was not ungenerous by comparison with average wages in earlier generations. Or, to take another example, Beveridge's poverty level of 1942 would seem to imply quite intolerable hardship, if it were to be adopted in the 1980s.

RELATIVE POVERTY

The relativity of what is regarded as poverty has long been recognised. Thus the point was made by a number of eighteenth-century writers, notably Adam Smith himself, who observed in a famous passage: 'By necessaries I understand, not only commodities which are indispensably necessary for the support of life, but whatever the custom of the country renders it indecent for creditable people, even of the lowest order, to be without.'[7] He illustrates the point by reference to conditions at different times and in different places. Leather shoes were one example. These had become a necessary of life in England, and in Scotland 'custom has rendered them a necessary of life to the lowest order of men.' Contemporary custom was, however, discriminatory, for he adds that the same order of women 'may, without any discredit, walk about barefoot'.

There can be no doubt that the poverty level must rise from time to time in a society in which average income is rising. Rowntree himself adopted a more generous standard for the 1930s than he had done for the 1890s, and he was more generous still in his estimate for the 1950s. These changes were made only after lengthy intervals, however. As we have seen in Chapter 1, Beveridge's recommended social insurance benefits were based on his estimate of the poverty line, which owed much to Rowntree's earlier work but was not identical to it.[8] It may be that he would have been prepared to raise this minimum after the passage of some time in an economy in which the average income of the employed was rising substantially, but, like many other social scientists of that period, he did not pay much attention to economic growth and its implications. Thus his attention was focused on the prevention of absolute poverty, as he had assessed it. This conclusion emerges clearly enough from his Report, in particular in the passage where he urges that 'want' (as judged by his poverty line) could have been abolished even before the Second World War by redistribution, even if the redistribution required had been provided only by members of the working class – although he did not, of course, recommend that other classes should not contribute.[9] 'Want' was undoubtedly given a static meaning in passages such as this.

Supplementary Benefit (SB) is commonly regarded as the official poverty level in Britain. On this basis the poverty level in 1980 was about twice what it had been in 1948 for those on short-term benefit and about two and a half times for those on long-term benefit. Thus what was regarded as an acceptable minimum by the postwar Labour Government had been greatly exceeded. Herein lies a substantial part of the explanation for the apparent failure of the welfare state to eliminate or even markedly to reduce the proportion of families with incomes below their respective poverty levels. The minima deemed to be needed – varying with size of family, type of benefit and certain other circumstances – had themselves greatly increased in real terms. In fact, these minima had risen over the trend roughly in line with the rise in gross average earnings and had gone up more than net average earnings after tax.

It has been recognised above that in setting any absolute poverty standard, even for a particular time in a particular country, some broad exercise of judgement is required. It is not to be supposed that such an exercise can be avoided by turning to a relative poverty standard. When, for example, the International Labour Office recommended in 1952 the adoption of a convention to the effect that the minimum income should be set at about two-fifths of the average,[10] it was choosing a ratio that was extremely arbitrary. Why not one third? Or one half? No wholly objective answer can be given to such questions. This is not to say that the choice is entirely arbitrary or to deny that, by careful inquiry and consideration, the range within which an appropriate choice may be deemed to lie could be narrowed. Suppose the initial assumption were that the minimum should be as generous as possible. It would still be necessary to consider whether those who would bear the cost in taxation would accept this burden or would try to restore their earnings after tax by pushing up their earnings before tax, thus adding to inflationary pressure. Even if the burden were made to rest on their shoulders, would this weaken incentives and harm production? And so on. These are exceedingly difficult empirical questions to answer and, side by side, there are questions of a different kind relating to equity between contributors and beneficiaries. The range of choice may be reduced, but an exercise of judgement is still ultimately required.

When the relationship between the chosen minima and average or median earnings has been determined, should this ratio be kept fixed thereafter, over an extended period, when real earnings are rising? If the ratio is to be held steady, it follows that the growing affluence of a country will do nothing to reduce poverty unless there is also a change in the distribution of income. An index of poverty, expressed in strictly relative terms, is really an index of inequality with particular reference to the share of the lower-income groups. It need scarcely be said that changes in this share deserve continuing scrutiny. It is more doubtful whether it is right to identify changes in poverty solely with changes in distribution so that the former cannot change unless there is change in the latter, no matter how much the standard of living of all income groups, both high and low, may have gone up. To do so would seem to depart somewhat from common usage.

Although it is undeniable that poverty levels must vary with time and place, it does not follow that a level, once chosen, will be meaningless unless it is promptly changed whenever earnings change. On the contrary, it is illuminating to apply a standard that is held fixed in real terms for, say, ten or twenty years, in order to see how the numbers in poverty by such a measure have altered. Let us refer to this as a *static* poverty level. In the USA an official yardstick of this kind has been available since 1962. (It is only a yardstick, not something that is used for operational purposes, and it differs therefore in this respect from the SB level.) It can thus be seen – to take an example – that the proportion of elderly people in poverty dropped from 30 per cent in 1969 to 6 per cent in 1979, after taking into account transfers in cash and benefits in kind, including Medicare and Medicaid. An interesting calculation for the UK was made by Fiegehan, Lansley and Smith,[11] which showed how large a difference can be made by keeping the poverty level hypothetically fixed for even a few years. Thus in 1971 4.9 per cent of family units were believed to have had incomes below the SB scale rate *plus* 30 per cent for average housing costs. But the proportion dropped abruptly to 0.5 per cent if the 1953/4 poverty level were applied. That is to say, when the bench-mark is held unchanged for rather less than twenty years, the proportion of families in poverty, measured by this constant scale, was reduced by nearly nine-tenths. It would, of course, be a great error to attribute this improvement simply to the welfare state. To a substantial extent it reflected the growth in national prosperity. Nevertheless, social transfers were also making their contribution. When the relativist approach to poverty is relaxed even to this extent, the verdict on the combined effects of growth and welfare benefits is seen to be a lot less bleak. We believe that, as a way of reducing widespread misunderstanding about the persistence of poverty, successive governments ought in the past to have included in their regular statistics calculations along the lines of that made by Fiegehen, Lansley and Smith. For the future, admittedly, the position will be affected by the changes in indexation mentioned on p. 56 above and more fully discussed in Chapter 5. For there is no longer any provision for raising benefits in line with earnings, and as long as this remains the case, we shall in effect have a static poverty level. This will not, of course, become an issue of any importance as long as output per head is stagnant or falling but would become one if growth were to be resumed.

The inclination to insist that poverty is a relative phenomenon was itself the product of a prolonged period of fairly steady economic growth. That this emphasis was carried further than was sensible by some commentators is scarcely open to doubt. Those who were more sophisticated preferred to leave some place for a static standard. To quote from an OECD report of 1976:

> Of course, the acceptance of a relative concept of poverty for practical policy does not mean that poverty is entirely a relative matter. For example, it would hardly be said that poverty had been reduced if all incomes were cut, but with larger proportional cuts being imposed on the richer members of society. Similarly, if all countries in the world were to achieve equal proportional growth rates over the next decade, leaving the relative positions of the poor and the rich unaffected, it would hardly be claimed that the former were just as poor at the end as they had been at the beginning.[12]

In short, we are to use two indices. The poverty standard is to rise with rising real earnings, but a minimum standard of living – with its static connotation – cannot be ignored when real average earnings are falling.

It is important to recognise that the emphasis on poverty as a relative concept was a feature of the period of well sustained economic growth. In the early 1980s the pace of growth has slowed down in some countries and has been halted in others; in others output is falling. It is one thing to insist upon having a relative minimum standard of living when the average income of those at work is rising in real terms; it is a different matter when bad times come and real earnings begin to fall. Consistency would then require that those commentators who were so resolutely committed to relativity in the past should now accept a decline in the real poverty level and in the real benefits related to it. Understandably, there has been little inclination to admit the force of this unpleasant logic, but rather a tendency to assert that any cut in real benefits would increase 'poverty' – although this may mean going back only to the standard accepted as adequate on a relativist basis a few years ago. It might have been wiser to have been less insistent on relativity in the past and thus to be able, without inconsistency, to maintain in a more direct way that those in the lower-income groups should be protected against cyclical recessions – with the value judgement clearly acknowledged. In short, the idea of a ratchet, which conceded something to the notion of a static poverty level, would have been more prudent. Although opponents of the 'poverty lobby' could still object that this would be unfair when real wages were falling the controversy would at least be less confused. We must, of course, be careful, not to over-dramatise the fall in real earnings that has occurred or is likely to occur. In Britain real earnings, even after deduction of direct taxation, rose by 15 per cent between 1978 and 1980 – a rise that was not well timed in view of the state of the economy. Any prospective fall in the immediate future can be expected to offset only part of this increase. It can also be fairly pointed out that, as a consequence of the change in the method of indexation, real short-term benefits fell behind on a strictly relativist basis (see p. 56). There are other countries, however, of which Sweden is an example, where benefits replace a very high proportion of earnings, and the fall in real earnings caused largely by the rise in energy prices has been substantial. It is scarcely surprising, therefore, that the level of real benefits is being viewed with a critical eye.

Enough has been said in this chapter to indicate the ambiguity of the word 'poverty' and the need for greater care in its use. To many people 'poverty' suggests hunger and homelessness, rags and squalor. In short, the word continues to evoke the emotional response associated with absolute poverty, indeed with bleak and heartrending destitution. Relative poverty is a different matter in affluent societies. For example, SB takes into account such extras as a TV licence, whereas the old Rowntree standard made no provision for luxury items, even if these luxuries had become conventional necessaries. Such an increase in the minima may be regarded as quite appropriate (and, indeed, highly desirable) in increasingly affluent societies. That is not the point at issue. What is misleading is to use the term 'poverty' in different senses without drawing attention to the differences. It is quite wrong to interpret poverty in a strictly relativist sense in one's statistics but to use it in a sense that suggests absolute destitution in one's rhetoric. If the concept that is being used is relative poverty – relative not just to a particular generation in a particular country but to current annual earnings – then the word 'relative' ought always to be inserted before 'poverty level'.

In some of the literature the extreme relativist approach has been carried very far indeed. This has been particularly apparent in the work of Townsend, notably in his *Poverty in the United Kingdom.*[13] His objective was to adopt a measurement of poverty which would endeavour to define the style of living which is generally shared or approved in each society and to find whether 'there is a point in the scale below which, as resources diminish, families find it particularly difficult to share in the customs, activities and diets comprising their society's style of living'. To this end he constructed a deprivation index. A person was said to be 'deprived' (Townsend's weights are attached): (1) if he had not had a holiday away from home in the last twelve months (53); (2) if he had not had a relative or friend at home for a meal in the last four weeks – adults only (33·4); (3) if he had not been out to a relative or friend for a meal or snack in the last four weeks – adults only (45·1);(4) if he had not had a friend to play or to tea in the last four weeks – children only (36·3); (5) if he had not had a party on his last birthday – children only (56·6); (6) if he had not had an afternoon or evening out for entertainment in the last two weeks (47·0); (7) if he did not have fresh meat on as many as four days a week (19·3); (8) if he had gone through one or more days in the past fortnight without a cooked meal (7·0); (9) if he did not have a cooked breakfast most days of the week (67·3); (10) if he lived in a household without a refrigerator (45·1); (11) if he did not usually have a Sunday joint (25·9); (12) if he lived in a household without sole use of a flush WC, a washbasin, bath or shower, a gas or electric cooker (21·4).

It must be emphasised that these items have not been listed simply in order to assess the money income needed to achieve a minimum. Townsend was sceptical of the use of monetary measures. He was postulating a pattern of consumption which he deemed necessary as the minimum and attached what he regarded as the appropriate weights to each item. These weights may seem to reflect a rather individual choice. For example, a cooked breakfast is held to be more important than sanitation. But, apart from these odd features of his list, the act of constructing it carries paternalism far beyond what is implied in the provision of, say, a national health service. As that distinguished socialist Bernard Shaw once said in his *Maxims for Revolutionists*: 'Do not do unto others as you would they should do unto you. Their tastes may not be the same.' In a devastating criticism of this approach, Piachaud concluded: 'There can be no doubt that Townsend's provisional deprivation index is of no practical value whatsoever as an index of deprivation.'[14]

It is possible, of course, to eliminate the paternalist element and to construct an index for what might be regarded as a tolerable minimum which would reflect the growing affluence of a society. This, after all, is what has been done *implicitly* by expressing the minimum as some fraction of median earnings after tax. If affluence were to increase steadily once more, this minimum would include more and more items that are now regarded as luxuries: video recorders, holidays on the Mediterranean, a new car every three years and so on. Only a curmudgeon would want to deny any group in the population its share in the fruits of affluence. Moreover, there are good grounds – admittedly, including a value judgement – for wishing to see the relative share of the lower-income groups increased. But it is doubtful wisdom to include too many luxury items in the minimum standard of living below which people are held to be 'poor.' For there is a grave danger that, in doing so, the anti-poverty campaign may lay itself open to ridicule. There is enough real hardship even in the developed countries and enough opposition to remedial measures for one to prefer the anti-poverty campaign to be conducted on a more sensible and more realistic basis.

It may therefore be helpful to introduce another possible index, which might be described as a *quasi-relative* index of poverty. This index would not remain unchanged for a number of years, as does the *static* poverty index. It would rise with rising earnings in a growing economy but not fully in proportion to the rise in real earnings. Continuous adjustments would therefore be made which would reflect growing prosperity and changing social habits but, because these changes would be at a reduced rate, the index would do less violence to what people normally understand by poverty. For it may be counter-productive in the long run to depreciate the linguistic currency by describing as poor those who may, by the standards of a few years ago, be reasonably well off. There would be more cause for grave concern if poverty were increasing or barely diminishing when measured by a *static* index or even by a *quasi-relative* index. An index of this latter kind would certainly help in assessing the effects of both growth and the welfare services. This index would be another bench-mark. another way of measuring progress. It is indeed abundantly clear that some additional bench-marks need to be employed. As we have seen, the fashion of concentrating attention almost exclusively on relative poverty, which leads to measures of inequality being used as measures of changes in poverty,[15] has caused much confusion and misunderstanding, especially perhaps in Britain. Some effort is now required in order to regain a sense of perspective in assessing past achievements and failures. Moreover, it is of some importance to observe that the preoccupation with relative poverty and the neglect of changes in the standard of living of the lower-income groups was essentially a feature of the period of high employment and well sustained growth. With continuing growth taken implicitly for granted, the benefits it brought could be scornfully denigrated and attention diverted to other things. With growth now arrested and with real national income even reduced in some countries, it may be realised that the standard of living of the poor, not just their relative position, is after all a matter of interest and importance!

So far we have been discussing the case for employing additional indicators simply as bench-marks. It would be an entirely different matter to use one or other of them operationally in order to determine the minimum level of benefits. Thus, it might be decided that the quasi-relative poverty index should be used in adjusting the SB rate so that the latter rose with average real earnings but less than proportionately. It could be held that in this way the sense of personal responsibility among those at work would be fostered and there would be more self-help on the part of those capable of helping themselves. Persons who felt themselves to be hard up when out of work or elderly would no longer be encouraged to regard themselves as the helpless and passive victims of 'deprivation'. And so on. The language might be that of Beveridge or indeed of Beatrice Webb. Thus we return to fundamental objectives and to fundamental disagreements about policy. We may, however, add a final reflection. This is that the scope for exercising self-help depends, by no means entirely but significantly, on the level of unemployment. Perhaps some future historian of our times will feel obliged to record that rather little stress was laid upon self-help and self-respect by policy-makers and academic commentators during the years of prosperity, but that the emphasis began to change at the very time that recession and shortage of jobs had made it increasingly difficult for many people to make adequate provision for their own future needs.

POVERTY AND MEANS TESTS

A. B. Atkinson has observed: 'In Britain nearly all postwar investigations of the extent of poverty have taken as their definition the scale of eligibility for the means-tested social security scheme of Supplementary Benefits (formerly National Assistance).'[16] This has indeed been the practice adopted, but it has been adopted in two different ways.

First, the SB level – or, rather, levels corresponding to specified differences in circumstances – has been used as the bench-mark for determining poverty in the way described in Chapter 3. It has been generally recognised that this bench-mark is somewhat arbitrary, but its choice has been justified because this is the official minimum. Sometimes, it is true, an unnecessary suggestion of mysticism has been introduced by saying that this is the minimum which 'society' regards as appropriate. We have already protested in Chapter 2 about this use of the term 'society' and need not repeat what was said there. It is enough to observe that the SB level has at least the merit of being official.

The next step is, then, to assess the number of families and the corresponding number of individuals whose incomes fall below the appropriate SB levels before the receipt of any benefits and after the receipt of *all* benefits, including SB. According to the calculations made by Beckerman,[17] 30·6 per cent of families in Britain would have been in poverty in 1975 if no benefits had been received and 22·7 per cent of individuals. As he concedes, a calculation of this kind does not allow for the indirect effect on pre-benefit incomes of the fact that people knew that benefits were to be provided and were contributing to their finance on a compulsory basis. He points out: 'In particular nearly 60 per cent of the individuals below the poverty line before transfers are pensioners and it is likely that in the absence of a national insurance pension many of them would have made some private provision for their old age.'[18] The pre-benefit figure must therefore be viewed with some reserve (see p. 183 below). His post-benefit figures show that 4.4 per cent of families were in poverty after receipt of benefits and 3·3 per cent of individuals. Fiegehen, Lansley and Smith also make a detailed assessment of the number in poverty after all benefits have been received.[19]

It may be asked why there should be any such residual families or individuals left in poverty. The explanation lies partly in the fact that the working poor were not entitled to claim SB, and that the other benefits available to them and actually claimed were not sufficient to rescue them from poverty. Another important explanation is that SB was not always claimed by those entitled to it – a problem to which we shall return below. It also appears to be the case that some of those who were claiming SB were not receiving all that they were entitled to. Fiegehen, Lansley and Smith have drawn attention to this somewhat puzzling fact (1977, p. 35).[20] To some small extent, the explanation in the past was the imposition of the wages stop, which meant that no one of working age was entitled to receive more in benefit than he or she had previously been earning. This wages stop has now been abolished. These authors believe, however, that the inclusion of this last group among those below the poverty line is due to changes in family circumstances since the last calculation of their entitlement or to misreporting of income or an inappropriate calculation of needs.'[21] It is also the case that some persons on SB had resources above their respective SB rates because some income and capital is disregarded in assessing needs (see p. 65 above). There are therefore statistical difficulties in making a calculation of this kind, but the approach appears to be the right one. That is to say, all benefits should be taken into account when attempting to assess the number left in poverty.

The second approach is rather different. It is to assess the number of the non-working poor as those who appear to be *eligible* for SB, including in their number *both* those who fail to receive this benefit *and* those who do. In *Social Trends* a table was published year by year which gave estimates of 'families and persons normally with low net resources', and these resources excluded receipts of SB. It is true that these estimates were not officially described as estimates of the number in poverty, but they were sometimes so regarded. For example, by this measure, 5 million families and over 8 million individuals appeared to be in poverty in 1975. This was a strange assessment, for the number in poverty according to this method of counting the poor comprises those with incomes below the SB bench-mark *after* the receipt of national insurance and other benefits but *before* the receipt of SB. What is really being measured, then, is the extent to which selectivity by means tests is being used in the structure of benefits rather than the residual number in poverty after all benefits have been received. Superficially this approach would appear to lend strong support to the plea for a reform that has been called 'Back to Beveridge'[22] or a 'New Beveridge'. For Beveridge, as we have observed above, wanted to have the non-means-tested benefits set at the poverty level so that the need to use means tests would be restricted to a limited number of special cases. If, then, by definition those receiving means-tested benefits were included in the number of the poor, the substitution of non-means-tested benefits would, *by definition*, reduce the number in poverty. Apart from this semantic play, there are, however, good and familiar reasons for regarding means tests with disfavour. First there is the problem created by the fact that some people may fail, for one reason or another, to claim the benefits to which they are entitled, when to do so involves a test of means. Secondly, means tests can be regarded as corrosive of self-respect and dignity. A real case can therefore be advanced for a 'New Beveridge', although it remains to be seen whether this case is strong enough to be conclusive. The first step, however, is to see why a departure from Beveridge occurred in the first place. Such an investigation is worth while not only for reasons of historical interest but also because, by looking back at the record of events, one can appreciate more fully the complexity of the problem and thus be better able to assess the case for a 'New Beveridge' today.

THE DEPARTURE FROM BEVERIDGE

Cedric Sandford was reporting a widely accepted view when he wrote: 'The explanation of the large and growing numbers of supplementary benefit claimants is very largely that the benefits under the national insurance scheme were never set at the levels that Sir William [Beveridge] had envisaged.'[23] This statement might be taken to mean that even after nearly four decades the standard of living provided by the national insurance benefits remains lower than the one that Beveridge recommended. Any such inference would be absurd, of course, for all these benefits, both national insurance and SB have doubled or more than doubled in real terms since 1948. Even if this error is avoided, however, and attention is concentrated on the *relationship* between national insurance benefits and SB, the true record differs from the one that came to be widely accepted. The postwar Labour Government fixed the means-tested national assistance cash rates at Beveridge's recommended figures in nominal money terms and fixed the national insurance rates at slightly higher figures. But the rise in prices between 1938 and 1948 was well in excess of what Beveridge had assumed in making his calculations, with the result that all the benefits were below the real level which he had estimated to be necessary to provide families of different sizes with subsistence incomes. This deficiency was to be made good only gradually in reviews carried out initially at somewhat irregular intervals. For some rather obscure reason, small differences were allowed to persist until 1980 between the national insurance benefit and the means-tested cash benefit. There could be no real case for such untidy divergences. No additional net cost was involved in removing them. Why, then, would it cost so much to raise the national insurance benefit to the minima set by supplementary benefit – that is to say, to the poverty level – as the 'New Beveridge' proposals require? The answer lies in the treatment of housing costs and, to a much lesser extent, in the provision of some other means-tested benefits for special purposes (heating, renewal of furniture and so on).

Beveridge had come down, after a detailed discussion of the matter, in favour of the view that cash benefits should be expected to cover housing costs. He was well aware, however, of the difficulties caused by differences in the cost of housing incurred by different families and drew attention to the problem of determining whether rents above the average reflected a preference for better houses or the imperfections of the housing market. The Labour Government, for its part, decided to treat housing costs as an additional claim that could be met subject to means tests. In this respect the arrangements adopted were more generous than those recommended by Beveridge.

It is this special treatment of housing costs that explains why the national insurance benefits, although now well above what Beveridge had recommended, are still below the current poverty level. These national insurance benefits are not meant to cover the housing costs of poor families. There is additional selective assistance for that purpose. It follows, then, that a large number of families will continue to be classified as poor when the poverty level is *defined* as cash benefit plus housing costs. This addition for housing costs adds substantially to the benefits.

With actual housing costs being met, it follows that there is no single poverty level for a family of any given size, but rather an indefinite number of levels which reflect the dispersion of housing costs around the average. This fact presents the proponents of the 'New Beveridge' with difficulties, which they have not indeed ignored but have failed to solve satisfactorily. What was suggested in the Meade Report was that insurance benefits should be raised by something like average housing costs,[24] but this would reduce by only about a half the number deemed to be in poverty. If, however, the insurance benefits were to be raised to cover the highest housing costs now met by means test, so that no one lost as a consequence of the change, the outlay required would be much larger, and the effect would also be to raise the vast majority of those receiving insurance benefits above the stipulated poverty level. A more radical approach would be to press ahead with the reform of the housing market in order to reduce differences in the cost of housing at any given standard of provision, and then to leave it to the recipients of benefits to allocate their money between housing and other things according to their preferences. To do so could also be described quite fairly as 'Back to Beveridge' – back to a different part of his recommendations!

These are difficult issues, and value judgements are involved, of course. It is abundantly clear, however, that on closer inspection the 'New Beveridge' would be a far more complex and dubious affair than might be supposed at first glance.

THE CASE FOR AND THE CASE AGAINST MEANS TESTS

That there is indeed a case against means-tested assistance must be conceded at once. In the past there was strong resentment at the inquisition entailed by the application of means tests, especially in response to the sometimes harsh procedures followed between the wars. An investigation carried out by Runciman[25] suggested, however, that this resentment was less general in the early 1960s among the actual recipients than some academic commentators might have been inclined to suppose. It is not, of course, to be inferred that the feeling of stigmatisation has been dispelled; its persistence even if less marked, together with the complexity of the arrangements, may have prevented a substantial number of people from claiming benefits to which they are entitled. Even if a sense of stigma did not have this effect, means-tested benefits could still be condemned on the ground that they undermine self-respect and self-reliance. This last point was one on which Beveridge laid much stress. It is a deontological point that would still deserve to be taken into account even if there were no objections to means tests of a more utilitarian kind, such as the high administrative costs involved. Means-tested assistance is certainly costly to administer. Administrative expenditure accounts for 12 per cent of S B expenditure as compared with only 4 per cent of the cost of national insurance outlays.

Estimates of the take-up of means-tested assistance were given in the annual reports of the Supplementary Benefits Commission, and in 1978 the latter body also published a special paper on the subject: *Take-up of Supplementary Benefits*. It would appear from these investigations that in 1977 about a quarter of the 4 million families believed to be entitled to benefit failed to claim their due and thus remained 'in poverty'. The sums believed to be unclaimed were substantial (see Table 4.1).

Table 4.1 *Estimates of take-up of supplementary benefit for 1977*

Group	*Total likely to be entitled (000)*	*Proportion receiving benefit (%)*	*Number eligible but not receiving benefit (000)*	*Estimated benefit unclaimed (£ million)*	*Average weekly amount of unclaimed benefit (£)*
Pensioners	2,280	73	610	100	3.10
Non-pensioners:	1,760	76	420	245	11.00
Sick	240	87	30	15	8.00
Unemployed	920	81	170	90	10.10
One-parent families	370	89	40	20	10.50
Others	220	19	180	115	12.60
Total for all groups	4,040	74	1,030	340	6.30

The total figure for non-pensioners has been rounded up in the Report in columns one and four, and the components do not, therefore, add to the total figure.

Source: Report of the Supplementary Benefits Commission 1978 (London: HMSO, 1978), Table 12.10.

With money falling rapidly in value, bench-marks are needed. It should therefore be observed that short-term SB, including the average housing allowances, came to £20.74 for a single person at 1977/8 rates and to £30.56 for a couple. Relative to these amounts, the sums believed not to have been taken up were by no means trivial.

These figures for unclaimed benefit are so high as to raise doubts about their reliability, especially in the case of non-pensioner families, of which 1·76 million are represented as failing to claim, on average, £11 a week. Common sense suggests that this is an absurd assertion. The Commission itself issued some warnings. One possible cause of difficulty is that the figures for incomes are derived from the Family Expenditure Survey (FES), and these relate to households rather than families in the SB sense. Thus some of those whose incomes are below the poverty level may be 'part of a household comprising more than one supplementary benefit unit, and sharing at least some consumption with other parts of the household, who may indeed include close relatives'.[26]

For example, children who are not students may be living comfortably at home without claiming. This report also observes: 'The major doubt concerned the availability for work of well over a third of those under pension age with an apparent entitlement, as there can be little doubt that most of them would be required to make themselves available if they claimed benefit.'[27] If the dubious 'others' group were omitted completely, the percentage of non-pensioners receiving benefit would rise from 76 to 84. But this is still a lower figure than might be expected, and the high estimates of unclaimed benefit for other groups remain disturbing. There are, however, further reasons for scepticism about these statistics.

These statistics show the position at a certain point in time and may therefore give a misleading impression. A large number of people become entitled to means-tested assistance every year, and a large number cease to be so. The time dimension is therefore important. It would be a quite unwarranted procedure to suppose that in 1977 the *same* 420,000 non-pensioner families failed to claim £11 a week over, say, fifty-two weeks and thus lost in every case as much as £572 a year! If, however, benefit is unclaimed only for a week or two, the incompleteness of take-up is a matter of small concern and may simply reflect the fact that people do not bother to claim. In referring to this group, the Supplementary Benefits Commission has observed: 'Unlike pensioners, whose situation is fairly static, their circumstances change from day to day and an examination of some recent sample cases where the amount unclaimed seemed particularly high indicated that they had only just become unemployed: they may even have been waiting for it to come through.'[28]

It is certainly not to be inferred from what has been said that incomplete take-up need cause no concern. The estimate of 610,000 pensioners who appear to have foregone £3.10 a week may exaggerate the problem even in their case, but it is scarcely in doubt that a number of old people do not obtain as much as is available to them. It is in this older age group that stigma may still have a strong inhibiting effect. Moreover, some may also be ignorant about their rights or uncertain about how to claim them. In the non-pensioner group the low take-up by single-parent families should also be noted. Unlike the unemployed and the sick, members of this group are less likely – in the nature of the case – to be moving on to and off the register after short intervals. It must be recognised, therefore, that incomplete take-up does present a problem, although it may be a much less serious one than figures such as those in Table 4.1 would lead one to suppose when the qualifications are neglected.

If there is a case against the use of means tests, there is also a strong, if less fashionable, case for selectivity of this kind. The use of means tests allows assistance to be directed to those most in need. By contrast, social insurance benefits go to everyone, irrespective of any unearned income they may receive or any capital they may possess. It is important to stress the case for means-tests because it has been somewhat obscured by the plea that national insurance benefits should be raised to the subsistence level. It is a plea that has a strong humanitarian appeal, but there is a real danger of being trapped by the semantics, for the term 'subsistence level' is in effect being given, at this point, a static rather than a dynamic interpretation. Over the years of economic growth, the scale rates (or cash payments) of SB have moved up closely in line with national insurance benefits, but assistance with housing has kept the poverty level above the insurance benefits. Suppose SB had risen less than national insurance benefits. The number in poverty, as measured by this yardstick, would now be lower, perhaps much lower. Indeed, poverty, in this conventional sense, could have been largely eliminated. But the standard of living of the lower-income groups would be still lower: there would be fewer poor people, but the poor would be poorer.

In effect, this is the kind of adjustment implied by the 'New Beveridge' proposals. National insurance benefits are to be raised to the poverty level at a position where this level happens to be at some point in time. But this is to revert to a static concept of poverty. The same amount of additional public money could be so distributed as partly to raise not only insurance benefits but also the poverty level itself.

An illustration may be helpful. In December 1976 there were 1,850,000 pensioners in 1,592,000 households in receipt of both pensions and SB and another 95,000 elderly people who received SB alone because, for one reason or another, they were not entitled to pensions. The average amount of SB claimed by those who were also pensioners was £5.92 a week, and the total sum over the year was £490 million. Suppose, now, that this £490 million had been added instead to the sum available for pensions. It would then have gone not to 1,850,000 people but to the whole body of pensioners, who amounted to 8,506,000. The households formerly in receipt of SB would then have been worse off, as Table 4.2 shows.

It may be objected that the 'New Beveridge' proposal would not result in a fall in anyone's income because total expenditure would be

Table 4.2 *The effect on poor pensioners of abolishing means tests*

	Number	*Average SB lost*	*Increase in pension*	*Fall in income*
Married couples	258,000	£6.23	£2.2	£4.01
Single	1,334,000	£5.85	£1.11	£4.74

Source: DHSS.

increased. No family would receive less than it was receiving before the change took place. All would be raised to the poverty level without being required to submit to any test of means. In reply it must be pointed out that even with public expenditure increased, more could be done to raise the standard of living of the poor by using means tests.

A quite different objection is that means tests are so destructive of self-respect that it would be better to scrap them or to restrict their use to very special cases, *even if* the poor had a lower standard of living as a consequence of doing so. There may indeed be irreconcilable differences of opinion on this score. It appears to be the case that some politicians and some academic students of the welfare state view all forms of means tests with deep dislike, and this dislike is not related solely to utilitarian considerations. Although much reference is made to the incomplete take-up of benefits, it is hard to believe that, even if take-up were complete and even if the cost of administering means tests were greatly reduced, selectivity would still be viewed with disfavour as undignified and demeaning. This moral viewpoint must be treated with respect. Yet it is not apparent that those who take so strong a line have accepted the consequences of doing so. Are they really prepared to accept a lowering of the standard of living of those receiving selective benefits below what would otherwise be possible because a larger part of any given volume of expediture would go to those who do not really need it in order to be rescued from poverty? We are not aware that this question has been answered.

The proposal to implement a 'New Beveridge' was not taken up in Britain by either of the main parties. That was not surprising perhaps, in view of the additional cost. What must seem strange at first sight, however, is that a new measure of a different kind was, in fact, adopted. This was the graduated pension scheme of 1975. Moreover, one of the main reasons given for adopting this was the desirability of reducing the number of poor elderly people who would otherwise have to rely upon SB. This objective will be achieved in due course, but the method thus chosen for its achievement is more costly, not less costly, than a 'New Beveridge' would have been. For graduated benefits means that a still higher proportion of any given amount of public money will go to those with incomes already above, perhaps well above, the level. It may be objected that the amount of public money that can be raised is not in fact given but will be larger precisely because, with graduated benefits, people will consent to paying graduated contributions which can be made to yield more than flat-rate contributions. It has not, however, been firmly established that graduated contributions would otherwise be impossible. Graduated contributions for flat-rate pensions are a long-established feature of the welfare state in the Netherlands, and the impossibility of attaining their acceptance elsewhere should not be taken for granted. In any case, graduated contributions may be of no help to the poor unless some redistributive mechanism has been built into the graduated scheme, as is the case in the USA. Creedy's detailed study of the British graduated pension has not, however, revealed any such mechanism.[29] What must be recognised is that from a political point of view, the graduated scheme had an immense advantage as compared with a 'New Beveridge'. Graduated contributions began immediately, but the payment of graduated benefits lies far in the future. Ultimately, these commitments will fall due – but *après nous le déluge*! Let us add at once that in our view it would be quite unfair to attribute such deliberate cynicism to the supporters of the scheme – which, it should be observed, has been accepted, at least tacitly, by all the main political parties. The fact remains that this is an improvident scheme.

It will be twenty years before these graduated benefits are paid in full; meanwhile, there will be large numbers of pensioners who have such small earnings-related pensions that they will have to depend upon means-tested assistance. It is to be anticipated, therefore, that a special supplement to the basic pension will be proposed on their behalf. An arrangement of this kind was adopted in the past in Sweden, when the second-tier national graduated pension was still immature, and this example may be cited in Britain. The procedure was broadly as follows. A supplement was provided in addition to the basic flat-rate citizen's pension, and every pensioner could then claim this supplement *less* any income that was already being received from the second-tier graduated scheme. The supplement was, therefore, selective up to a point, but it was not fully means-tested, for no deductions were made for any private income, not even income in the form of occupational pensions. If a similar supplement was ever to be adopted in Britain, it would be possible to make it rather more selective, and therefore cheaper, by also deducting occupational pensions. At the moment, however, there seems no likelihood that a new scheme of this kind will, in fact, be introduced.

A substantial and perhaps increasing number of families will depend upon means-tested assistance for the foreseeable future. It would be helpful if the opponents of selectivity would accept this fact and assist in what is the really relevant undertaking: that of making the provision of means-tested assistance more efficient. The first step should be to simplify the arrangements. The range of means-tested benefits in Britain is very wide, and these benefits involve the application not of one but of some 1,500 different scales for the testing of means.

Assistance with housing is the really important item. Under the confused arrangements which have evolved over the years, with no coherent plan or rational structure, this assistance is available both as a form of SB and as assistance provided by the local authorities. There are many cases in which potential beneficiaries can choose between assistance from one source rather than another, and great skill may be required in order to make the right choice. As though this were not bad enough, the test of means is applied at different levels in different places, and this is confusing. It is also inequitable. As Buchanan put it in a well-known article on 'Federalism and Fiscal Equity', fiscal equity requires 'equal treatment for persons dissimilar in no relevant respect';[30] and the location of a person's residence is not a relevant respect. Fortunately, reform is now imminent.

After prolonged discussion, an important measure of simplification was proposed in an official consultation paper, *Assistance with Housing Costs*. At that time about 2 million households were being assisted through SB and another 3 million or so were getting rent rebates, rates rebates and other allowances from the local authorities, subject to a wide variety of conditions. This diversity is partly the consequence of the devolution of authority to local government, but the price has been high in terms of confusion and administrative cost. The Supplementary Benefits Commission had repeatedly recommended that the scheme should be rationalised,[31] and this is what was officially proposed in the consultation paper. A new housing benefit would be introduced, which would include both rent and rates. It would be administered by the local authorities, which would, however, apply a standardised means test with standardised rules for tapering off the benefit to those with rather higher cash incomes. Thus this benefit would no longer be provided at all through supplementary benefit. Any tenant who was fully dependent on SB for cash income would simply pay no rent or rates if he was a local authority tenant. Tenants in private accommodation would be given cash allowances by the local authority. The administration would thus be greatly simplified and a saving achieved in this respect. Moreover, it would not be necessary to apply for SB for assistance with housing costs. This would come from the local housing office, which might convey less sense of stigma and should also reduce the risk that full potential benefit might not be claimed through ignorance – as may happen today, with the jungle of intertwined regulations. The local authorities would then be reimbursed from the central government. The substance of these proposals was contained in a new Bill introduced by the Conservative Government in November 1981. It is only to be expected, of course, that views will differ about the scale on which assistance is provided; but there can be no serious doubt that the machinery for its provision would be greatly improved by a reform of this kind.

Even with this simplification, assistance with housing would be far from simple. The actual rent and rates of every claimant would still be met – unless they were absurdly high – an ill-conceived arrangement which would seem to rest on the assumption that practically no one can ever move from one house to another. It is of interest to note that in Sweden individual housing costs are not met. The procedure in dealing with a pensioner – whose means-tested housing allowance is built into the pension itself – is to allocate a sum corresponding to average housing costs in the locality where the pensioner lives. This average rent is then compared with his income from all sources, and he will receive all or part of his rent according to this test of means. In the case of families, there are specified bands for rent. The beneficiaries may, in the event, spend more on housing than their allowances, or they may spend less. In this respect the Swedish arrangements are less paternalistic than the British.

As a first step towards reform, regional or local averages might replace individual housing costs; or it might be better to proceed boldly to a national average, possibly with some temporary supplementation for those living in London. The next step would be to follow the course recommended by Beveridge himself, including an allowance for housing costs in the supplementary benefit cash payments, which would be raised by the appropriate average amount.

Some beneficiaries might in the event spend more on housing and some less. That degree of freedom of choice could be left to them, as it is in Sweden. It may be objected that the housing market is so imperfect – with such wide differences in rents for similar housing, with waiting lists here and surpluses there – that assistance should be offered on an individual basis, hand-tailored to match every family's own peculiar needs. If it must be accepted that the housing market is in so unsatisfactory a condition almost four decades after the end of the war, that in itself is a condemnation of the maze of controls, subsidies and tax concessions. There is no escape from the fact that there is an urgent need to reform this market by freeing its operation in order to allow it to work more effectively. This reform could, of course, leave room for selective temporary assistance to poor families with particularly high housing costs in order to allow time for the market to adjust such disparities.

The condition of the housing market has unfortunate implications for other proposals designed to provide protection against poverty. As we observed above, this complication seriously affected the coherence of the recommendations put forward in the Meade Report, for the recommendation in that report that non-selective benefits should be raised to the poverty level, as set by SB, encountered the formidable complication that there is no single poverty level appropriate to families of a given size. There is, rather, a vast multiplicity of poverty levels under the SB arrangements, with cash benefits supplemented by the particular housing costs actually incurred by every family, as we have noted. As long as this state of affairs persists, a limit is set to what can be achieved by any attempt to abolish selectivity or – more realistically – to streamline its operation. If this is true of the 'New Beveridge' proposals, it is also true of the recommendation that a negative income tax should be adopted.

It should be observed that a great deal of progress has been made in reducing housing subsidies, and this has been reflected in an increase in the housing allowance component of Supplementary Benefit. This allowance (which includes local authority rates) has gone up from 25·3 per cent of the total benefit available to a married couple in November 1976 to 27·7 per cent in November 1981. For a single person the corresponding figures are 30·8 per cent and 37·7 per cent. With these increases continuing, SB (including housing costs) can be expected to reach an all-time high in real terms in 1982. To this extent the effect of cutting subsidies has been to transfer the cost in public money from one account to another. That is only what was to be expected as part of the process of change to a less restricted and subsidised housing market.

It should also be observed that the indirect cost of subsidising owner-occupiers through tax allowances is very large – the equivalent of about 5p on the income tax. If direct subsidies are to be reduced so, in fairness, should indirect ones. Or a tax should be imposed on the annual value of a house, as used to be done. Unfortunately, this is an issue that governments of different complexions may not wish to face, for a large proportion of floating voters are owner-occupiers. The value of the maximum tax allowance has, however, been reduced by not raising the total sum (£25,000) against which tax relief can be claimed on mortgage interest. The real value of this allowance was reduced in this way by about two thirds between 1974 and 1981. Thus a partial adjustment is being made gradually, its pace depending upon the rate of inflation. This is not the way in which changes should be made, as we have stressed elsewhere, but it may at least be better than no change at all.

There is a final point of some importance to be made in concluding this section. Whatever changes in the administration of means-tested benefits may be devised, it is important that their administration should be such as to heal the old scars of stigma. There is a real danger, however, that these scars could be reopened by an unduly rigorous attempt to prevent abuses on the part of those who claim benefits. No one can seriously deny that such abuses take place. Some of those who are receiving SB – or, indeed, unemployment insurance benefit – are undoubtedly working on the sly. It is right that an attempt should be made to prevent abuses of this kind lest the whole system fall into disrepute. It is also desirable, however, to ensure that the investigations are carried out without unduly severe inquisitions in which the onus of proof is placed too firmly on the shoulders of the recipients by over-zealous investigators. This is so on general grounds. It is also so because in the case of means-tested benefits the effect could be to strengthen the feeling of distaste with which quite genuine applicants may regard the investigation of their means and may add to the difficulty of improving the take-up of benefits even by those fully entitled to receive them.

Once more Swedish experience is relevant. Means tests are quite widely used in Sweden but do not appear to convey any sense of stigma. As was recorded in Chapter 3, means-tested assistance with housing is built into the pension and a *higher* proportion of pensioners receive means-tested assistance in Sweden than in the UK. There are also a variety of means-tested benefits for housing and for other purposes which are provided to those below pension age, but these are not described as benefits for 'poor' families. Other countries such as Britain and the USA have something to learn from the way in which means tests are administered in Sweden.

WELFARE BENEFITS AND INCENTIVES

Selective benefits given subject to means tests are open to criticism on the ground that such benefits weaken the incentives to get work, to do well at work and to change jobs in search of better prospects. It is necessary to add at once that any cash transfer, even if there is no means test, can have this effect. (This is so on the assumption, in economist's jargon, that neither leisure nor a higher standard of living is an 'inferior' good.) It must be recalled, of course, that selection is still imposed even if it relates not to family means but to continuing membership of some category – the unemployed, the sick, the retired. Selection by means tests is likely, however, to be rather more harmful to incentives, other things being equal. How much incentives will be affected in either case will depend partly upon the ratio of benefits to earnings, partly upon the tax structure and partly upon the various conditions determining the right to benefits. It will also reflect less quantifiable factors such as the satisfaction that people take in their work and the manner in which they respond to the uncertainties of the future.

Consider the possible effects on incentives to work of the FIS, the means-tested benefit for low-income families with children described in Chapter 3. These supplements range from tiny sums to about a fifth of gross average earnings, depending on the amount of gross income from work and the number of children in the family. It should also be observed that entitlement to FIS is a passport to such other means-tested benefits as rent and rate rebates, school meals and prescription charges. The loss of FIS together with these other benefits, and the increasing liability to direct taxation, implies a severe net penalty at the margin as income rises – the poverty trap. It is possible for a family receiving an extra £1 per week in earnings to lose *more* than that amount.

Take, for example, the case of a man with a non-employed wife and two young children aged 4 and 6 living in a council house for which he is paying average rent and rates. In his case, if he had received earnings in April 1980 between £42 and £59 per week (roughly between a third and a half of average male manual earnings), there would have been a net loss from each extra £1 of earnings. The net gain from the extra £1 would have been less than 50p until earnings rose above £86 per week. The progression is not, of course, in a straight line, as entitlement to various means-tested benefits ceases or falls at different points in the earnings scale. The number of families that are very severely affected by the poverty trap is fortunately very small, although the problem can certainly not be dismissed out of hand. A DHSS analysis based on data from the Family Expenditure Survey[32] estimated that about 50,000 families with children at the end of 1977 might in theory have been liable to derive no increase in net incomes from a £1 rise in earnings. In practice, the number would have been very much lower; entitlement to FIS and the associated benefits are awarded for fifty-two weeks at a time, so the effects of a change in earnings are unlikely to be felt immediately. There were, in any case, only some 100,000 families in total receiving FIS in early 1981, out of some 6 million families with dependent children and a family head in full-time employment. That the number is so small is partly a reflection of the low take-up rate of FIS. Estimates made by the Family Finances Survey[33] put this as low as 50 per cent, contrary to earlier figures of around 75 per cent based on the Family Expenditure Survey. Even with full take-up, however, the number would not be large – only some 1·7 per cent of all families.

Other countries also experience problems with selective benefits, differing, naturally, with the characteristics of the benefit structure. In some states in the USA, for example, means-tested aid to families with dependent children, together with food stamps and help with medical costs, may give a woman with several children a higher net income than the minimum wage for full-time work.[34]

Attention is more often directed to the possible effects on employment of *unemployment pay*. It is frequently asserted, with a greater display of confidence than of evidence, that people are 'better off on the dole'. On a more serious plane of discussion it has been suggested that the rise in unemployment in Britain in 1966 was to be largely explained by the introduction of the earnings-related supplement to unemployment benefit. As unemployment rose subsequently in the late 1970s and 1980s to heights unprecedented in the postwar period, no such explanation could be offered, for benefits were not then increased but were falling a little in real terms.

What effect would unemployment and other benefits be likely to have on the behaviour of recipients on the assumption that a job was available at average earnings or some specified fraction of average earnings? Standard unemployment benefit in 1980 was equivalent to only some 15 per cent of *all* average male earnings for a single person and 24 per cent in the case of a married man (see Table 3.3, p. 48). It is true that some modification of these figures is called for. First, the more relevant comparison is usually with *manual* earnings, for unemployment is higher among the less skilled sectors of the workforce. Secondly, unemployed persons can normally expect to earn well below average manual earnings, as Department of Employment inquiries have shown. Thirdly, it is more informative to compare benefits with *net* earnings rather than with gross. Making these adjustments, the replacement ratios are raised to 26 and 39 per cent of net manual earnings for an average single and a married manual worker respectively, and rise further to 37 and 56 per cent when compared with, say, two-thirds average earnings. Fourthly, the presence of children has an important effect; the replacement rates at two-thirds average earnings rise very substantially to 72 per cent when there are two children and to 83 per cent when there are four. The very high replacement ratios sometimes quoted in Parliament and the press, showing that those out of work are about as well off as the employed, have usually related to a man, his wife and two children or more, and such cases, though obviously important, are not the most typical. A high proportion of the unemployed are without children. Moreover, formerly the earnings-related benefit was usually included in these comparisons, though it was received by only a fifth or less of the unemployed.[35]

There is, however, an important addition to benefits yet to be made. This is for housing assistance and various other benefits, subject to means tests, for which the unemployed may also be eligible. The average allowance for housing made by SB was equivalent in 1980 to nearly a third the cash benefit received in the case of a single person and to nearly a quarter in the case of a married couple. Thus the ratios of total benefits to average *net* manual earnings will be raised to over a third and over a half respectively. In the case of those who could expect to earn two-thirds of average earnings, the ratios will become nearly three-fifths and four-fifths for single persons and married couples respectively. In the case of families with children the ratios will be still higher. These high replacement ratios may, it is true, give an exaggerated impression in some cases, for employed workers can also receive means-tested assistance with housing from their local authorities.

High replacement ratios – especially those that are high relative to low earnings – do not mean that the benefits would support an 'extravagantly comfortable standard of living'. Nor is it a question of being better off when unemployed, but rather of *how much more* a worker must earn – 10 per cent, 20 per cent or whatever – so that it will really be worth his while to search actively for employment and perhaps to move to another home. There is no escaping the fact that the net additional gain is often small. The reward for working could, of course, be greater if the ratio of take-home pay to gross income could be increased. This is partly the familiar question of allowances against income tax and of the rate of tax. It should be observed that the ratio is also affected by his contribution to national insurance itself. This begins when earned income exceeds a relatively low minimum level (w_m), equivalent to about a fifth of average earnings, and is then levied at 10 per cent on all earnings. That is to say, there is no tax allowance. The tax is $c\,w_i$, where c is the rate and w_i stands for earnings with $w_i > w_m$. If the minimum were also treated as an allowance, the tax payable would be $c\,(w_i - w_m)$. This may not constitute a large quantitative difference, but it adds something to the total of disincentive effect.

Even before the small reductions in real unemployment benefit and before the massive rise in unemployment in the early 1980s, it seems highly improbable that many people left their jobs for a life on the dole on the assumption that they would be able to evade official pressure to take new employment. But those who had lost their jobs may well have taken more time over finding new ones than they would have done if benefits had been less. In particular, there would be an obvious temptation to remain in a relatively depressed area, in the hope that something might yet turn up, rather than migrate. In any case, the cards were stacked against mobility by housing problems – in turn largely a reflection of mistaken policies. With unemployment benefits on a less generous scale, structural and frictional unemployment might have been less. We must also take seriously the complaint that labour, even unskilled labour, was often hard to find, even in some of the special development areas. When the economy was prosperous and labour was scarce in much of the country, a case – not a decisive case, for value judgements are involved – could be made out for lower replacement ratios for the unemployed as an incentive to speed up job search and, if necessary, migration. There were, of course, other ways of stimulating mobility, such as special grants towards the cost of moving. Perhaps most important of all was the need to reform housing finance and to reduce local authority waiting lists for homes in areas of labour scarcity. Although the need for this reform remains the situation is different in other respects when jobs are hard to get because the whole economy is depressed.

Even in recession, some of the unemployed find work, and it may be that more people would think it both possible and worth while to take up at least part-time work if they were not deterred from doing so by the penalty they might incur from a loss of means-tested benefits. It is true that some earnings from work are disregarded when entitlements to SB are worked out, but the amounts are small and hardly likely to encourage an unemployed man to search actively for work. Any earnings his wife may bring home, above a very small amount, are also taken into account, and this may help to account for the fact that the wives of the unemployed are substantially less likely to be employed than are the wives of the employed.[36] A case can therefore be made for some increase in the amount of income disregarded – with this specified amount regularly adjusted for changing prices.

Sickness benefits share many of the characteristics of unemployment benefits but have received less attention and aroused less controversy. Admittedly, the standard flat-rate benefits– which since 1982 have been the only form of state sickness benefits – give low replacement ratios, although these may be increased by supplementary benefits. This is not very often the case, however, because large numbers of workers have additional occupational sick pay. In some cases earnings may be made up in full for at least a limited period; then it is possible to be as well off when sick as when at work. To what extent this delays return to work cannot be assessed. The proportion of unskilled manual workers covered by occupational sick pay is lower than for all employees. Low-paid workers also have inferior sick-pay cover. If their wages are made up, they are more likely to receive only 'basic wages' rather than their total earnings when at work.[37] Unskilled manual workers, however, have higher rates of sickness absence than do white-collar workers, which may be due in part to the poorer health standards of the low-paid. The fact remains that for workers as a whole the average number of days of certified sickness absence in the UK increased from 12·2 to 18·8 in the case of male employees between 1954–5 and 1978–9 and from 15·9 to 19·2 in the case of women. The rise, which was common to all developed countries, was, of course, caused by a number of factors – improved methods of diagnosis and treatment of illness, better health education and lower tolerance of minor states of ill health, higher expectations as to job satisfaction, an increase in the employment of married women with family commitments. Nevertheless, it is generally considered in all these countries that improved sick-pay arrangements, which frequently replace nine-tenths of earnings or even more, have contributed to higher rates of sickness absence.[38] The mass unemployment of the late 1970s and early 1980s has, however, brought the rising trend to a halt with increased fears of job loss (see pp. 52–3 and 156).

A rather different case is that of the *retired pensioner*. If he chooses to draw his pension at 65 but continues to work on a part-time basis, his pension will be reduced by 50 per cent for every £1 earned above a certain limit and by 100 per cent above a higher limit (roughly two-fifths of average male manual earnings), which is no longer to be adjusted for rising earnings. The number of pensioners who have their pensions reduced by the earnings rule is small, but that may be precisely because they restrict their work income to keep within the allowable limits. Apart from any disincentive effect this may have on the amount of time worked, another question arises: the doubtful ethics of withholding income to which the recipient has earned a right by reason of the contributions he has made or those made on his behalf by a former employer. This is a matter of particular concern in the USA.[39]

It is not merely the readiness to search for work and the incentive to increase earnings from work that may be affected in a variety of ways by both social insurance and means-tested benefits. The inducement to save may also be weakened. This effect is very clear when a means-tested benefit is denied to anyone possessing capital above a specified amount, as is the case with SB. No benefit will be paid to those with more than a modest £2,000. It is scarcely surprising that most claimants are reported as having no capital. If this is so, it is not necessarily because they have been unable to save; they may have chosen not to do so, or they may have spent their savings or given them away in order to claim benefit. Fortunately, it would be wrong to judge the case for selectivity through means tests simply by reference to the British SB system with all its quirks. Thus the amount of capital to be disregarded completely could be raised to a more reasonable figure and indexed. Capital above this amount could be deemed to earn a notional rate of return – notional in order to avoid the troubles of collecting actual figures. But the notional rate should be related to an appropriate market rate on small savings. It should not be a penal notional rate of 25 per cent, as it has been under SB, which is so much above what can be earned that it is only sensible to spend or to give away any excess capital – unless one expects to be on SB for only a short period. House ownership, it should be observed, is already given favourable treatment with regard to SB – in line with the general bias in the British treatment of assets. For houses are excluded from assessments of capital, and assistance is even provided with rates, upkeep and mortgage interest payments. It would be possible to arrange for the value of a house to be turned into an annuity, but equity between home-ownership and other forms of capital does not appear to be an objective.

Capital ownership is not penalised in the same way under the national insurance arrangements. In no case is there any restriction on property ownership or income from property. Whether or not saving is discouraged by the knowledge that social security benefits, especially pensions, will be received is a different matter. For example, Feldstein[40] came to the conclusion that while social security programmes for old age may on the one hand reduce life-time savings for retirement at a given age, the incentive which such programmes provide for retirement at an earlier age may have a positive effect on saving during working life in order to provide for a longer retirement period. The two effects may cancel each other out, and the net impact on savings may be indeterminate. In some cases, however, 'recognition effect' induced by the prospect of a public transfer income in old age may be sufficiently strong to increase an individual's total savings, forced and voluntary.

NOTES

1 B. Abel-Smith and P. Townsend, *The Poor and the Poorest* (London: Bell, 1965).
2 R. Berthoud *et al.*, *Poverty and the Development of Anti-Poverty in the UK* (London: Heinemann, 1981).
3 *Public Expenditure on Income Maintenance Programmes* (Paris: OECD, 1976).
4 B. S. Rowntree, *Poverty: A Study of Town Life*, 2nd edn. (London: Macmillan, 1902), p. 86.
5 B. S. Rowntree, *Poverty and Progress*, 2nd edn. (London: Longman Green, 1950).
6 M. Orshansky, 'Counting the poor: another look at the poverty profile', *Social Security Bulletin*, vol. 28, no. 1 (1965).
7 Adam Smith, *The Wealth of Nations* (1776), ed. R. H. Campbell, A. S. Skinner and W. B. Todd (Oxford: Oxford University Press, 1976), pp. 869–70.
8 G. C. Fiegehen, P. S. Lansley and A. D. Smith, *Poverty and Progress in Britain 1953–73*, National Institute of Economic and Social Research, Occasional Paper No. 29 (Cambridge: Cambridge University Press, 1977), pp. 133–4.
9 *Report on Social Insurance and Allied Services*, Cmnd 6404 (London: HMSO, 1942), p. 8.
10 International Labour Office, *Convention 102*, concerning minimum standards of social security (Geneva, 1952).
11 Fiegehen, Lansley and Smith, *Poverty and Progress in Britain 1953–73*, p. 27.
12 *Public Expenditure on Income Maintenance Programmes*, p. 63.
13 P. Townsend, *Poverty in the United Kingdom* (London: Allen Lane, 1979).
14 D. Piachaud, 'Peter Townsend and the Holy Grail', *New Society* (10 September 1981), pp. 419–21.
15 Berthoud *et al.*, *Poverty and the Development of Anti-Poverty Policy in the UK*, p. 33.
16 A. B. Atkinson, *The Economics of Inequality* (London: Oxford University Press, 1975), p. 190.
17 W. Beckerman, 'The impact of income maintenance payments on poverty in Britain', *Economic Journal* (June 1979).
18 ibid., p. 288.
19 See *Poverty and Progress in Britain 1953–73*.
20 ibid., p. 35.
21 ibid.
22 A. B. Atkinson, *Poverty in Britain and the Reform of Social Security* (Cambridge: Cambridge University Press, 1969).
23 Cedric Sandford, *Social Economics* (London: Heinemann, 1977), p. 160.
24 J. E. Meade, *The Structure and Reform of Direct Taxation* (London: Allen & Unwin, 1978), p. 276, note to Table 13.1.
25 W. Runciman, *Relative Deprivation and Social Justice* (London: Routledge & Kegan Paul, 1966), part 3.
26 *Take-Up of Supplementary Benefits*, SBC Discussion Paper (London: HMSO, 1978), para. 3.9.
27 ibid., p. 23.

28 *Supplementary Benefits Commission Report* for 1978, DHSS (London: HMSO, 1978), p. 104.
29 J. Creedy, *State Pensions in Britain* (London: National Institute of Economic and Social Research, 1982).
30 J. M. Buchanan, 'Federalism and fiscal equity', *American Economic Review*, vol. 47, 1957.
31 D. Donnison, 'A rationalisation of housing benefits', *Three Banks Review*, no. 131 (September 1981).
32 See *Social Trends*, no. 11 (London: HMSO, 1981), pp. 74–5.
33 OPCS, Social Survey Division: Family Finances, Occasional Paper 26 (London: HMSO, 1981).
34 S. Danziger, R. Haveman and R. Plotnik, 'How income transfer programmes affect work, savings and the income distribution: a critical review', *Journal of Economic Literature*, vol. 19, no. 3 (1981).
35 A. B. Atkinson and J. S. Flemming, 'Unemployment, social security and disincentives', *Midland Bank Review* (Autumn 1978).
36 R. Layard, D. Piachaud and M. Stewart, *The Causes of Poverty*, Background Paper for the Sixth Report of the Royal Commission on the Distribution of Income and Wealth (London: HMSO, 1978).
37 Evidence of Low Pay Unit to Royal Commission on the Distribution of Income and Wealth (1978); Metropolitan Pensions Association Survey (London: 1981).
38 International Social Security Administration, *Absenteeism and Social Security*, Studies and Research No. 16 (Geneva: ISSA, 1980).
39 M. R. Colberg, *The Social Security Retirement Test: Right or Wrong?* (Washington, DC: American Enterprise Institute, 1978).
40 M. Feldstein, 'Social Security, induced retirement and aggregate capital accumulation, *Journal of Political Economy*, vol. 82 (1974).

CHAPTER 5

Cash Benefits in a Changing Economy

INDEXATION FOR INFLATION AND GROWTH

If social security is to mean what the term implies, benefits ought surely to be adjusted for changes in the value of money. This proposition would appear at first sight to be incontrovertible, but it was one that neither Beveridge[1] nor Keynes[2] was prepared to accept. Their rejection of indexation for price changes – by which is meant the adjustment of benefits in line with an appropriate index of prices – did not, of course, reflect indifference to the real standard of living of the beneficiaries. Rather, it reflected their refusal to assume that the rate of inflation should be taken, in this context, as given – as an independent variable. On the contrary, they feared that indexation would greatly weaken political resistance to inflation and would encourage those who were thus protected against the consequences to acquiesce in the falling value of money. It is of interest to note in passing that Friedman[3] adopted a very different position. Although a hard-liner in his opposition to inflation, he recommended the widespread indexation of all payments, not just social benefits, for price changes on the grounds that uncertainty about the future price level would not then lead to anxiety about the real standard of living, and that this reassurance would make it unnecessary to build a large margin for protection against possible future inflation into demands made for increases in money income.

Inflationary pressures can originate in many different ways, and it certainly cannot be assumed that if social benefits were unprotected, the resistance to inflation would then be decisive. In short, prices may rise anyway, with or without indexation, even if the rate of increase proved to be different in the two cases. Social benefits may then need to be protected for political reasons, and a value judgement may require them to be so protected on humanitarian grounds. Indeed protection is obviously needed if an inconsistency in social policy is to be avoided. The really contentious questions are rather different.

Granted that, as a general principle, cash benefits should be raised as the value of money falls over time, should this adjustment always be complete? Or are there circumstances in which *some* erosion of real values may be tolerated and may even be appropriate? There are two parts to the answer. First, it is necessary to ask whether the rise in prices is accompanied by a fall in average real income per head. The clearest case is a deterioration in the terms of trade caused, for example, by a steep rise in the price of imported oil. Real income is then bound to decline, or at least to be lower than it would otherwise have been if a unit of exports still bought the same amount of imports. As modern economies operate, the fall in real income is likely to express itself initially as a fall in the value of money. If indexation were so comprehensive as to apply to payments of all kinds, and if the price index used were not adjusted for the terms of trade, the outcome in a mature economy heavily dependent on imports could only be cumulative inflation, with monetary outlays being raised in a futile attempt to offset the fall in real income. The attempt would be futile because real expenditure must clearly be reduced somewhere in the economy, either in the public or in the private sector, or in both. The second point is, then, a distributional one. Should any part of the inescapable fall in real expenditure be borne by the recipients of social security benefits? Or should these beneficiaries be given full protection, which will increase their share in national income? The answer given may be that this group is one that should be fully protected because its members are on average poorer than the rest of the community. It may be, however, that their share is thought to have been high enough before the change and therefore that it should not be increased. In Sweden this question has been faced explicitly, and the price index used for indexation now *excludes* the rise in the price of energy – an exceedingly interesting development in indexation policy which does not appear to have received much attention elsewhere.

Whatever recommendation is made, whether for full or partial indexation, it is crucial that its implications should be fully accepted. It would be an empty gesture to maintain that benefits be protected if, at the same time, it were not recognised that the burden would then be shifted somewhere else. This is not just a plea for honest dealing. For there is the further point that useless attempts to sustain real expenditure everywhere will only build up inflationary pressures, and the policies needed to check inflation may then cause unemployment and loss of output. Thus real income may decline not only as a direct consequence of the adverse terms of trade but also because domestic production has fallen below capacity – an additional and really unnecessary secondary loss of the kind so widely experienced in oil-importing countries since 1973/4. Thus if it is agreed that social benefits cannot be allowed to suffer from an inflationary scramble, the additional tax burden should not be resisted by corresponding increases in pay demands. In practice such consistency may be lacking.

A different example is that of an inflationary gap caused by a government deficit which is met by an inflationary rise in the money supply. The central government is to this extent imposing what amounts to a concealed tax – the 'inflation tax' as it has been called – for it is adopting the ancient practice of financing part of its requirements by depreciating the value of money. This inflation tax is bound to fall somewhere. Again, it may be held that the implicit levy should not fall on social benefits – a 'levy' that would take the form of reductions in the real value of benefits as prices rose. The first duty of the social scientist is, again, to insist on the need for consistency. If the other parties concerned, including the unions, accept the need for a full indexation of benefits, consistency requires them to moderate their own demands accordingly, especially when their members are relatively well paid, or to press for a cut-back in some other items of public expenditure apart from social benefits.

It is always difficult to identify all the places where the 'inflation tax' has fallen during any period of rising prices. Clearly, those holding fixed-interest securities and even ordinary shares have been 'taxed' in this sense in recent years; but there are less clear cases. The difficulty arises because the incidence of the 'tax' shifts around so much as now one group and now another succeeds in gaining an increase in money income. It is important to observe that the social benefits themselves cannot in practice be fully protected. Suppose that some benefit is fixed at, say, £40 a week at one particular date and is then raised in a year's time to £44 in order to offset a 10 per cent rise in prices. Between these two dates the real value of the benefit will have declined and will soon start to decline once again after the second review has taken place. (These falls and recoveries are illustrated by the saw-edged lines in Figures 3.3 and 3.4.) If the pace of inflation were steady, it could be said that the real value of benefits roughly at the mid-point between reviews should be the figure that is made to conform to the target for real benefits. But prices do not rise at a steady pace, and benefits will naturally depreciate more when the rate of inflation is accelerating. Reviews made more frequently than once a year would help, but at the cost of somewhat higher costs for administration. In some countries there is a threshold above which the rise in prices will bring about an automatic increase (e.g. 3 per cent for pensions in Sweden). Even this is not full protection. Another possibility is for benefits to be adjusted in line with the *prospective* increase in future prices rather than with the increase that has occurred over a past period; but the difficulty then is that any finance ministry will feel almost bound to be over-optimistic in its public forecasts of future inflation, and beneficiaries may suffer as a result. In short, it must be recognised that the 'inflation tax', with its shifting incidence, will fall to some extent on social benefits, even when the case for their indexation has been accepted in principle and implemented as fully as is practicable.

In 1980 and 1981 prices were rising in Britain and real national output per head was falling. In other developed economies too prices were rising and output was stagnant or rising quite slowly as compared with earlier years. For the greater part of the postwar period, however, real output was rising as well as prices. Before the oil crisis of 1973/4 instability meant variations in positive rates of growth of output in the developed nations, with very few instances of cyclical declines when a drop in real output was recorded. Over this period real gross earnings more than doubled, even in slowly growing Britain. The standard of living of those at work was thus raised substantially, and it was thought appropriate to accord a share of this growth to the recipients of social benefits. This was something that could be achieved by discretionary increases in real benefits from time to time or, in a more automatic way, by the indexing of benefits to average earnings, which were then rising faster than prices. (See pp. 53, 112 for a discussion of the procedures followed in a number of countries.)

In looking more closely at the problems raised by indexation, it is convenient to begin with a welfare system that provides flat-rate rather than graduated cash benefits. This, of course, has been the case in Britain, apart from (a) the graduated supplements to unemployment and sickness pay introduced in 1966, which in the case of the unemployed, however, were received by only a small proportion, and (b) the graduated pension scheme of 1959, which never provided significant benefits. If, then, the objective were to protect people against poverty, and if it were held that a benefit level, once determined, could be kept fixed (not for ever but for, say, two or three decades), there would be no case for any interim increases in the real value of benefits. Clearly, this raises again the basic question: how is the term 'poverty' to be interpreted? In Britain, as has been observed above, the practice was gradually adopted of raising both social insurance benefits and means-tested cash benefits on a scale which kept them roughly in line over the trend with the *gross* earnings before tax of male manual workers. It is true that the relationship was not precisely preserved in the short run. It should be noted that there was no statutory obligation to do so, and it is an interesting aspect of social history that this form of *de facto* indexation came into force. The relationship thus gradually adopted was, of course, only roughly observed, with impending elections often providing a stimulus to change.[4]

Thus the beneficiaries of the welfare state were allowed to share in the growth of the economy. Indeed, their share was increased. For personal direct taxation was absorbing a larger and larger proportion of the gross incomes of the employed population, and most workers were brought within the net of direct taxation. As a consequence, the main social benefits increased as a proportion of *net* average earnings after tax. The effect on replacement ratios – the replacement of earnings by benefits –

has been discussed above (see p. 48). It can reasonably be asserted that if benefits are to be linked to an index of earnings in order to preserve some chosen relationship between these benefits and the standard of living of the average worker, the link should be with take-home pay. It may, of course, be thought proper to increase this ratio above the level at which it may stand at some point in time; but, if so, this increase should ideally be made in a deliberate manner and by an explicit amount, not implicitly and by an amount not deliberately determined. Why gross earnings rather than net were chosen in practice as the appropriate basis of indexation is not altogether clear. The explanation may, however, lie in the fact that in the early years the average worker was paying little income tax, so that the choice between gross and net earnings was to that extent less important, although even in those days all employed persons were paying another direct tax to which no personal or other allowances were attached – the national insurance contribution itself. It may be, then, that the practice of adjusting benefits to gross earnings, once loosely adopted, simply persisted. In some countries the decision to act in this way was more explicitly taken – although the *reasons* for the choice remain obscure.

In 1972 the Conservative Government accepted an explicit obligation to index for prices, although rather more than that was achieved in practice over the subsequent years. In 1975 the Labour Government introduced legislation which established rules for indexation, and these rules differed from the previous practice. Short-term benefits were in future to be adjusted for prices only. If, then, earnings rose in relation to prices, the ratio of short-term benefits to earnings would decline unless some ad hoc adjustments to the former were to be made beyond what the legislation of 1975 required. In the event, real earnings, both gross and net, rose by about 15 per cent between 1978 and 1980, although unemployment was also growing. For a single person the ratio of *short-term* benefits to net manual earnings fell beween 1977 and 1980 from 26·1 per cent to 23·3 per cent; for a married man with two children, it went down from 50·6 per cent to 45·0 per cent. In 1981, when real disposable earnings dropped a little, the real value of short-term benefits also fell because full price indexation was not maintained.

It was also decreed in 1975 that *long-term* benefits should be raised in line either with prices or with gross earnings – now the gross earnings of *all* workers, not those of manual workers – whichever yielded the larger increases. Thus a ratchet was introduced which allowed these real benefits to rise but prevented them from falling. It was a provision that attracted some criticism, and it was dropped by the Conservative Government in 1980. Thereafter long-term benefits were to be indexed only for prices. The beneficiaries would not share in any subsequent growth unless special action were taken to that end. As real wages did not rise much in 1981, the change imposed no loss. As real wages fell in 1982, pensioners should have done better than the average wage-earner. In fact, pensions also fell slightly in real terms – by about 3 per cent – although in principle price indexation was to be applied. Such errors are scarcely surprising when benefits are fixed early in each year but the new scales do not come into operation until November.

It should now be apparent that indexation policy, previously fairly stable for some twenty years, has been in a state of flux since the onset of the oil crisis. This is true not only of Britain but of some other European countries as well. In Britain the breaking away from older procedures has not as yet resulted in a new arrangement that can be confidently expected to last for an extended period, and this may be the case in other countries as well. Thus when the recession is over and growth is resumed, it will be necessary to consider afresh whether the recipients of social benefits should share in this growth and, if so, in what way. Admittedly, the view may be advanced that real benefits need to be reduced in relation to real net earnings in order to ease the burden on the working population. If so, the desired change could be brought about quietly and with less political fuss – though with the obvious sacrifice of open government – if real benefits were merely stabilised for a few years while real earnings were rising. This may be one of the reasons why the Labour Government decided in 1975 that short-term benefits would be automatically adjusted only for prices.

What has just been said applies not only to national insurance benefits but also to supplementary benefits. If, then, SB is taken as determining the conventional poverty levels appropriate to various types of claimant, it follows that *Britain is now applying a static indicator of poverty*. Thus a resumption of growth could be expected gradually to reduce the number of people deemed to be in poverty, as has occurred in the USA in the past but did not occur in Britain where the poverty level moved upwards roughly with rising gross average earnings (see pp. 54–7 above). It is true that in the case of all benefits, both national insurance and means-tested, it would be quite possible to continue with automatic indexation for prices only, as is done in Sweden. In the case of the short-term social insurance benefits, recent practice has done rather less than this, but it must be assumed that at some point the fall in real short-term benefits will be deemed by the government then in power to have gone far enough. In short, there could be general price indexation over the whole range of benefits – possibly qualified for changes in the terms of trade. The real value of benefits need not, it is true, be held unchanged indefinitely, for discretionary increases could occasionally be made with no automatic indexation except for prices. Such an arrangement could conceivably be permanent, with the flat-rate benefits indexed only for prices but adjusted in real terms by discretionary action from time to time. This would, however, have the advantage of lumpy rather than more even adjustments.

If, however, it were decided to index benefits for growth – on the assumption that growth is resumed – how could this best be done in the light of experience? In attempting to consider this question, it is necessary to draw attention to an important feature of previous arrangements in most EC countries, including Britain, which appears to have received little attention. This feature was the linking of benefits to *average* income per worker, without regard to any changes that might occur over the years in the relative numbers in these two groups – contributors on the one hand and beneficiaries on the other. Demographic changes have in the past added substantially to the increase in real expenditure on benefits, as the proportion of the population that is of retirement age has grown in relation to the population of working age.[5] It is relevant here to recall that pensions are by far the largest of the cash transfers. Demographic changes of this kind are now a matter of grave concern in continental European countries and in the USA. In the USA, for example, there were three people of working age to every retired person in the late 1970s. By 2020 the ratio may be only two to one. This is the 'greying of America' which is causing so much concern. It would appear that the 'greying of Britain' did not receive as much attention as it deserved when the graduated pension scheme of 1975 was designed. Apart from these demographic developments, there may be changes in the ages at which people retire or changes in the proportion of people, especially women, in paid employment. The percentage unemployed may also change and may do so not only in a short-term, cyclical manner but over longer periods as well.

The effects such changes may have on a pay-as-you-go scheme can now be illustrated. If the population is ageing and benefits are indexed on *average* gross earnings, the *total* tax burden carried by the working population in order to pay for these benefits must increase. Can it then be concluded that the proper relationship for indexation would be a link between *total* benefits provided and the *total* income of the population of working age? The beneficiaries would still share in the growth of output but would no longer do so disproportionately.

Let b_i represent the flat-rate social transfer received in year i, and let m be the desired relationship between b_i and average gross earnings per head, e, so that:

$$b_i = m\bar{e}_i \qquad (1)$$

Let R_i be the number of people receiving social benefits, Q_i the number paying social insurance contributions at the rate k. For simplicity, assume that these contributions take the form of a proportional contribution on all earnings. Then:

$$R_i b_i = k\bar{e}_i Q_i \qquad (2)$$

$$b_i = \frac{k(\bar{e}_i Q_i)}{R_i} \qquad (3)$$

If the ratio of R to Q remains unchanged over time, there will be no conflict between (1) and (3). If, however, the number of beneficiaries (R) rises relatively to the number at work (Q), then it will be necessary to increase k if the fixed relationship between benefits and gross earnings implied by (1) is to be retained.[6] Alternatively, the benefit-earnings ratio, m, could be reduced.

The ratio of R to Q alters over time for three reasons. (i) Demographic factors change the proportion of the total population that falls within the active age groups – the dependency ratio. (ii) Changes occur in the proportion of those in the active age groups who are either currently employed or deemed to be available for paid employment. Moreover, some fraction of the inactive age group is, in fact, employed. Changes in the proportion of those over normal pensionable age who are at work may be of some importance.[7] Indeed, the upper cut-off point which determines when people are deemed to be no longer active may become increasingly arbitrary. The dependency ratio must therefore be adjusted in order to take account of these complications. (iii) The proportion of the occupied population that is in employment varies – as we have had occasion to know in recent years. Variations in the proportion of the population in employment that are brought about by all these factors will obviously be reflected in the funds available for the payment of benefits if k is unchanged. (The self-employed are ignored here for the sake of simplicity.)

Changes of the second and third kind occur for cyclical reasons, as good times alternate with bad. It does not follow that there should then be offsetting changes in k or m. If unemployment rises or the participation rate declines, k need not be increased nor need m be reduced, for it may be sensible to allow the social security account to run into deficit with the deliberate intention of helping to sustain monetary expenditure. Traditionally, the social security system has been so used as an automatic or built-in stabiliser. Indeed, it was proposed in the past, when the main features of employment policy were being discussed and determined, that the contribution rate should be *reduced* as unemployment rose and unemployment benefits increased.[8] This proposal was not adopted, but by maintaining m and by not increasing k in the way that balanced accounts would have required, the system was allowed nevertheless to exert a stabilising effect in the USA and in Continental European countries, as well as in the UK. The basis of Keynesian policy, of which this was a part, was to be challenged in due course by the monetarist school. Whether or not monetarism is accepted, it is clear that the role of an automatic stabiliser had to be assessed afresh in a situation such as that of the late 1970s and early 1980s, when rising unemployment was accompanied by rising prices. At this point we are in danger of being engulfed by a difficult controversy about macroeconomic policy. Let us simply assume that deficits and surpluses will occur from time to time.

Apart from cyclical fluctuations, in (ii) and (iii), these arguments in the equation could alter on a longer-term basis. There may also be important changes in (i) – that is to say, demographic changes, as we have noted. There has been a large increase in Britain in the number of people of pension age as a proportion of the total population, from 13·7 per cent in 1951 to 17·1 per cent in 1979, and many other countries have experienced similar changes. If one goes further back, the changes are even more startling; in 1931, for example, as assessed by modern criteria, people of pension age made up 9·7 per cent of the population and in 1901 only 6·3 per cent. For the rest of the century, the ratio of pensioners to active population may not change much and there should even be a slight decline in the first decade of the next century. It is expected that this will be followed however by a substantial rise towards the end of the second decade. These projections are necessarily speculative, but it is only prudent to recognise that adverse changes could occur.

Prospective demographic changes must clearly be taken into account in assessing future commitments. It does not follow, however, that it would be appropriate to adopt a formula for indexation so designed as to maintain over an extended period some steady relationship between total benefit expenditure and total income from work. Regular annual changes in k or m in order to ensure a smooth adjustment to the changing demographic pattern would imply very fine tuning indeed – and, moreover, fine tuning in harmony with what can be only speculative forecasts of dubious reliability. Further, the desirability of short-term adjustments alone for the second and third kinds of change listed above is at best doubtful. It would seem better, therefore, to rely upon discretionary changes in k or m when this appears to be appropriate in order to cope with changes under these headings rather than to attempt to achieve adjustment by means of automatic indexation.

If it were decided that changes in benefits should be linked to changes in some index of average earnings, it would still be necessary to decide whether this should be an index of *gross* earnings or of *net* earnings after tax. It has been the general practice to use gross earnings in those countries where benefits have been indexed for earnings. Not only has this been the practice followed, but the consequential effect has been that the ratio of benefits to take-home pay seems almost to have escaped attention.[9] In recent years official statistics for the latter ratio have been published from time to time in Britain, and the point is no longer wholly neglected. It remains true, however, that the proper basis for indexation has not been much discussed, partly because wage indexation has been suspended during the recession years. When economic growth is resumed, however, this will again become a relevant issue.

There are really two points to be decided. The first is the determination of the appropriate relationship between the more important benefits and the income of the average worker. It is surely clear that this relationship should be with take-home pay. This would clearly be seen to be the case if benefits were themselves untaxed, as in the case of the US federal pension. In Britain pensions are assessed for tax, but no tax has to be paid unless there are other sources of income. The gross pension can therefore be properly compared with net average incomes if the objective of policy is to establish an appropriate relationship between the standard of living provided by the pension and that provided by average earnings.

The second issue is how to maintain this relationship. A fair approximation could be achieved by changing benefits in line with average earnings *less* income tax, as illustrated by the relationship: $b = m\bar{e}\,(1 - t)$. This relationship, as stated, is obviously oversimplified because it ignores allowances against tax and also the fact that social insurance contributions themselves also reduce take-home pay. But it is intended to do no more in the present context than serve as an illustration. There is, however, a further point that needs to be added. This is that the acceptance of an arrangement which linked benefits to take-home pay would not necessarily mean that beneficiaries would be worse off than they would be if the link were with gross earnings. That would depend partly upon the initial target relationship chosen. Thereafter the outcome would depend upon changes in the ratio of net to gross average earnings. If this ratio were to fall, the growth of benefits would also be correspondingly lower; but this would not be inequitable. If, however, a future government were to succeed in reducing the rate of growth of total public expenditure in relation to GNP and were then to lower direct taxation, the recipients of social benefits would be better off than they would be with their benefits linked to gross earnings.

So far attention has been confined to flat-rate benefits. Graduation introduces additional complications. Under a graduated scheme benefits will be linked by some formula to earnings in the year before retirement or to life-time earnings or to earnings over the best years. (For example, graduated pensions in Britain are based on earnings in the best twenty years, as we noted in Chapter 3.) It follows, therefore, that the amount of benefit available from a graduated scheme immediately after retirement will depend partly upon the date of retirement, for the general level of real earnings is always changing over time. Consider the respective positions of two people whom we assume to have stood at exactly the same spot in the pecking order throughout their working lives. To take an obvious example, suppose that both have always received average earnings. Both will then get the same proportion of average earnings in the form of a graduated pension. If, however, their ages are different, so that their dates of retirement are widely separated, the one who retires at the later date will receive a larger pension – on the assumption that real earnings have been rising during the intervening period. In this sense a graduated scheme reflects growth quite *automatically* in a way in which a flat-rate scheme does not. This, however, is not the end of the story, for it is possible that a graduated pension already in payment may or may not be adjusted subsequently for any further growth in earnings that takes place. In the USA and in Sweden there is no such adjustment. Nor did the pension legislation of 1975 make provision for adjusting in this way the new British graduated pension, as distinct from the basic pension. When a person draws a graduated pension for the first time, he can expect this benefit to be held steady – or roughly steady – in real terms, provided there is price indexation. But he cannot anticipate any future growth, in real terms, in this graduated pension, although the real wages of those still at work may be rising. The position has been different in France. Pensions are graduated, and new pensions, as they become payable for the first time year by year, do therefore reflect, to an extent determined by the particular formula used, any change in real earnings that may have taken place. But pensions already in payment are also linked to an index of earnings. Thus there will be further increases in their real value if real wages continue to rise – and declines if the latter fall. In West Germany a broadly similar arrangement has applied.

It is an arrangement that may seem the more attractive because it is generous to the elderly, but there is a danger that objectives may be confused at this point. One of the arguments for a graduated structure of pensions is that differences in benefits are appropriate in order to allow for the fact that, during working life, different people have grown accustomed to different standards of living, so that a flat-rate pension would mean greater hardship for those who have been well off than for those who have been badly off. This, it may be felt, is to carry to the point of absurdity the neglect of self-help and the assumption of complete dependence on the state in retirement. The objection is considered elsewhere (see pp. 122–3 below). Let us leave it aside for the moment, however, for our immediate concern is with consistency. If it is really maintained that different habits of expenditure acquired in working life justify graduation in benefits, then habit should be accommodated thereafter by *constancy* in the real value of the graduated benefits. Further increases in the benefits provided, in line with rising real earnings, are not easy to justify.[10] Increases in the real value of flat-rate benefits or of the poverty line are a quite different matter, for the reason for providing such benefits is different from that advanced in defence of graduated pensions.

FUNDING AND PAY-AS-YOU-GO

OFFICIAL SCHEMES

Modern social security schemes are mostly financed on the pay-as-you-go or assessment basis. That is to say, current expenditure is met almost entirely from the current contributions of employers and employees, together with whatever subvention, if any, the state provides from its general revenue. It is true that small funds are usually held, but the income derived from them contributes only marginally to the current outlay on benefits. For example, interest received in Britain amounts to less than 4 per cent of total revenue and expenditure. The fact that receipts are not accumulated in a great fund but are passed on at once to beneficiaries has important consequences for the economy as a whole. More specifically, there are important consequences for indexation.

Pension schemes that are strictly funded are described as cash-purchase or money-purchase schemes. Suppose each person contributes a constant proportion of his pay, k, over his working life, and suppose, again for simplicity, that his pay remains unchanged at w and that the rate of return earned by the fund also remains steady at r. Then the value of his first contribution at the point of retirement after n periods will be $kw\,(l+r)^{n-1}$. The second contribution will be worth $kw\,(l+r)^{n-2}$. And so on. Given these assumptions, the series can be summed, and the accumulated value of his contributions assessed. In fact, his income, w, will almost certainly change from time to time over his working life, and the contribution rate can also be expected to vary. There may also be changes in r. The calculation of the accumulated value of his contributions will then be more complicated but will still depend upon four variables: his past income in each contribution period, the proportion of his income put into the fund by himself or his employer or both, the varying rate of return on the fund, and the length of his working life. Under this system he will not know in advance just how much he will receive on retirement. Moreover, his accumulated contributions must, in effect, be turned into an annuity to give him a pension. This will involve an actuarial calculation about life expectation after retirement and will also depend upon the rate of return relevant to that period of retirement, and this rate will not be known in advance. Moreover, the value of the annuity may be reduced over the years by inflation.

A pay-as-you-go pension is different. Its main features were indicated above. Under such a scheme, the pension will depend mainly upon the number of contributors at work *during the period of retirement* when it is being paid, upon the contribution rate and upon the number of pensioners receiving benefits. No pensioner has any claim to a share in an accumulated fund. There is no such fund or only a very small one. The pension will depend on current contributions from those still at work. They must be prepared to pay his pension, just as in the past, when he was at work, he helped to pay the pensions of those who were then retired. The whole system rests on an implicit understanding, which was described as follows by Samuelson: 'Let mankind enter into a Hobbes–Rousseau social contract in which the young are assured of their retirement subsistence if they will today support the aged, such support to be guaranteed by a draft on the yet unborn.'[11] This was a pleasing way of describing the arrangements. But a metaphor about a contract is not a contract!

What are the attractions of the pay-as-you-go system? One attraction, from the point of view of a government introducing a new pension scheme, is that it can, if it chooses, provide the new pensions immediately to those now retired or on the point of retirement. This is what is referred to as 'blanketing-in'. Or the government may compromise and provide full pensions after, say, twenty years, with scaled-down pensions in the interim. If the pension were fully funded, about forty years' contributions might be required to earn a full pension. Blanketing-in is obviously attractive to the pensioners who will benefit from it and may win their political support for the government, especially when there is full blanketing-in. The fact remains that the money must come from somewhere, and the contributions levied from those at work will have to be correspondingly higher. But the contributors are likely to be a less well organised pressure group than the pensioners and may in any case feel sufficiently sympathetic towards the elderly not to resent the levy. What has been said about interdependent utility functions is relevant here, as is Browning's hypothesis that public choice is likely to create a bias in favour of pensioners (see p. 40 above).

The second advantage, and a more important one, is that pensioners may be better protected against inflation. If pensions are fixed relative to average earnings, whether gross or not, these pensions will keep pace with rising prices as long as wages, whether gross or net, rise at least as fast as prices. In the event wages rose much more than prices prior to the depression of the early 1980s and benefits also went up in real terms, as we have seen (Chapter 3). It is necessary to add at once that there is some compensation for inflation in fully funded schemes, for the rate of return on the fund will also to some extent rise with inflation. Thus the yield on Government bonds, which was about 3 per cent in 1948, had been roughly quintupled by the early 1980s. The protection has been far from complete, however, because the rise in the accelerating rate of inflation was not foreseen, and funds invested in long-dated, fixed-interest securities in the past are now earning rates of return on initial cost well below the rate of inflation. Even in recent years the rate of return on bonds will prove to be negative unless inflation is reduced. It is true that pension funds are also invested in shares and property, but here too the return has not matched inflation for a variety of reasons. In short, the rate of accumulation of a fund will depend upon what is happening to the rate of return on capital, whereas in a pay-as-you-go scheme it will reflect what is happening to average earnings, given the rate at which contributions are levied. Finally, under a pay-as-you-go scheme, a person may be told that the pension he will receive on retirement will be some stated percentage of his final or average income. Provided this promise can be kept, his future position will be less uncertain. Enough has been said to explain the popularity of pay-as-you-go arrangements since the war. Moreover, it is easy enough to show, as a matter of fact, that pensions received under such schemes have risen more than pensions in private occupational schemes which are based substantially – though not exclusively as we shall see – on funding.

Benefits must be paid for – a fact that may not have been given sufficient weight in the euphoric period of economic growth when commitments for the future, especially with regard to pensions, were somewhat lightly accepted. The position must be looked at again when account is taken of the factors described in the previous section. Given adverse demographic factors, together with a fall in the proportion of the active population that is employed, the pay-as-you-go arrangements look less secure. For it cannot be taken for granted that the contribution rate, k, can be raised indefinitely in order to preserve some fixed relationship between gross earnings and benefits, still less a rising relationship, as in the British graduated scheme of 1978. Clearly, a new formula relating benefits to *net* earnings could help, as we have seen. We must also allow for the fact that real wages have not only ceased to rise in some countries but have actually fallen. Admittedly, it does not follow that funded schemes would now offer more to the pensioner, for the real return on capital has been meagre. The point is rather that the assumptions on which pay-as-you-go schemes were based appear to have been too optimistic, and some of the undertakings previously made now look less secure.

In Britain the introduction of the graduated pension scheme in 1978 had the effect of helping the financing of social security in the short run but only at the cost of incurring an onerous obligation for the future. The contributions being made for these pensions which will not be fully paid until 1998, are not being accumulated now in order to meet this obligation later. On the contrary, these contributions are simply flowing through the system and are being used almost entirely to pay flat-rate benefits. (This is also what happened to the contributions paid under the older and more modest graduated scheme introduced in 1959.) It can indeed be argued that it would have been wiser to resort at once to full blanketing-in without any twenty-year waiting period. To do so would have been regarded by many as improvident; but it would have brought home to everyone immediately the burden of the obligation that was being incurred – and it might then have seemed prudent to scale down that obligation. There is nothing provident about postponing full payment for a period of years and diverting meanwhile the contributions collected for another purpose. That is not prudence; it is profligacy.

In Sweden there was also a waiting period of twenty years for the second-tier pension, but a fund has been accumulated meanwhile which will go at least some way towards meeting the obligation. The State Reserve pension scheme introduced by Sir Keith Joseph for Britain in 1972 was to be fully funded, and forty or so years were to elapse before full pension rights could be earned. This was a money-purchase scheme which implied uncertainty about the future real value of pensions; but it was at least an honest scheme, unlike those of 1959 and 1975.

The accumulation of a large state fund would, of course, have other effects on the economy. The funds thus at the disposal of the state could be used for back-door nationalisation – a possibility that was viewed with favour by an earlier Labour administration and disregarded, rather inexplicably, by Joseph. A more general effect would be to raise the flow of total savings available for investment. It is true that an official pension scheme might reduce the flow of private savings that people would otherwise try to accumulate in order to maintain their incomes in old age. Admittedly, the evidence suggests a complicated reaction, and private savings might not fall precisely in line with the pension rights acquired, but some fall might be expected. However, this fall would be offset by a rise in public savings if the official scheme were fully funded. If it were not funded, total savings (public plus private) would probably be reduced. We must not, therefore, compare the respective advantages and disadvantages of funding and pay-as-you-go arrangements on the assumption that the level of output would be unchanged under both schemes. It may be inferred that with more savings there would be more investment and therefore higher output.

In Britain social security contributions are used to finance all the insurance benefits. Although there is no separate item for pensions, the latter can be said to absorb roughly 70 per cent of what is contributed by employers and employees together. If this sum had gone into an accumulating fund in 1979, and if everything else had been unchanged, the addition to savings would have been equivalent to about three-fifths of the fixed investment by all industrial and commercial firms. If these additional savings had been absorbed into additional investment, the rate of return would presumably have been substantially reduced. It is important, therefore, not to compare the *actual* rate of return on invested funds with the *implicit* rate of return on pay-as-you-go schemes without allowing for the fact that the former would have been reduced if there had been more funding.

PRIVATE OCCUPATIONAL SCHEMES

So far attention has been confined to official pension schemes, but account must also be taken of occupational benefits, for the receipt of such benefits makes a substantial difference to the incomes of those not employed and thus has important implications for both the scale and the distributional pattern of the state benefits that may be thought appropriate. In Britain occupational pensions were equivalent to about 4 per cent of total personal income before tax in 1980, when state pensions for the retired and for widows amounted to 5½ per cent. The occupational benefits have been growing fast – at about 4½ per cent a year in real terms – and their growth will continue. It has been estimated that if total personal income rises on average at 1½ per cent a year until the end of the century, occupational pensions may then contribute something like 7 per cent of the total.[12] The official graduated pension scheme has been devised so that it is linked to the occupational schemes up to a specified maximum. In other countries occupational schemes have also been taken into account in fixing targets for the replacement of income after retirement – for example, in France, Sweden, the Netherlands and Germany.

A possible terminological confusion must be mentioned at the outset. Occupational pension schemes may be public or private. Public occupational pensions must not be confused with official national pensions, for the former are derived from special schemes for civil servants, teachers and so on. In Britain these occupational benefits have been paid in addition to the basic state pension. In some countries (for example, the USA) public servants do not receive Federal pensions. (It is true that some retired public servants in the USA do, in fact, get jobs in the private sector and thus acquire rights to the federal state pension as well – the 'double-dippers' as they are called – but this is not what was contemplated when the federal scheme was devised.) In most countries occupational public schemes, established at an early date and expanded on a generous basis, have been important pace-setters both for private schemes and for the national schemes themselves.[13] These public occupational pensions are financed on a pay-as-you-go basis with the tax-payer carrying the burden. However, it is not with such public occupational arrangements that this section is primarily concerned but rather with private occupational schemes. (It is necessary to add that some of the nationalised industries in Britain have their own funded schemes – for example, British Rail – and this adds to the danger of terminological confusion.)

Nearly all private occupational pensions in Britain have now been put on a final- or average-salary basis. That is to say, those who belong to these schemes expect to receive on retirement some specified proportion of their final year's salary or of some average of salaries previously received. There is, however, no obligation to protect the value in real terms of pensions in payment, and real pensions have, in fact, been eroded by inflation. It is true that supplements are paid. When these are on a contractual basis, the additions provided usually amount to something like 3 to 5 per cent a year. Non-contractual supplements have been provided. The fact remains that pensions in payment have not been fully protected against rising prices, and no private pension fund has felt that it could guarantee such protection; for these funds cannot rely upon the compulsory levies of the national schemes to support them, and it cannot be assumed that the future return on the assets they hold will keep pace with inflation. To guarantee full protection would, therefore, be to accept an obligation which, in the event, they might be unable to fulfil. So much is understandable. But it would also have been understandable if the pension funds had said that they could not even guarantee to provide pensions that constituted some specified proportion of final or average salary. As we have observed, a strictly funded money-purchase scheme yields benefits which depend upon the real rate of return on its assets, and this return is uncertain. To promise, say, 60 per cent of final income as a pension which, in many cases, will become payable at some remote date in the future, would also seem to imply a commitment which it may not be possible to meet. Why, then, has the acceptance of such a commitment now become the general practice?

In making an actuarial assessment of the future obligations and future income of a fund, an assumption has to be made about the rate of return on the assets held, and this has been done on a very conservative basis, usually of 3 per cent. In the event, the rate of return actually earned has been substantially higher over the recent inflationary years, and the pension funds have gained accordingly. Three groups of potential beneficiaries may now be distinguished: those who are still employed members of the fund and expect to remain so, those who have already retired and those who have left. It is only to be expected that the interests of the first group will carry most weight in influencing decisions about benefits. The

1975 legislation afforded some protection for the third group but has subsequently been felt to be inadequate, and the matter is under review.

Pensions already in payment have been supplemented, as we have observed, but in part this supplementation has come from the ordinary revenue of firms. It must be recognised, however, that these pensions could have been increased to a greater extent from the resources of the pension funds themselves if the commitments accepted on behalf of the first group had been on a smaller scale. But it is the current body of employees whose interests are bound to receive more attention. It is true that pension funds are run by trustees, not by the management of the firms themselves, but the management appoints these trustees. Some of the trustees are themselves employees who are not members of the firms' management teams, but it is only realistic to expect them too to be more concerned about the interests of the currently employed group of members, to which they belong, than those of the other groups. This is not to say that there will be no sympathy for the latter groups, but rather that their interests will not come first. Even so, the protection of pensions in payment will one day be a matter of much concern to those not yet retired. They might therefore be expected to attach a good deal of weight to the supplementation of pensions, as well as to the proportion of final salary that is to be replaced at the point of retirement. To do so, however, without extending any more generous arrangements to former employees already retired may be thought to be too difficult. This is one explanation. There is another, as the Committee on the Value of Pensions observed:

> It is relevant to note that retiring employees, given the alternative of a pension of fixed amount or a reduced pension which would be increased at a fixed rate each year, tend to select the higher initial amount. Employers unable to finance increased pension costs may thus have difficulty in negotiating lower initial pensions with the aim of preserving their real value.[14]

The evidence on which this observation is based was not presented by the Committee responsible for the report. Presumably, it reflects in a broad way the experience of fund managers, and we have no contrary evidence to set against it. It may be that a more systematic testing of opinion would lead to some modification of the view expressed, but this is only speculation. Moreover, there is some evidence on related questions of choice that seems to lend it support. People on the point of retiring show a marked preference for taking as much of their future benefits as the Inland Revenue will allow in the form of lump sums, with a reduction in annual pension. Furthermore, it is relevant that in the market for annuities fixed-sum annuities are generally greatly preferred to increasing annuities, which start with lower payments. No doubt this tells us something about time preference. It may also reflect the composition of whatever other assets beneficiaries may hold, for these assets may include items of capital which afford protection against inflation, such as houses. Without speculating further, we can at least record the fact that occupational pensions in payment could have been raised more over recent years in order to provide better protection against inflation if there had been less emphasis on providing pensions that would afford high replacement ratios at the time of retirement.

Any assessment of the future solvency of pension funds must involve difficult technical issues that lie beyond the scope of this volume. What must be noted, however, is that trustees can exercise their discretion with little legal restraint or supervision. This has not so far resulted in serious disasters, but that was scarcely to be expected in times of prosperity. In hard times there could be serious difficulties.[15] Indeed, a sharp fall in inflation, with lower rates of return in money terms on assets held, could seriously affect the financial position of the funds. Admittedly, contribution rates could be raised, but this might not always be possible on a large enough scale. Employees would resent higher contributions for unenhanced benefits, and trade unions could be expected to demand more pay as compensation. In a declining firm with a shrinking number of employees this source of additional finance would be particularly limited; nor could the firm easily afford the employer's contribution. In some countries – for example, Sweden – there are institutional arrangements for insuring obligations, and the case for following suit in Britain needs to be examined. A substantial proportion of pension schemes in Britain are, of course, already run by insurance companies or mutual assurance societies, and in their case the normal insurance guarantee applies to the fund.

There is another institutional change that should, in principle, help pension funds to provide better protection against inflation. This is the provision of indexed bonds now available to them, though not on an unlimited scale. It is interesting to observe that these bonds were not an immediate sell-out in 1980/1, as was widely predicted. The return they offer is much lower than that on ordinary government bonds, and if inflation were to be brought under control and reduced, the latter could yield a higher real return than indexed bonds. In short, there was a choice between a secure but modest return and a potentially high but uncertain one. If inflation should persist or increase once more, these previous investments in unindexed bonds could prove to have been a mistake.

One of the advantages claimed for funded pension schemes is that they provide a large flow of savings for investment and are thus helpful to economic growth. It is true that if there were less deferred pay – for that is how occupational pensions can be described – and correspondingly higher current pay, presumably more saving would be done voluntarily by individuals. The net effect of the institutional arrangements cannot therefore be precisely assessed but can reasonably be assumed to be substantially positive.

The pension funds which provide about a third of total personal savings have great potential power in the capital markets, in particular in the markets for shares and real property, for there is not much investment in fixed-interest securities. The pension funds have been criticised for not using this power in a more enterprising way. This criticism may be largely unfair, but it is only to be expected that increasingly insistent demands for official control will be made. The defenders of these funds can urge that official interference might well involve greater risks for the pensioners if this were to lead to a significant part of their resources being directed into whatever projects commended themselves to the government of the day.

A question that may now be posed is whether some pay-as-you-go arrangement could not be devised for linking private occupational pensions directly to the earnings of those at work without undermining the solvency of the schemes. In fact, the French have devised just such an arrangement.[16] Each firm belongs – indeed *must* belong – to a federal scheme. Contributions are paid to those organisations, and it is they that are responsible for paying pensions. Not only does this avoid any complication when a future pensioner changes jobs, but the fact that a large number of firms are grouped in this way obviously provides a much higher degree of security than a single firm, acting in isolation, could provide for an unfunded scheme. As contributions are proportionate to wages, resources have been available to raise benefits in line (roughly speaking) with earnings – as in the official pay-as-you-go schemes. With rising unemployment during the depression, however, these federations have appeared less strong, and the need to raise the contribution rate, if benefits are still to be raised with earnings, has led to tension and uncertainty. In short, though ingenious and attractive in several respects, the French model may look rather less secure in the 1980s than it did in the 1960s. It should be noted further that these schemes contribute nothing of significance to national savings but, by their very existence the benefits they offer may reduce the rate of saving by individuals.

GRADUATED BENEFITS AND LIFECYCLE EXPENDITURE

As was pointed out in Chapter 2, the case for the provision of graduated benefits by the state rests on somewhat shaky foundations. It is one thing to provide a minimum as protection against poverty – perhaps even a generous minimum. It is a different matter to project into retirement some of the inequality of working life. Private people, for their part, will naturally wish to have some such protection. Everyone will want to enjoy a standard of living which, if lower than before retirement, at least bears some relation to it. But they could be left to act accordingly. It is not apparent that this is the responsibility of the state.

One of the reasons given for the adoption of a graduated scheme in Britain in 1975 was the uneven distribution of occupational pensions. Until recent times these schemes had been designed mainly for salaried employees, and even in the 1970s the proportion of manual workers covered was smaller, and their pensions, especially pensions already in payment, were much smaller. The state, it was said, had to step in to fill the gap and to ensure a more equitable arrangement.

Occupational pensions have traditionally been described as deferred pay. How, then, is one to interpret the assertion that manual workers should also have good graduated pensions? Does that mean that more of their pay should be deferred? Or that they should have more pay in total? If the first answer is given, this raises at once the further question of whether manual workers themselves would endorse this view. If the second answer is given, then legal insistence on graduated benefits – whether in an official scheme or in a contracted-out scheme – is somewhat analogous to minimum wage legislation, and the final benefit, when everything is taken into account, may be somewhat dubious.

There are, however, some good reasons for wishing to belong to a graduated scheme or to remain within such a scheme. If this were not so, one would expect protests to be made. For official and occupational provisions combined replace very substantial proportions of previous income received when at work. Indeed, it is not impossible to be better off after retirement, especially when account is taken of the saving of expenditure on national insurance contributions, travel to work, meals out and so on. No doubt many people may be content to have their life-cycle expenditure substantially influenced by such pension arrangements. Others, however, might prefer something different. This is a matter over which diversity of preferences is to be expected; yet the protests appear to have been few.

One explanation is that future pensioners can and do take offsetting action by accumulating smaller independent savings than they would otherwise. In so far as their pensions will come ultimately from a pay-as-you-go official scheme, the proportion of national income saved is probably reduced as a result; in so far as their pensions come from funded occupational schemes, the role of the institutional investor grows at the expense of the private investor. There are two important consequences of attempting to adjust lifecycle expenditure.

However, there are reasons for believing that few people would opt out of official graduated or occupational schemes even if given the chance to do so. A person who did so would not, of course, have to contribute any more, and his gross pay would rise accordingly. But it would be a bad bargain unless he were also to receive: (a) the contributions that would otherwise be made on his behalf by his employer; (b) the tax remission his employer would receive; (c) access to an investment fund which enjoyed the same tax privileges as a pension fund.

These reflections prompt the suggestion that some provision might be made for opting out not only from the state scheme (apart from the basic pension) but from private occupational schemes as well. After all, one of the claims made for occupational schemes is that they offer variety. In fact, this is so only to a limited extent. A real regard for private preferences would require more provision for the exercise of more independent judgement in the shaping of lifecycle expenditure. Obviously, the administrative cost would make it necessary to restrict choice to a limited number of packages, but some variety at least could be permitted on condition – a crucial condition – that the government agreed to complementary provisions with regard to taxation.

The general assumption usually implicit in discussion of these matters is that private people, if left to themselves, would make too little provision for old age and that they would see their mistake only when it was too late. This assumption may be realistic enough for some people. But there may well be others who, without being in the least short-sighted or improvident, would prefer to contribute a little less for their retirement in order to have more cash available at an earlier age, when family responsibilities have to be met.

NOTES

1 J. Harris, *William Beveridge: a Biography* (Oxford: Oxford University Press, 1977).
2 D. Moggridge (ed.), *Collected Writings of John Maynard Keynes*, vol. 27: *Activities 1940–46* (London and Cambridge: Macmillan and Cambridge University Press, 1980).
3 M. Friedman, *Monetary Correction* (London: Institute of Economic Affairs, 1974).
4 H. Heclo, *Modern Social Politics in Britain and Sweden* (New Haven, Conn.: Yale University Press, 1974).
5 *Public Expenditure on Income Maintenance Programmes* (Paris: OECD, 1976).
6 T. Wilson, 'The finance of the welfare state', in A. T. Peacock and F. Forte (eds), *The Political Economy of Taxation* (Oxford: Blackwell, 1981), p. 110.
7 K. Judge, 'State pensions and the growth of social welfare expenditure', *Journal of Social Policy*, vol. 10 (1981).
8 *Employment Policy*, Cmd 6527 (London: HMSO, 1944).
9 T. Wilson (ed.), *Pensions, Inflation and Growth* (London: Heinemann, 1974).

CHAPTER 6

The Welfare State and the Health Services

The demand for medical care and its supply have some special characteristics which have been mentioned in Chapter 2. Illness strikes with uncertain incidence, sometimes mildly but sometimes with devastating consequences in the form of medical costs as well as lost income.[1] When medical services are provided on the market, insurance cover may be bought, but the cost is high if this cover is to be reasonably comprehensive. Some may be too improvident to pay for this insurance. Others may be too poor to do so. Of course, the cost must be met somehow, for there is no such thing as a free hospital bed, any more than there is a free lunch! The payment may be made voluntarily, either directly or through an insurance policy, or it may be under compulsion, through taxation. This latter alternative has been supported on the ground that some redistribution of the costs between income groups is appropriate and that the desirable degree of equality of access to medical care is greater than the desirable degree of equality of total income. It has been opposed on the ground that it not only restricts freedom of choice between different forms of treatment but also limits supply to what the government's budget can bear, although many individuals might be prepared willingly to pay more.

Whatever the system used – whether wholly public, or wholly private or some combination of both – it is clear that medical services are different from many others, at least in degree. In particular, the consumer is often inadequately informed about his need for treatment and is generally very ill-informed about the form that treatment can best take and its probable efficacy;[2] nor is it easy for him to shop around and test different possibilities – even in less extreme cases when his illness is not such that death may cut short the shopping around. These are real difficulties and are not to be dispelled by moving from private to public medicine or vice versa. They hold good, if to varying degrees, no matter in what way health care is provided.

In looking at the various approaches which different countries have adopted to the provision of health care, an over-simple distinction is frequently made between private and public health care models, as exemplified by those of the USA and the UK. In practice, neither country conforms strictly to either description; there is a small but growing market for private health services in the UK, and in the USA the Federal and state governments together are responsible for over two-fifths of total private and public expenditure on health care. Between these supposed extremes there is a wide variety of health systems in Western Europe, which combine, in varying patterns, compulsory health insurance, the free provision of some services, charges for others and the public and private supply of facilities. All countries have accepted some national responsibility for health, but there is enormous variety in the ways in which these responsibilities are met. Health, perhaps more than any other area of the social services, demonstrates Wilensky's proposition that 'The welfare state is at once one of the great structural uniformities of modern society and, paradoxically, one of its most striking diversities.'[3]

DIFFERENT MODELS OF HEALTH SERVICE PROVISION

This section summarises the main features of the systems by which health services are provided in the UK, the USA and some other countries; the lessons to be learned from these different models will be taken up in later sections of the chapter. We begin with a 'public' model: the National Health Service (NHS) which came into operation in 1948 in England and Wales and, with small differences, in Scotland and Northern Ireland. The aim was to provide a comprehensive system of health care, free at time of use and guaranteeing equality of access to every individual, irrespective of age, sex or place of residence. It is true that free services did not necessarily mean the public *supply* of these services by an agency of central government, for the services could still have been supplied by municipal or private sources. As Abel Smith has observed: 'The removal of the money barrier [did] not make it necessary to nationalize health services.'[4] Nor need some nationalization of supply necessarily have entailed monopolistic supply. The postwar Labour Government, however, came down firmly in favour of linking public supply to public financing.

Public supply inevitably raises difficult questions concerning legislative and administrative centralisation or devolution, equitable distribution and the efficient use of resources and, in the case of health, some particularly sensitive problems raised by the monitoring of professional standards of performance. Various experiments have been tried over the years in order to find workable solutions to these problems. The first model, the so-called tripartite structure introduced in 1948, owed much to the need to secure the co-operation of the various long-standing components of the medical services, which were then brought together in order to form the new system and which viewed 'nationalisation' with varying degrees of hostility. First, the voluntary and municipal hospitals, which had already been brought under government control as an emergency wartime measure, were absorbed into the NHS. Secondly, as some sop for losing permanent control of their hospitals, the elected local authorities were left to provide, and in large measure to pay for, local health services such as maternity and child welfare, immunisation and home nursing. Thirdly, a somewhat uneasy compromise was worked out with general medical, dental and ophthalmic practitioners and pharmacists working outside the hospital service, all of whom had been strongly opposed to any suggestion of government employment, whereby they made their services available, under contract, to local committees largely composed of members of their own professions. There was no compelling logic for this hybrid system of centralised, devolved and quasi-private provision; it was essentially a political compromise.

The weaknesses of this division of functions came under increasing attack: services, it was alleged, were frequently duplicated or triplicated; co-ordination was poor; administration was excessive; and services were of very uneven standards. After prolonged deliberations the Joseph plan for comprehensive reorganisation was put into operation in 1974. This brought the hospital and local health services together in a three-tier administrative structure organised on a regional, area and district basis; the general medical practitioners once again retained a large measure of independence under their own Family Practitioner Committees. The consumer's interest and involvement in the operation of the NHS was to be served through the appointment of Community Health Councils (CHCs).

The reorganised structure again came under attack. The various health authorities and management teams at different levels of the structure were appointees acting, in principle, not as representatives of any particular interests but as participants in corporate decision-making and management. The local authorities, trade unions and other lay interests, as well as the medical profession, were consulted before appointments were made, but it was soon claimed that the medical members of the various bodies were, by virtue of their standing and expertise, exerting more than their 'due' share of influence. Conversely, the professionals were critical of what they saw as a top-heavy management structure, excessive red tape and the undue weight exercised by lay administrators and financial advisers. As the CHCs were largely appointed bodies, their links with the community were often tenuous. Some of them were allegedly ineffectual, others dominated by political minorities. Whatever the rights and wrongs of these charges and counter-charges, there seems little doubt that the reorganisation had been less effective than had been expected in bringing together in a working partnership the different branches of the health professions, the various lay interests and the consumers of the service.

The Royal Commission, in the Report published in 1979, was of the opinion that 'we need not be ashamed of our health service' and that there are many aspects of it of which 'we can be justly proud.'[5] It did, however, go on to recommend a further overhaul and simplification of the administrative structure. Some of its proposals were novel but impractical or contentious. One of the most remarkable was that the delivery of health services should be fully delegated to the regional health authorities, which were actually to be made responsible to a committee of the House of Commons, not to a Minister. General practitioners were to be given the option of salaried employment. The CHCs were to be strengthened. In 1979 the Government responded with a consultative document, *Patients First*, which, while accepting the need for slimming the administrative structure of the NHS, rejected the specific proposals of the Royal Commission. Subsequently, the Government brought into effect, as from April 1982, a new structure which will retain the regional health authorities in their existing form but will combine the responsibilities of the former area health authorities and district management teams in new district health authorities which, it is hoped, will bring management closer to the recipients of the service and into line with the Conservative Government's philosophy of local responsibility. At the same time it is hoped that considerable savings will be made in administrative costs. It remains to be seen whether the changes will be anything more than symbolic, for 'symbolic action' is 'the tribute political necessity pays to Party ideology'.[6]

Some space has been devoted to the administrative problems of the NHS that are in some ways unique to a nationalised health service, which combines public financing with public supply by central government. Other health-care systems follow various different lines, which can be touched on only briefly. As has been stressed above, there is a danger in doing so of indulging in oversimplified polarisation between 'public' and 'private' medicine. Even in the UK, with its largely zero-priced health services and the nationalised provision of medical facilities, there is a sizable private market in non-prescribed drugs, in dental and ophthalmic treatment and in insurance for hospital treatment outside the public sector. Conversely, although the USA is commonly cited as the prime example of a 'private' system, government revenues finance 40 per cent of total health expenditure from private and public monies. It is true, however, that government intervention in the USA is highly selective in the groups for which it caters and that its activities differ from the British model in that assistance largely takes the form of the subsidisation of health insurance or the reimbursement of medical costs. Only for special categories of people does government at any level go so far as to *provide* medical facilities. There are, for instance, Federal facilities for service veterans and for small groups of the Indians and Esquimaux, state mental hospitals and local government maternity and child welfare services.

In the USA the two big programmes, accounting for over four-fifths of public expenditure on health, are Medicare and Medicaid, which date only from the mid-1960s. Medicare is primarily a compulsory hospital insurance (HI) programme for elderly or disabled social security pensioners. It is financed out of a payroll tax levied on employers and employees, together with a federal government subsidy. A pensioner may voluntarily take out Supplementary Medical Insurance (SMI), which is subsidised by the federal government and covers part of the cost of drugs and surgeons' and physicians' fees when these are incurred during the treatment either of hospital patients or of out-patients, up to 'reasonable' limits. The patient is still left with quite heavy premiums and deductibles to pay under SMI, as well as the full cost of hospital or nursing-home care, when his HI entitlements run out. It is reckoned that HI and SMI together cover on average some 40 per cent of the medical bills of the elderly, who constitute about 10 per cent of the total population. Some elderly people take out further (expensive) private insurance; others continue to be covered by their former employers' health insurance plans; many have to fall back on means-tested Medicaid.

Medicaid, the largest of the federal government health programmes, is designed to help with the medical expenses of the recipients of various federally supported, means-tested assistance programmes for the elderly, for the sick and disabled and for families with dependent children. About half the states extend Medicaid to the 'medically indigent' (that is, people who would be on assistance if they did not receive help with their medical bills), and in total nearly 10 per cent of the population are helped in this way. Medicaid is jointly financed by the Federal and state governments, the former providing between 50 and 80 per cent of the cost, according to the tax-raising capacity of the different states. Like Medicare, it operates on a reimbursement basis, and the efforts of the Federal Government to tighten its control over the price and the quality of the services supplied by private or public hospitals and medical practitioners do not appear to have met with much success.[7] Nor does the system of internal review by the medical profession itself, introduced in the mid–1970s in the hope of exercising some control over expenditure under these programmes, appear to have been particularly effective.

For the great bulk of the population, however, there is no government assistance with the high costs of medical care. Over the years 1946–69 the price of medical services increased by 129 per cent, while the general price rise was only 69 per cent.[8] (There is no reason to suppose that the relative price effect has changed much in the ensuing years.) The potential patient may find it difficult to turn his 'want' into an 'expressed demand' for medical care at the time when he needs it. Rationing is to a large extent determined by the purse, and, not surprisingly, there is evidence to suggest that the consumption of medical services is correlated with income.[9] As might be expected, extensive use is made of private insurance in order to obtain some protection, although the cover thus obtained is not comprehensive. About four-fifths of the non-pensioner population have insurance at least against the heavy costs of in-patient hospital treatment; about 50 per cent are covered for physicians' or surgeons' fees and for drugs or X-ray and other diagnostic procedures, whether in hospital or at home; less than 10 per cent have any dental insurance. Private insurance rarely covers the whole cost of treatment, so there may still be considerable medical bills to be met. For the majority of employees insurance is provided through company group plans, largely as the result of collective bargaining. For those not covered in this way (and these are likely to be the poorer non-unionised workers), private purchase of care at time of use or private insurance may be very costly, and unless their incomes are low enough to qualify them for Medicaid, their only resort may be municipal or charity hospitals which, with some notable exceptions, provide low-quality amenities and medical attention. The whole system favours in-patient treatment – which, of course, raises costs further and may not reflect the patient's individual preferences.

At various positions on the spectrum between the so-called 'public' and 'private' models of the UK and USA lie the health-care systems of most western European countries, shaped by their different historical, political and social roots. Nearest to that of the UK perhaps is the Swedish system. Comprehensive medical and dental care is now available to every citizen or resident of Sweden, although charges at time of use, except for in-patient hospital treatment, play a larger, if still limited, role than in the UK. Nominally the Swedish system works on an insurance basis, but contribution records are irrelevant when it comes to obtaining access to services, and contribution income makes up only a very small proportion of the revenues of the health service. Unlike that of the UK, the central government in Sweden does not *supply* or even finance the actual facilities; this is the responsibility of the twenty-five county governments that for over a century have had the power to raise a local income tax, four-fifths of which is spent on their hospital services. Most out-patient treatment is provided by hospital out-patient departments or local health centres, and the great majority of doctors have been salaried employees of the county councils since the early 1970s. The strong financial standing of the counties has resulted in vast hospital-building programmes and operational costs, which in turn have pushed up Swedish health expenditure to about 10 per cent of GNP. The health-care systems in other Scandinavian countries follow broadly the same pattern.

To take a rather different example: in West Germany the first compulsory health insurance scheme for workers was introduced in 1883 and has subsequently been widened until it now covers over 90 per cent of the population. The financial arrangements are handled by some 1,400 independent health insurance funds organised on an occupational basis. Contributions from employers and employees, which are earnings-related, provide the main source of income for the funds and at any given level of income are higher for manual than for salaried workers because of the greater sickness risk in the case of the former. The funds reimburse the private practitioners and the local government, voluntary and private hospitals which provide the services, according to scales of fees negotiated between government, the funds and the suppliers of the services. Remuneration on a fee-for-service basis for out-patient and hospital care has pushed up both the amount of treatment prescribed and the length of hospital stay and hence the overall cost of the service.

In other countries different variations on these themes are to be found. In France 98 per cent of the population is covered by compulsory insurance, which is largely financed by employers' and employees' contributions and is handled by some 120 social insurance funds. The patient, however, is usually left to pay his own medical expenses and to claim reimbursement from his fund. Whereas in West Germany this form of insurance covers virtually the whole of medical care, this is not the case in France, where, increasingly, additional private insurance is being taken out to cover the patient's share of doctors' and hospital bills. Social aid, as in West Germany, continues to provide medical care for poor people with no insurance rights.

The Netherlands has an interesting two-part arrangement. Insurance against heavy medical costs, such as those incurred by long-term illness or permanent disability, is compulsory for the whole population and provides unlimited free health care. For less costly, routine medical care lower-paid workers are required to take out insurance with one of some seventy sickness funds which handle the heavy risk insurance, but such insurance is voluntary for higher-paid workers, the self-employed and the elderly. Some 70 per cent of the population is covered through the sickness funds, and the majority of other workers choose to take out private insurance against routine medical costs. Small contributions are payable for the compulsory insurance, but the greater part of the cost is met out of general tax revenue.

In the UK it is often argued that a national health scheme financed out of general taxation is preferable to private health insurance, which would be so costly as to put it beyond the reach of large sections of the population. However, the experience of the Continental schemes would appear, at first sight, to contradict this view. It may be natural to ask whether mutual assurance societies could not be expected to do the job of financing health services quite satisfactorily – where 'mutual' means that the associations are non-profit-making co-operatives. On closer inspection, however, much is seen to turn on the meaning given to the term 'insurance'. Insurance in these countries is not actuarially comparable with that used in private insurance. It is true that the higher contributions exacted in West Germany from those groups that are more liable to sickness is a partial concession to the actuarial principle, but it is only partial. In all these countries the contributions paid are proportional to earnings, and this represents an obvious difference from the practice that would be followed if individuals were left to insure themselves as private individuals. For this form of financing clearly permits a measure of redistribution which is not actuarial in the strict sense, although it may obviously be highly desirable on social grounds. In short, these Continental arrangements can be regarded as examples of 'social insurance' (so-called) against the risk of sickness. Indeed, as the state requires these contributions to be made, the arrangements can be described as official health schemes financed by earmarked taxes imposed on workers and employers, though with an administrative framework that is very different from that of the NHS. Suppose the British social security plan instituted in 1948 had been so designed that the NHS was financed from contributions to the same extent as cash benefits instead of being financed by general taxation. It would then have been possible to say that the NHS was financed on the basis of 'social insurance' in the same sense as that in which the financing of cash transfers is described.

What, then, are the differences? First, the fact that the NHS is financed from general revenue means that the cost is met in a somewhat more progressive way than would be the case if the cost were met entirely from a proportional tax on earnings paid by employees, together with a proportional tax – of still more uncertain incidence – paid by employers.

The second point is that administrative costs may be different under these two different arrangements. It could be argued, on the basis of economies of scale, that the administrative costs of the unified NHS system must be less than those incurred in running a number of separate insurance institutions. This is not, however, a point that can be established *a priori* one way or the other.

Thirdly, the creators of the NHS believed, on what appear to have been largely doctrinaire grounds, that the *supply* of medical services should also be nationalised. In the countries described above the supply of health care has been left in the hands of sub-central levels of government and of voluntary bodies and private suppliers. Again, an exceedingly difficult assessment of the outcome would need to be made before a confident verdict could be given. Economies of scale *may* be present, at least in some parts of the service. Apart from economies of scale in hospitals, medical centres and the like, there is the exceedingly important problem of monitoring medical costs – a problem which, in the nature of the case, is difficult to resolve under *all* systems of organisation. Direct control by central government offices is, of course, out of the question. Some form of decentralisation is essential, and the successive reforms of the structure of the NHS described above can be regarded in part as attempts to achieve a more satisfactory outcome. The question, then, is whether monitoring is or is not more effective when the bills are paid by a number of insurance organisations, but we are not in a position to hazard an answer to this question.

The fourth difference is the acceptance of the view in these Continental countries that not all medical costs need be covered by their respective schemes. To a marginal degree this point is also accepted under the NHS, in that charges are made for prescriptions, glasses and dentures, but the range of charges could be extended. That is to say, there could be full cover, as in the Continental health services described above, against the heavy hospital charges, with more limited assistance with expenditure on other items. Additional private insurance could then be taken out voluntarily to cover these excluded risks. An objection to this arrangement is that it would place a burden on the lower-income groups, although the cost could be met on a means-tested basis in the case of those who were really poor. A possible advantage would be that, given that there is a limit to what people will pay in taxation, the proportion of public money available for the extension and improvement of hospital care would be rather greater.

The fifth difference is that the NHS imposes a penalty on the expression of different preferences for expenditure on health care. Some people would clearly wish to devote more of their income or capital in order, say, to obtain earlier treatment for arthritic hip joints or in order to have better hospital accommodation than their local NHS hospitals can provide. This they may indeed be able to obtain in private institutions or through private insurance – some 2¾ million people and their dependants are covered in this way. But in exerting their preferences they are paying twice. That is to say, they have to pay the cost in these institutions but are not given any rebate because they are not making a claim on the resources of the NHS to which they have contributed as taxpayers. It is true too that in some NHS hospitals a compromise is permitted in the form of amenity beds provided in return for special charges, but the scale of such provision is limited. When the financing is done through a Continental insurance scheme the funds thus provided can be supplemented from private insurance, which means that these patients do not pay twice. It need scarcely be said that this is a highly controversial issue. There is a strongly, though not universally held opinion in Britain that all medical services should be supplied on a strictly egalitarian basis. It is a view that must be treated with respect in the case of catastrophic illness, when it is a question of life and death or dealing with very painful illnesses. But a cool assessment of the extension of this principle is also appropriate. If the supply of skilled medical attention is limited, there is clearly much force in this contention. If the supply of doctors is limited and, given long training periods, cannot quickly be increased, then it would be ethically wrong to allow those whose illnesses may be less acute to divert to their care, by virtue of the mere size of their purses, some of the attention that is urgently needed by poorer people whose illnesses are much more acute. The supply situation is changing, however, and soon the supply of doctors in Britain may exceed the demand for their services, as this is limited by the funds at the disposal of the NHS. Moreover, the provision of amenity beds and the like would not really seem to raise the same ethical question. It would rather appear to be the case that by catering more fully for supplementary private demands in this way, the NHS might add a little to the funds at its disposal which could then be put to good use.

If an attempt is made to assess the respective merits of the health systems in different countries, the global statistics are of limited assistance. Sweden and West Germany spend about one and a half times as much, in relation to GNP, as does the UK. Moreover, GNP per head is substantially higher in these countries. The amount of health care provided – as measured crudely by doctors or hospital beds per thousand – is greater (see p. 157 below), and it appears to be the case that the standard of amenity in hospitals and in the surgeries of private practitioners is higher. To what extent these better provisions explain the higher cost is impossible to judge, for, once again, there is the difficult question of the efficiency with which health expenditure is monitored and the extent to which health costs have risen in relation to other costs. The answer can be expected to vary from country to country. Even a detailed comparative investigation into these matters – which we are not competent to make – could be expected to produce no more than incomplete and tentative answers. But it is a fair criticism of the various investigations into the NHS that the approaches have been unduly parochial and that little attempt, it would seem, has been made to derive what lessons may be learned from the experience of other countries.

DEMAND AND SUPPLY IN A ZERO-PRICE HEALTH SERVICE

When, as is the case in the UK, medical services are supplied in the main at a zero or low price in cash, the potential demand is indefinitely large. In such circumstances 'Rational consumers will go on demanding health care until the "marginal utility" approaches zero'[10] – that is to say, until further units of the service confer no additional utility. In fact, demand will be restricted by the cost in terms of time and inconvenience to the patient. If demand still exceeds supply, some form of rationing will be required; this will be discussed below. For public choice – that is to say the choices made by government and its agencies – in this case will determine supply, not unsatisfied demand expressed through the market, and public choice will also determine the various forms in which health services will be supplied.

Given the rapid advances in medical science and the restraints on resources, the NHS has operated in large measure as a 'crisis' service, heavily orientated towards *curing*, with the aid of expensive new medical techniques, rather than *preventing* illness or *caring* for the chronically sick. Yet, with a growing number of elderly people long-term care requires more emphasis, which was acknowledged when geriatric and psychiatric services were safeguarded against the full rigours of the cash limits imposed on expenditure in the later 1970s. The biggest cuts then fell on deferrable capital expenditure, such as the renewal of hospital stock, in which economies are easier to make than in the case of current expenditure on treatment and care. The allocation of resources between different uses has not always been made as explicitly as these last statements imply. Allocations were in large measure incremental, so that what was spent in year 1 more or less determined what was spent in year 2 – although in the longer term the changes following on from proposals made by the Resource Allocation Working Party[11] should bring about a more efficient allocation policy. Revenues are to be allocated between regions according to a formula worked out on the basis of population figures, adjusted for age, sex and marital status and standardised fertility and mortality rates. Adjustments are to be made for the high costs of providing medical services in London, for teaching activities and for the movement of patients between different areas. There is a separate population-based formula for calculating capital expenditure in England. The Royal Commission on the NHS, which reported in 1979, considered the formulae 'an important step towards determining a rational and equitable system of allocating resources', although it was critical of their actual constitution (which is, in fact, under the scrutiny by the DHSS at the time of writing).[12]

At the individual level, it is not only the overall supply of resources which determines whether the patient's wants with respect to health care are satisfied but also the manner in which these wants are expressed and converted into demands. Apart from the school medical service and emergencies such as road accidents, fires and so on, when the consumer has little choice but to submit to medical examination and treatment, it is up to the potential patient to express initially his desire for medical care. This want is often met by self-medication bought in the market rather than by a visit to the doctor. Thus it has been estimated that 30 per cent of all drug sales by value were direct over-the-counter purchases of non-prescription drugs.[13] A potential patient will naturally be discouraged from seeking medical attention if the costs involved in gaining access to such attention are greater than the anticipated return. There are, in fact, considerable deterrents to converting wants into demands by making a visit to the general practitioner, who, in the majority of cases, is the patient's first contact with the health service. If the general practitioner operates an appointment system, as is generally, the case, it may take several days to obtain an appointment, by which time the condition which stimulated the original want may have righted itself. The potential patient may prefer to take the risk that his possible requirement for medical attention may not turn out to be self-eliminating rather than wait for an appointment and then for treatment. The opportunity cost to the patient in work time lost or leisure forgone may sometimes not be taken adequate account of by the medical practitioner, although the latter may be very conscious of such costs to himself when asked to make home visits. The position may be different, of course, when the patient is paying for the service. In this case he will have more opportunity to change his medical practitioner, so there may be pressure on doctors to pay more heed to their appointment systems. On the other hand, in a nil-price system, at any given intensity of demand for medical attention, the patient may be willing to incur *greater* opportunity costs in lost time and inconvenience in obtaining medical care. This problem does not disappear if the patient is using private health services, provided he has bought medical insurance, especially when the insurance cover is unrestricted and there are no deductibles. This is a case of 'moral hazard' – to use the jargon.

In the first instance it may not even be the doctor himself but his receptionist who decides between competing claims on the time which the doctor makes available for consultations and who acts as a gatekeeper between the patient and the attention he is seeking. There are other ways too in which the doctor may ration his services to the patient – for example, short consultation time especially perhaps for less vocal and less demanding patients, the use of ancillary staff, repeat prescriptions and so on. There is no guarantee that such rationing procedures produce a fairer distribution of medical resources than would a pricing system.[14]

When the patient succeeds in seeing his medical practitioner, it is the latter who decides whether or not the individual's want for medical attention should be converted into a further demand on the health services: medication or investigation or treatment at the out-patient department of a hospital or a specialist consultation. Thus the doctor is in a strong position.[15] Not only does he know more about the supply side of the market than does the consumer, but he also knows more about the 'mix' of services that it is appropriate for the consumer to demand. There are few doctors, however, who will send the patient away without at least a prescription for a drug, which in many cases may be no more than a *placebo*. Pressure is being put on medical practitioners by the DHSS to limit their prescribing habits, but a patient's expectations may carry more weight than any official exhortation, particularly with a busy practitioner who does not have the time to offer his patient the alternative of simple advice or moral support. The patient is, by and large, willing to allow the doctor to determine what health care he may call on, although some patients are more vocal and more persistent than others in turning their wants for medical attention into specific demands and in influencing the way in which those demands should be met. (These are problems which are not confined to a zero-price system.)

In most cases the general medical practitioner cannot recommend hospitalisation, for this is the function of the consultant to whom the patient is referred. There are therefore two screening or rationing procedures to be gone through, and this imposes further restrictions on the consumer's freedom of choice. Whether or not in-patient treatment is recommended will depend not only on the seriousness of the medical condition and the persistence of the patient but also on the amount of the service available. It is necessary to add that even in a market system like that in the USA the suppliers may play a crucial role in shaping demand. For example, if a doctor knows that a patient has medical insurance, he may be less reluctant to press the need for expensive treatment such as surgery.

In the case of in-patient care any shortfall between demand and supply is generally measured by the length of the waiting lists for hospital beds. If the supply of beds is increased, however, it does not necessarily follow that the waiting list will be proportionately reduced. Doctors may then adopt different criteria for determining the need for hospital treatment; either more patients will receive it, or the length of the in-patient stays will go up. The knowledge that supply has increased will also affect the patients' demand for treatment at a zero price: hence the difficulty of reducing the length of the waiting list. In other ways too the waiting list is a very imperfect indicator of unmet need. Some patients die before they reach the top of the list. In some cases the medical condition cures itself; in others, when treatment or surgery is elective, the fact of being on a waiting list does not necessarily mean that the demand will still be there when the supply becomes available. In economic jargon, demand and supply are not independent functions. The waiting list remained remarkably stable for many years at about the 500,000 mark, despite a more than twofold increase in the number of patients receiving hospital treatment in any year. The list lengthened in the mid-1970s and peaked at 750,000 in 1979 before falling again to something over 600,000 in 1980. Industrial action among hospital staff was an important factor in accounting for the rise in numbers. In turn, patients may have been discouraged from seeking treatment, especially of an elective nature, by their knowledge of resource constraints. Doctors too may have pursued more conservative policies in referring their patients for hospital consultations which might result in a decrease in demand for in-patient treatment.

The truth of the matter, however, is that we have no firm basis for estimating what has been called the 'iceberg' of untreated sickness below the tip which actually receives attention.[16] Although this metaphor begs the question, such surveys as have been carried out suggest that unmet 'needs' (as these might be assessed after more rigorous investigation by the medical profession) could overwhelm the NHS. Some filtering of demand is obviously necessary, whether achieved by the market or in other ways. In either case we have no means of knowing whether, and if so to what extent, the health status of the nation as a whole suffers as a consequence. We may assume, however, that for any population of a given size and composition, the want for medical attention will rise with continuing improvements in the information available to patients, with a lowered tolerance of minor illnesses and with improvements in the identification of new treatments for disease. It may be that the greatest scope for containing the demand for health care lies outside a health service, whatever its form – for example, in wiser expenditure on food and alcohol, in the control of environmental pollution and so on.

This is not to say that there is no room for increasing the supply of medical care, and this might be achieved by the more economical use of given resources. There is evidence of excessive demands for drugs on prescription on the part of patients, as well as of over-prescribing on the part of doctors. There is evidence too that some drugs prescribed are at best harmless but ineffective, at worst positively harmful.[17] Not all members of the medical profession are likely to respond to the DHSS guidelines on prescribing, which they may regard as government intervention with their clinical freedom. Admittedly, the cost of drugs should not be looked at in isolation. Account must also be taken of the alternative cost of hospital care for patients who might otherwise be cured or treated in their own homes with the aid of drugs.

Any further steps that could be taken to control the use of hospital beds would appear to offer the greatest scope for economy in finance and manpower. The NHS has already gone some way towards making more intensive use of the stock of hospital beds, though admittedly with a disproportionate increase in the number of hospital personnel employed.[18]

More intensive use of primary care as a substitute for hospitalisation may offer more scope for reducing expenditure. Even if this increases the demand for the services of general practitioners, home nurses and other ancillary medical staff and for welfare services like home helps, there are big offsetting economies for the NHS in hospital 'hotel' and overhead costs and in the servicing of capital required for building and equipping the marginal hospital bed. The answer, however, is not as clear-cut if account is also taken of an appropriate part of the capital and revenue costs of maintaining the patient's own home and of the labour of the relatives involved. There are opportunity costs too if family members have to forgo earnings in order to stay at home to look after a sick person. These costs have already been acknowledged by the Government through the introduction of attendance and invalid care allowances (see Chapter 3).

THE COSTS AND FINANCES OF HEALTH CARE

A question sometimes asked in Britain is: can the country 'afford' a free national health service? The implication here is that spending has been wildly extravagant. Conversely, it has been said from time to time that the service is grinding to a halt for lack of money, and frequent predictions of bankruptcy have been made. What are the facts?

Expressed as a percentage of the gross national product, expenditure fell during the early 1950s after an initial rise when the large unmet demand for health care was unleashed (see Table 6.1). From the mid-1950s to the late 1960s the rate of growth was slow, especially in view of the rapid advances in medical technology over this period. Between the late 1960s and the early 1980s the pace accelerated, but the UK still spent a smaller proportion of her GNP on the health services than did other

Table 6.1 *Expenditure on the NHS as a percentage of GNP at factor cost, 1950–80*

1950	*1955*	*1960*	*1965*	*1970*	*1975*	*1980*
4·2	3·5	3·9	4·2	4·5	5·4	5·9

Source: National Income and Expenditure (London: HMSO, various years).

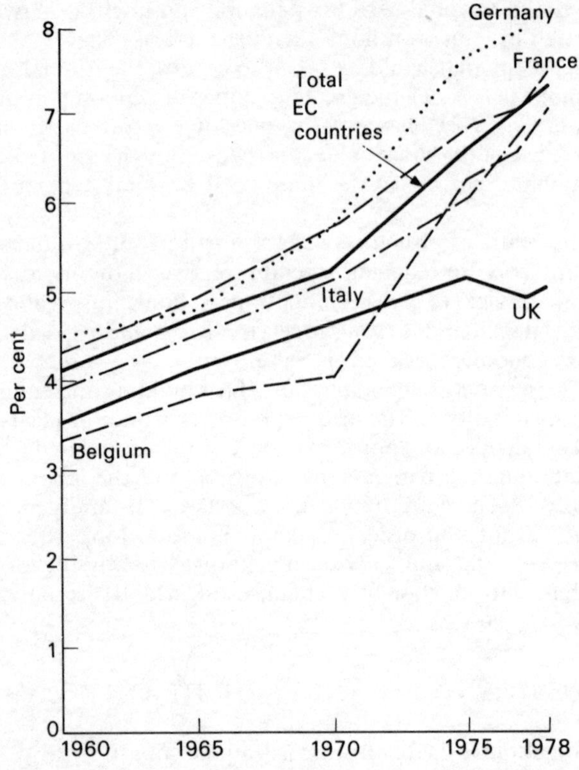

Figure 6.1 *Health care expenditures as a percentage of gross domestic product: various European countries, 1960–78*
Source: Office of Health Economics, *Trends in European Health Spending* (London: OHE, 1981).

EEC countries, as Figure 6.1 indicates. Nevertheless, expenditure in Britain, as in these other countries, has for many years been growing faster than the GNP, a matter that may occasion particular concern in times of low or nil economic growth. Advances in medical science clearly require changes in practice; whether or not technological developments require growth at a rate higher than that of the GNP is another matter. Such considerations are all the more relevant when we consider that with the major infectious diseases under control, increased expenditure on health care no longer has much to show in the way of an investment return in the form of additional output from those who would otherwise have died or been incapacitated. The great bulk of health expenditure is now consumption, given in particular the large demands made by the elderly and chronic sick.

The Guillebaud inquiry into the cost of the NHS perceived this change in emphasis, although it also held that the 'wealth-producing' as well as the 'health-producing' function of the NHS should be kept in mind. 'In so far as it improves the health and efficiency of the working population, money spent on the National Health Service may properly be regarded as "productive" – even in the narrowly economic sense of the term'.[19] (It may be observed in passing that this is a dubious use of the term 'economic': see Chapter 1.)

The question is frequently raised of whether the NHS is under-funded, especially when UK expenditure in relation to GNP is compared with that of other countries. To spend more does not necessarily mean that the medical care provided is correspondingly 'better'. Account must be taken not only of total supply but also of the distribution and the effectiveness with which it is used. It might be supposed, on general grounds, that in a private market consumers would exercise some control over private costs, but we cannot be sure. A patient does not always have the necessary information on which to base rational choices and generally leaves much of the decision-making to the providers of the service. The widespread availability of private insurance may also be important in so far as it encourages patients to make use of medical services, as is thought to be the case in the USA. The medical personnel, for their part, are reimbursed on a fee-for-service basis and have every incentive to maximise the service provided – and hence the cost. The insurers must pass back the higher costs to the consumers in the form of higher premiums, which are spread over such a large a number of beneficiaries that they are unlikely to restrain demand for coverage.[20] In Sweden, where services are free or virtually so and where, as it happens, the revenue available for health expenditure has been very buoyant, one might again, on general grounds, expect that emphasis on cost-effectiveness would be weak. Health expenditure per head is very high, but we are not in a position to determine whether this is reflected in the standard of service. The fact that expenditure is much lower in the UK does not necessarily mean that the service provided is correspondingly inferior.

High health costs are a common concern of all Western countries, the UK included, and in the late 1970s some countries began to take steps to control their rate of growth. In West Germany, for example, new charges were introduced for pharmaceutical products and for certain types of dental treatment, and a national agreement was reached with the medical profession so that scales of remuneration became fixed which had previously been negotiated by the profession with the insurance institutions. In the Netherlands it was decided to reduce the number of hospital beds from five to four per thousand of the population. In France, the *ticket modérateur*, the charge which the patient must pay for medical consultations, was raised in 1977 to make patients responsible for about a third rather than a quarter of the cost of each consultation. One result of this was an increase in the number of people taking out voluntary insurance against this charge, with a resulting increase in administrative costs. Complete reinsurance against the cost of *le ticket* was ruled out by legislation; 5 per cent of the charge had to be met by the patient – if only to make him more cost-conscious. The UK tried to reduce expenditure primarily by the imposition of cash limits; this has the disadvantage that it may prevent services being supplied even when people are willing to pay for them. It is true that certain health charges were increased in 1979 and 1980, but these relate only to prescriptions and dental and ophthalmic charges and make only a very modest contribution to NHS revenue. The more distant future is naturally more problematical. The Office of Health Economics at least is confident that even if health expenditure does not decline in relation to GNP, it will at least cease to rise.[21] Governments will make serious attempts to cut back their expenditure on health, partly because of a growing view that much expenditure is wasteful and in some cases unnecessary, reinforced by the recognition that, particularly as people get older, it may become necessary to accept lower standards of 'wellness'. In their view, which we are not competent to assess, new developments in pharmaceuticals are likely to increase expenditure on drugs but to decrease overall health expenditure in relation to the GNP because of resulting economies in medical treatment. In view of the lengthy training periods involved, however, there would be time lags before the supply of medical personnel could be adjusted for a decrease in demand, if this should indeed occur.

The breakdown of expenditure on the health and personal social services in the UK (see Table 6.2) has shown relatively little change over the past decade. Most notable, perhaps, has been the increase in expenditure on the personal social services, which doubled between the years 1969/70 and 1970/1 and had trebled by 1976/7. These services largely complement the health services for certain groups in the population, such as the elderly and the mentally ill and mentally handicapped. The health authority services, however, account for over three-fifths of total expenditure, and here, of course, it is the hospitals that are the big spenders, as they are in every country. Only 16 per cent of the patients receiving medical attention in any year become hospital in-patients. The high unit cost per patient, however, explains the efforts that are being made to shift more of the responsibility to the primary care teams: general practitioners, health visitors, home nurses and paramedical staff. The figures explain also the concern of the DHSS to control the drug-prescribing habits of both general practitioners and hospital staff. As long, however, as members of the medical profession

Table 6.2 *National health and personal social services in Great Britain: expenditure 1976/77*

Service	*Percentage of expenditure*
Health authorities[1]	
current	57·1
capital	5·6
General medical	5·1
Pharmaceutical	7·9
General dental	3·5
General ophthalmic	1·0
Welfare foods	0·2
Other	2·8
Personal social services	16·2
Central administration	0·6

[1]Excluding capital expenditure financed by loans.
Source: DHSS, *Health and Personal Social Service Statistics, 1978* (London: HMSO, 1980).

have the clinical freedom to prescribe what medication or treatment they see fit, control over expenditure is difficult in the extreme, unless the profession is prepared to co-operate in the exercise. Much of the weakness of planning and management in the NHS has been attributed to this unrestricted clinical freedom. Doctors are only rarely penalised in any cases of over-prescribing that come to light. There are no sanctions against doctors who carry out costly but unnecessary surgery or investigations on patients, and the profession as a whole is rarely exposed to the malpractice litigation which appears to be endemic in some other countries, notably the USA. This underlying conflict between clinical freedom and cost considerations was spelled out as early as 1956 by the Committee of Enquiry into the cost of the NHS. 'Even in matters of medical practice, such as the prescribing of drugs, doctors should be aware of the cost, although it does not follow that this knowledge should affect their action when deciding what is best for their patient.'[22] This is scarcely a precise statement; perhaps its interpretation might be slightly facilitated if the word 'always' were to be inserted before 'follow'.

A closer look at hospital expenditure itself (see Table 6.3) suggests other possibilities for more effective resource use. Only three-fifths of the total cost is accounted for by direct treatment, while general services (including catering and cleaning) amount to two-fifths of the total. The hospital service is the largest hotel and catering industry in the country. Would more cost-effective use be made of the very sophisticated and highly costly equipment and techniques if hospitalisation were to be

Table 6.3 *Hospital services: breakdown of expenditure, England, 1978/9*

Service	*Percentage of total expenditure*
Direct treatment:	
Medical/dental staff	9
Nursing staff	33
Medical and surgical supplies, equipment and services	9
Medical and para-medical supporting services (radiology, etc.)	9
General services	
Administration of records	7
Catering	7
Domestic/cleaning	7
Estate management	12
Other	8
Less direct credits	−1
	100[1]

[1]These figures do not add up to 100 owing to rounding up.
Sources: Health Services Costing Returns: Year ended 31 March 1979 (London: HMSO, 1981).

reduced? Could more patients be treated as out-patients, or at least as day-patients, returning home to sleep and perhaps being looked after by their families at home at weekends, a practice which is already being encouraged? The therapeutic value of bed rest is in any case a controversial question. The considerable variations in length of hospital stay between different hospital regions – from 8·2 to 10·8 days in acute specialities in 1978 – at least gives some credibility to suggestions that further economies might be made here.

The NHS is nominally a contributory insurance scheme, and the national insurance payroll tax paid by employers and employees contains a small element which is earmarked for the health service. In another and much more important sense, it is a citizen's service; benefits are available irrespective of whether or not any contributions have been paid, and the greater part of the cost is met out of general tax revenues. It started as a free service, and while charges have subsequently been levied, it is in practice still virtually free. Patient charges, as Table 6.4 demonstrates, met less than 2 per cent of the total cost of the health services in 1976/7. Hitherto they had never reached as much as 3 per cent, although with the increases introduced in 1982, the intention is that they should cover 5 per cent of expenditure.

The development of the NHS has been influenced in various ways by the structure of its finances. The heavy reliance on central government

Table 6.4 *National health and personal social services: sources of finances 1976/77*

Type of service/source of finance	*Percentage of total*
Central government services	
Consolidated fund	73·7
NHS contributions	8·2
Charges to recipients	1·8
Miscellaneous	0·2
Personal social services	
Rates and consolidated fund grants	14·4
Charges to recipients	1·7
	100·0

Source: *Health and Personal Social Service Statistics 1978* (London: HMSO, 1980).

funds has meant that the Treasury and the DHSS have played a decisive part in determining the size of the NHS grant and its allocation to different geographical regions and to different areas of medical need. Thus it has been possible to make special concessions to services for particularly needy groups, such as the elderly, the mentally handicapped and the mentally ill. In other countries where health insurance contributions (as in West Germany or France, for example) or local taxes (as in Sweden) provide a larger part of the revenue for the health services, central government is very much less able to influence the allocation of resources. At the same time, the heavy reliance in the UK on general tax revenues has meant that the NHS has continuously had to jockey with other claimants, such as defence and education, for a share of the government monies available. This has been one of the main causes of the low rate of capital investment in the NHS. Deferable expenditure is obviously more liable to cuts when different departments are pressing their claims for money. The NHS has little or no earmarked money of its own.

Increases in patient charges might have provided another obvious source of additional finance and, it is argued, might have done something to restrain total demand. Although its distribution by income classes may have changed, there is no evidence from other countries that this has been the case. Hospital care is far and away the most expensive item, and it is unlikely that boarding charges, even if they were introduced, would be sufficiently high to make any substantial contribution to revenue. A different argument is that charges might have the incidental advantage of encouraging patients to demand service of a higher quality. Charges, accordingly to Seldon,[23] would give the lower-income, and normally less articulate, sections of the population a larger voice in determining the standard of service they receive; they would at least have the sanction of withdrawing their purchasing power if they were not satisfied with the product. The Royal Commission, on the other hand, was in no doubt that charges should be gradually phased out; it rejected an insurance-based system and stuck firmly to general revenue financing.[24]

One of the fears in the UK has been that financial considerations might affect the patient-doctor relationship, a sacrosanct principle of the NHS, and charges for medical consultations have not been as strongly urged. Moreover, as long as some 50 per cent of the population are exempted from charges on grounds of age, health or low income, charges for these items will never bring in much revenue.

A noteworthy feature of NHS financial arrangements are the methods used to reimburse the general practitioners. Dentists and opticians are remunerated on a fee-for-service basis. This may encourage unnecessary treatment and may put up costs if the practitioner attempts to maximise his income. In Germany this method of remuneration is widely thought to have encouraged doctors to increase the number of treatments they prescribe. In the USA too reimbursement on this basis for both hospital and medical services is one of the factors that have contributed to inflation in health expenditure. In this case the patient might be expected to exercise some control over the amount of treatment prescribed and its cost, but widespread insurance, together with the patient's dependence on the doctor, weakens any possible resistance. Similar charges are frequently levelled against the dental profession in this country; hurried NHS treatment, long waiting times for appointments, together with relatively high charges, encourage the use of the private market. The savings on price may not be sufficient to offset the opportunity cost involved in waiting for NHS appointments and the often inferior quality of the end product. At the same time the methods used to restrain demand on the NHS dental services may also effect supply. Many dentists choose to practise privately not only because of the higher financial return but also because of the greater freedom which this gives them to carry out whatever procedures they think best for the patient, however sophisticated and costly, without resort to time-consuming applications for approval from the local Dental Board. However, the suggestion has been made by the Government that in order to encourage regular inspections and preventive care, dentists should be reimbursed on a capitation basis for children under 16.

The remuneration of general practitioners consists of three elements: a basic practice allowance; a capitation fee for each patient on their lists; special payments for many services, such as the certification of absence from work or screening for cervical cancer, together with expense allowances for ancillary staff. Capitation fees make up just over half of a doctor's income and fees, apart from a loading for patients over 65 years of age, take no account of the amount of service given to the patient. In some cases this may lead to the dilution of services in order to maximise list size, and the Government has attempted to exercise some control by imposing limits on the number of patients that any doctor may accept. Nevertheless, there are complaints, not completely without foundation, about the number of patients seen at any surgery session, the brevity of consultations and the restrictions placed on the more time-consuming home visits. The payment of NHS hospital staff on a salaried basis (apart from some consultants who combine NHS service with private practice) is more neutral in its effects, although there may be some inducement to minimise workloads by cutting back on treatment of an elective nature, by restricting consultation time or by delegating responsibility to ancillary staff. The Royal Commission in 1979 in fact proposed that a salaried service for general medical practitioners be introduced, but on an optional basis. As it is, the doctors have so far had an open-ended budget on the grounds that their service is 'demand-determined' and that cash limits could not be operated, as in the case of the hospitals and community health services.

ASSESSMENT AND EVALUATION

The objectives of the NHS were defined, as we have seen above, as the provision of a comprehensive and free service equally available to all that is designed to prevent illness and to promote better health, as well as to diagnose and treat illness. In quantitative terms the record of the NHS is in many ways impressive. More people are receiving more comprehensive treatment and at less cost than in many other countries. Over the period 1948–80 the number of general practitioners increased by 26 per cent, hospital doctors by 168 per cent and consultants by no less than 218 per cent.[25] Over the period 1969–77 alone there was a threefold increase in the courses of dental treatment provided under the NHS, and the number of prescriptions dispensed per person rose from 5·5 to 6·5. The number of patients receiving hospital treatment increased by some 18 per cent, although the number of beds actually decreased by some 12 per cent. More intensive use was made of hospital beds, although at the expense of increases in medical personnel. At the same time there were parallel expansions in the domiciliary health services, as Table 6.5 shows. What has not received comparable attention is preventive medicine – screening, regular medical check-ups and so on – and health education. These are the areas in which lie some of the greatest opportunities for the cost-effective use of resources.

It is difficult, however, to measure the extent to which this increase in

Table 6.5 *Health visitor, home nursing and chiropody services, Great Britain, 1966–79*

Service provided	*Cases attended (thousands)*					
	1966	*1971*	*1976*	*1977*	*1978*	*1979*
Health visitors	11	5,158	4,358	4,400	4,385	4,498
Home nurses	991	1,265	3,132	3,314	3,469	3,577
Chiropody services (persons treated)	554	1,122	1,549	1,630	1,730	1,760

Source: Health and Personal Social Service for England 1978 (London: HMSO, 1980).

the volume of services provided at virtually zero price at time of use has achieved equality of provision, and even more difficult to assess the outcome of this provision in terms of improvements in health status, which is, of course, the more valid measure of the achievements of the health services in any country. We shall therefore confine ourselves to raising a number of specific questions. Do individuals enjoy equality of access to health care? Is access affected by regional and class differences in availability of resources, as the evidence collected by the Black Committee suggested?[26] Do different individuals and different social classes make appropriate use of the services open to them? In what ways, if any, can we assess whether the NHS has improved the health of the people? It is instructive to compare, as far as may be, the achievements of the health services in other countries in these respects.

EQUALITY OF ACCESS?

Individuals, of course, have very different needs for health care, and in order to achieve equity of treatment some will need greater access than others to the health services, irrespective of their ability to pay for them. A useful distinction may be made here between horizontal and vertical equity.

Horizontal equity means 'equal access to care and equal resource provision for a patient with a given condition of given severity *regardless of where he lives*' (italics added).[27] This, of course, requires that the regional inequalities which we will discuss in the next section have been ironed out. Even then, whether or not patients with like conditions will make like demands on the health services will depend on the information at their disposal and their willingness to make use of it. Even if they do convert their want for attention into a demand by visiting their doctor, much will depend on the individual doctor; there is a wide range of choice open to the individual GP or consultant as to the drugs, medical procedures or surgical techniques he may prescribe. Patients with ailments of the same degree of severity may find themselves faced with very different diagnoses and prescribed very different treatments, which in turn may make very different calls on medical resources, according to the decisions made by their respective GPs or consultants.

Vertical equity requires that 'individuals suffering from different disorders receive appropriately different services.'[28] Views, again, differ as to what is appropriate. While the NHS offers a high-quality service in emergencies and provides for non-urgent cases reasonably well, even if after a considerable waiting period, there is some doubt about the appropriateness and quality of care given to chronic cases, which include geriatric and mentally ill patients.[29] If such a complaint is valid, equity of provision would require that the geriatric and mental health services received an even larger proportion of the health budget than they are currently receiving, in spite of government action to protect these sectors of medicine against the cutbacks in health service expenditure. The standards of amenity and care enjoyed by these classes of patient suffers by comparison with that afforded to acute patients in all the countries with which we have been concerned. In the USA in particular there is very great concern about the shortage of adequate and reasonably priced nursing-home care for elderly patients who have used up their entitlement to in-patient hospital treatment under Medicare health insurance arrangements.

Table 6.6 *Estimated current expenditure per head on health and personal social services by age groups, England, 1978/9, as percentage of average expenditure at all ages.*

	Expenditure (£ at 1980 currency prices)					
Services provided	*All ages*	*0–4*	*5–15*	*15–64*	*65–74*	*75+*
Hospital and community health services	100	109	43	57	196	474
Family practitioner services	100	114	114	71	114	229
Personal social services	100	150	117	33	117	600
Total	100	117	61	58	167	447

Source: Based on *The Government's Expenditure Plans 1981/2 to 1983/4*, Cmnd 8175 (London: HMSO, 1981), Table 2.11.4.

Whether or not they are receiving health services in appropriate relation to their condition of health, different groups in the population make very different demands on the NHS. Table 6.6 demonstrates the inequalities in the use made of the health and personal social services as between different age groups, and in particular the heavy use made by persons over 75. This is supported by evidence from the General

Household Survey for 1978. Persons over 75 were found to consult their general practitioners twice as often as persons in the age groups 15 to 64, and patients of 65 and over (some 15 per cent of the population) accounted for 25 per cent of all prescriptions. Further, geriatric and psychiatric patients occupy about half of the hospital beds at any one time. The inequalities in resource consumption will widen before the end of the century, as persons over the age of 75 and over the age of 85 grow both in absolute numbers and as a proportion of the population, as Table 6.7 shows. The extent to which the elderly receive all the health care they need depends partly on their own initiatives. The initial decision about whether or not to seek medical attention rests to a large extent with the individual old person, who may discount his need for

Table 6.7 *Projected elderly population, UK, 1976–96*

	Persons aged 75 and over		*Persons aged 85 and over*	
	Numbers (thousands)	*% of total population*	*Numbers (thousands)*	*% of total population*
1976	2,842	5·07	520	0·33
1986	3,407	5·96	612	1·07
1996	3,498	5·91	740	1·25

Source: Office of Population Censuses and Surveys, *Population Projections of 1974–2014* (London: HMSO, 1976).

health care as this might be assessed by a detached and unbiased expert, or may have insufficient knowledge about either the ageing process or the health and social welfare facilities available to mitigate its discomforts, or may be unwilling to incur the time and other costs involved in seeking attention. Self-referral, the responsibility of the individual to turn the initial want for a service into a demand for attention, entails the danger that some people, and not only the elderly, may not be receiving all the medical attention which the unbiased expert would judge to be necessary. However, the individual's freedom of action must be respected here – if he is physically and mentally competent, he may be receiving all the service that he wants.

TERRITORIAL INEQUALITIES

Individual inequalities in access to and the use of health services are, of course, closely linked with regional inequalities in the provision of service. Again, 'equality' and 'equity' have to be distinguished. To ensure equity on a territorial basis, it would not be sufficient to allocate hospital beds, doctors, dentists and so on to areas in strict proportion to their population size. Areas, like individuals, have different levels of need depending, for example, on the age composition of their populations, on their industrial bases and consequent environmental pollution, perhaps even on the nature of their water supply. (For example, a positive correlation has been found between the incidence of heart disease and soft water.) Declining inner-city areas have very different health needs from remote rural areas and both, although for different reasons, may require higher than average inputs of medical services per capita to achieve equality with less disadvantaged areas. There are limits, however, to the speed with which such changes can be effected. The hospital stock of the country, for example, has remained more or less fixed since the inception of the NHS, when the question of where the hospitals happened to be located depended largely on local voluntary effort and bore little relation to varying local need. Hospitals have suffered more than the housing stock or schools from restraints on capital spending, and nearly half of the hospital stock at 1976 was built before 1918.[30] Of course, slow replacement rates inhibit any moves to redress regional imbalances as well as adding to the operating costs and detracting from amenity. Wide regional variations remain in the distribution of hospital beds, ranging from between 6·1 and 9·2 per 1000 population in England to up to 11·4 in Scotland in 1978. Similarly, there were considerable differences in average length of patient stay – from 8·2 to 10·8 days – and in the cases treated per available bed – between 11·6 and 17·9. The marginal additions to hospital stock have set limits to any regional redistribution of resources that might have been possible. We might, of course, take the view of medical authorities like McKeown[31] or Cochrane[32] that the future of modern medicine does not lie in sophisticated medical technology or long spells of hospitalisation, in which case the sluggish growth in hospital building might not be a bad thing! Or, going back a century and more, we might agree with Florence Nightingale that 'the very first requirement in a hospital [is] that it should do the sick no harm' and come to the same conclusion!

A centralised service such as the NHS has, however, given the DHSS the opportunity to effect some change in the regional distribution of more mobile resources like medical personnel. An inducement scheme to attract medical practitioners to under-doctored areas was in operation for many years, and GPs were debarred from setting up practice in areas which were considered to be adequately served; such moves went a considerable way towards improving the distribution, and the average GP list size in England in 1979 varied only from 2,371 to 2,140 as between regions. More serious is the uneven distribution of dentists, which varied from 3,000 to upwards of 5,000 persons per practitioner. Interference with personal choice is a *concealed* tax on the practitioners concerned, as it cuts into their total satisfaction not only with their work but also with their lifestyle. The proximity of a lively teaching hospital, the attractions of the cultural life of a large city, perhaps the alternative lure of rural leisure pursuits have all to be taken into account. The incentives to move have to provide a sufficiently large reward to compensate for loss of these other satisfactions. The particularly low average size of GP lists in Scotland – below 2,000 – is a function partly of the low population densities in the Highlands and Islands and partly of the high output of doctors from Scottish universities. The small list sizes in these areas may, however, be more than counterbalanced, in terms of workload, by the distances to be travelled to visit patients, the absence of night and weekend emergency medical services and the distance from hospital facilities which may require the doctor to carry out many investigations and treatments that a town doctor would refer to a nearby hospital. On the other hand, the greater variety of the work in a country practice may be an inducement in itself! It is obvious from the population ratios that dentists are attracted by the more lucrative practices in London and the home counties. The regional imbalance may in turn hide much greater local variations.

The peculiar position of general practice in London, for example, was recently revealed in a report commissioned by the London Health Planning Consortium. It found that the wealth of charitable and teaching hospitals in the capital had led to the decline of general practice in many districts. Although London might appear well provided for in terms of numbers of doctors, this was deceptive. The doctors who practised there were found to be older, to have smaller lists and to practise less efficiently than the national average. Seventeen per cent of the GPs in inner London had lists of 1,500 or less, compared with 7 per cent nationally; 10 per cent were over 70 years of age, compared with 3 per cent nationally; and twice as many worked on their own as in group practice, which is widely considered to give a better service. With their remuneration, and hence their superannuation, closely related to the size of their lists, many of these doctors could not afford to retire and leave room for younger men. As the exceptionally large number of acute beds are axed in the planned remodelling of the capital's hospital services, London is also likely to be faced with a shortage of primary care. The Royal Commission considered that one of the first priorities of the NHS was to improve the quality of such care in the declining inner-city areas and recognised the particular difficulties of London.

Distributional problems are, of course, more difficult to tackle where the supply of medical services is less centralised than in the UK. In West Germany, for example, the stock of doctors is large by European standards; the regional distribution, however, varies from 63 per cent above to 16 per cent below the national average ratio of doctors per

100,000 population. The rate of growth is rapid, and the Federal Government has found it difficult, for constitutional reasons, to bring either the output or distribution of doctors under control.[33] France is attempting to deal with a similar threatening 'surplus' of doctors, however that may be defined, by restricting the number of places in training schools. In Sweden the National Board for Health and Welfare has taken advantage of the growing surplus of doctors from the medical schools in the 1970s to restrict entry to the more popular medical specialities and the more sought-after hospitals in the larger cities in order to direct doctors to the less popular specialities like geriatrics and to the remoter rural areas. West Germany is also well endowed with hospital beds, but the regional variation ranges from 10·26 to 17·40 beds per 1000 population. More important, this large hospital stock is not used efficiently, if efficiency is measured by the length of hospital stay; in 1974 the average length of stay in acute cases was 17·2 days, as compared with the English figure of 9·5 days in 1977. When the hospitals are owned by the Land (regional) and local government, by voluntary bodies or by private organisations, it is obviously difficult for the central government to secure the efficient distribution or use of resources. France has enacted legislation to create a public hospital service, provided by public hospitals and approved private hospitals and organised on a four-tier basis offering services of different degrees of specialisation from the large regional centres down to the small rural hospitals. Sweden has almost completed a similar territorial reorganisation of the hospital service.

THE HEALTH SERVICES AND SOCIAL CLASS

The removal of financial barriers to health would, it was hoped, bring about greater equality in use of medical facilities and a more standardised quality of service, with resultant improvements in the health status of the lower socio-economic groups. Views differ as to what has actually happened. Rein was of the opinion that the lower social classes enjoy services of comparable quality to those enjoyed by the higher social classes and make greater use of them.[34] The 1978 General Household Survey showed that, among a sample of some 30,000 households, the unskilled manual workers consulted their general practitioners on average four times a year, compared with three consultations made by members of the professional classes. Perhaps this was to be expected, since 60 per cent of manual as compared with 48 per cent of professional workers reported some chronic illness. In its Report, *Inequalities in Health*, the Black Committee found the greatest class inequalities in the use of preventive health services, in particular antenatal care. At the same time the working classes were found to make more use of hospital in-patient treatment. It is suggested that this is because working-class patients are more ill when they seek medical attention and are less likely to have suitable domestic arrangements for domiciliary care. There appears to be general agreement that occupational class differences in the use of services depend, among other things, on the distribution and quality of services available as between different areas, as well as the greater skill of the middle classes in pressing their demands for service. To combat this it has been suggested that new hospitals should be sited in working-class areas and that medical staff should be trained to communicate more effectively with members of the lower socio-economic groups.[35]

Deaths from all causes are higher at any age the lower the occupational group and this is particularly the case for diseases of the respiratory system and infectious and parasitic diseases. The risk of death before retirement is two and a half times as great among unskilled manual workers and their wives as among professional men and their wives. Absence from work on grounds of illness or injury was reported by three times as many unskilled manual workers as professional workers and employers and managers in 1977, and the average number of work days lost showed even wider variations. The differences between occupational classes have in some cases even widened; for example, between 1930 and 1970 infant mortality rates declined by some 75 per cent in classes 1 and 2, while the comparable fall in occupational class 5 was only 60 per cent. Differences in income, nutrition, housing and education have to be taken into account, and it is not possible to say how much weight should be given to differences in the use made of health services and in the quality of such services available to different occupational groups. It is the case, however, that in classes 4 and 5 the antenatal services are not used as widely, nor from as early a stage in pregnancy, as among the professional and salaried classes.

Less attention has been given in other countries to class differences in the use of health services or in standards of health; regional variations have attracted more attention. However, there is evidence from the USA of inequalities in the use of medical services by different income groups.[36] Using data from the Health Interview Services, Wilson and White[37] also found substantial differences in the percentages who had not visited a doctor within the previous two years as between both racial and income groups. These differences declined over the period 1964 to 1973 but without any decline in morbidity, as measured by the proportion of these different populations reporting limitations of activity due to chronic illness. The investigations carried out for the Low Incomes Commission in Sweden in the late 1960s showed higher incidences among the lowest of three income groups of a wide range of physical and mental disorders, such as chest and heart conditions, circulatory diseases, insomnia, nervous conditions and, above all, of untreated dental conditions (this was before the introduction of dental insurance).[38] French studies, reported by Black,[39] showed higher mortality rates among manual workers than among administrative and professional workers and similar differences in infant mortality rates, although the differences in the latter were declining. In none of the examples given is it possible, however, to do more than speculate about the role played by the health services among a wide range of social and environmental factors.

THE 'OUTCOMES' OF THE NATIONAL HEALTH SERVICES

So far we have been discussing in the main individual, regional and social class access to the *inputs* of health care. Such information tells us little about the effect that the NHS or any other health system has had on the health of the recipients of the services, although by attaching importance to inputs some positive correlation is implicitly assumed. The NHS was originally designed 'to secure improvement in the physical and mental health of the people'. The question of how this can be measured, however, poses some very difficult problems indeed.

One of the hoped-for outcomes of the NHS when it was first inaugurated was a reduction in the number of working days lost due to sickness absence. In this sense, it was thought, the NHS would be wealth- as well as health-producing. Such expectations, shared by other countries, have not been fulfilled, however. The number of days of certified sickness (excluding influenza) increased from 12·2 per male employee in 1954/5 to an all-time high of 18·8 in 1978/9, with comparable increases for female employees from 15·9 to 19·2.[40] The rise followed a period in the early 1970s when rates of sickness absence appeared to have stabilised. In fact, these figures, which are based on a DHSS sample inquiry, may underestimate the days of work lost for a number of reasons: short spells of absence are normally not included in the figures, as they do not attract sickness benefits; half of all married women have exercised their right to opt out of the national insurance scheme; large numbers of employees, non-industrial civil servants and members of the armed forces, for example, are outside the national insurance scheme. On the other hand, the figures include permanently sick or disabled people unlikely ever to return to the workforce. Looked at more closely, the figures show a substantial increase in the number of short spells of sickness, especially among young workers, and also in the number of very long spells of sickness, as well as large differences between regions and between industries. These problems are by no means confined to the UK; Sweden probably has the highest sickness absence rate in Europe, at 23·5 days per employee (1977 figure).

Medical factors that we have already noted undoubtedly contribute to this general rise in absenteeism: more sophisticated methods of diagnosis; a greater public awareness of the nature of diseases and of the potential for treatment; a lower tolerance of states of minor ill-health, especially perhaps of nervous and mental conditions. There is, however, general agreement among international experts in this field that medical factors are only *part* of the explanation.[41] Absence may be due to many other causes – the degree of job satisfaction, for example, which in turn may depend upon the quality of the working environment, the organisation and pace of production or the status of the job. Family and other responsibilities may be another cause of absence, especially if there are no alternative arrangements for taking paid or unpaid leave; the increase in the number of married women with families in employment is obviously relevant here. Some analysts, both in the UK and elsewhere, see another cause for increased absence in the arrangements for sick pay. In Sweden, for example, there is some debate about how far the higher sickness allowances introduced in the mid-1970s, together with liberal conditions concerning the production of medical certificates, have contributed to the very high rates of absence. Similarly, in the UK the question has been raised of whether the combination of benefits from the state scheme and from occupational sick-pay allowances, to which four out of five workers are entitled, have influenced rates of absenteeism. A new question, which came much to the fore in the late 1970s and early 1980s was the possible effect which high unemployment rates might have on sickness absence. High levels of unemployment were in fact already deterring people from taking sickness absence for fear of losing their jobs.[42] Doherty's study of national insurance and absence from work (before the withdrawal of earnings-related supplements to the state benefits)[43] lent support to the disincentive hypothesis and also suggested that 'job security influences decisions about sickness absence just as strongly as direct financial disincentives.' There appears, then, to be no direct positive correlation between the standard of health-care provision and the health of the workforce, as measured by rates of sickness absence. Here, of course, it is extremely difficult to isolate medical from other factors. Improved health education and greater health awareness may, in fact, have the opposite effects from those anticipated on productive capacity, particularly since the more obvious causes of ill-health, like infectious diseases, have been brought under control.

Can we make more positive assessments about other possible outcomes of the development of the health services? In the virtual absence of morbidity figures, the only reliable (if crude) indicators are the figures for infant, perinatal and maternal mortality and for average life expectancy, although these are a function of many other factors apart from the availability of health services. Between 1901 and 1977 life expectancy at birth in the UK improved in the case of males from forty-eight to seventy years and in the case of females from fifty-two to seventy-six years. The big improvements had, however, occurred *before* the NHS came into being, these were largely the result of the control of the major infectious diseases, which in turn owed more to simple medical procedures such as immunisation and to improvements in environment and general living standards than to costly health services. These cost-effective procedures continue to play an important part in our health services and have contributed in large part to the disappearance of smallpox and diphtheria and to the fall in the number of notified cases of tuberculosis from nearly 60,000 in 1951 to some 10,000 in 1979. The infant and maternal mortality rates have been falling too since the beginning of the century, although at slower rates in recent years.

Table 6.8 *Physicians and hospital beds: selected countries (latest years)*

Country	*Year*	*Population per physician*	*Year*	*Population per hospital bed*
Belgium	1978	444	1976	110
England and Wales	1977	659	1977	120
France	1976	613	1976	90
Italy	1974	485	1976	100
Netherlands	1977	583	1976	100
Sweden	1976	563	1976	100
West Germany	1977	490	1977	80
Japan	1976	845	—	—
USA	1976	595	1977	160
USSR	1977	289	1977	80

Source: *World Health Statistics Annual* (Geneva: WHO, 1980).

In attempting to estimate the outcomes of the NHS, an instructive exercise is to compare the British figures with those of other countries at comparable levels of economic development. First, we must look at inputs (see Table 6.8). The overall UK record here is poor, although there is some evidence, as we saw above, that in the UK these inputs are more evenly distributed over different parts of the country. More important, of course, are the outcomes. Table 6.9 shows that as far as life expectancy is concerned, England and Wales are in the middle range, with the Netherlands, Japan and the Scandinavian countries performing particularly well and wealthy West Germany and the USA falling behind. In Figure 6.2 we can see that the UK has lost her early lead over other countries and that the fall in British infant mortality rates over the past three decades has been unimpressive by comparison with that of

Table 6.9 *Life expectancy at birth: selected countries (latest years)*

Year	*Country*	*Life expectancy* *Male*	*Female*
1976	Belgium	68·9	75·5
1977	England and Wales	70·2	76·3
1976	France	69·9	77·9
1975	Italy	69·8	76·1
1978	Netherlands	72·0	78·7
1978	Sweden	72·5	79·0
1978	West Germany	69·2	76·0
1978	Japan	73·2	78·6
1977	USA	69·4	77·3

Source: *World Health Statistics Annual* (Geneva: WHO, 1980).

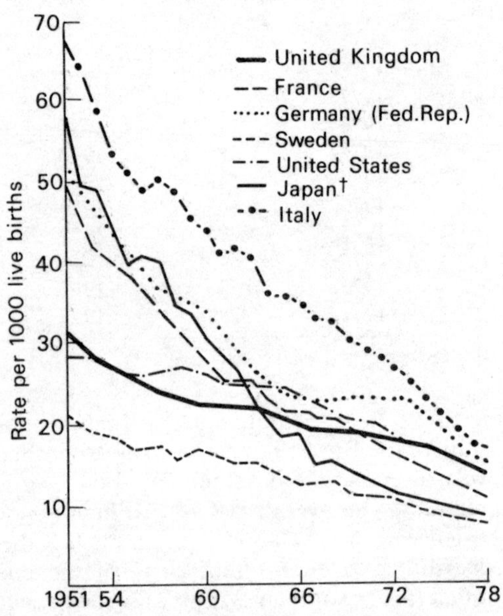

Figure 6.2 *Infant mortality rates:* international comparison*
Notes: *These include deaths under one year of age; † = includes deaths of foetuses of over seven months' gestation.
Source: Office of Population Censuses and Surveys.

many other countries. The leaders and the laggards are the same countries again. Differences in health-care provision, in particular the greater development and more intensive use of antenatal services, is part of the answer, but important contributory factors here, as in the case of life-expectancy rates, are, of course, differences in living standards and lifestyle, and in the case of the USA account has also to be taken of racial inequalities with respect to access to health care and standards of living. Overall, however, there has been growing concern in all these countries that the improvements in indicators such as mortality rates have not been commensurate with the increase in real expenditure on health services over the past few decades.[44]

NOTES

1 K. J. Arrow, 'Uncertainty and the welfare economics of medical care', *American Economic Review*, vol. 53 (1963).
2 V. R. Fuchs, 'The contribution of health services to the American economy', *Millbank Memorial Fund Quarterly*, vol. 44 (1966); reprinted in M. H. Cooper and A. J. Culyer (eds), Health Economics (Harmondsworth: Penguin, 1973).
3 H. Wilensky, *The Welfare State and Equality* (Berkeley: University of California Press, 1975), p. 1.
4 B. Abel-Smith, *Value for Money in Health Services* (London: Heinemann, 1976), p. 44.
5 *Report of the Royal Commission on the National Health Service*, Cmnd 7615 (London: HMSO, 1979), para. 22, 11.
6 R. Klein, 'Health services', in P. M. Jackson (ed.), *Government Policy Initiatives 1979–80: Some Case Studies in Public Administration* (London: Royal Institute of Public Administration, 1981).
7 K. Davis and C. Schoen, *Health and the War on Poverty: A Ten Year Appraisal* (Washington, DC: Brookings Institution, 1975); S. A. Levitan, *Programs in Aid of the Poor for the 1980s* (Baltimore and London: Johns Hopkins University Press, 1980).
8 C. M. Lindsay and J. M. Buchanan, *The Organization and Financing of Medical Care in the United States* (London: British Medical Association, 1969).
9 R. Andersen, B. Smedby and O. Anderson, *Medical Care in Sweden and the United States* (Chicago: Chicago University Press 1970).
10 M. H. Cooper, *Rationing Health Care* (London: Croom Helm, 1975), p. 25.
11 *Sharing Resources for Health in England*, Report of the Resource Allocation Working Party (London: HMSO, 1980).
12 *Report of the Royal Commission on the National Health Service*, para. 21.41.
13 Cooper, *Rationing Health Care*.
14 P. Foster, 'The informal rationing of primary medical care', *Journal of Social Policy*, vol. 8, no. 4 (1979).
15 J. G. Cullis and P. A. West, *The Economics of Health* (Oxford: Martin Robertson, 1979).
16 S. Israel and G. Teeling-Smith, 'The submerged iceberg of sickness in society', *Social and Economic Administration*, vol. 1, no. 1 (1967).
17 A. L. Cochrane, *Effectiveness and Efficiency* (London: Nuffield Provincial Hospital Trust, 1971); *Report of the Committee of Enquiry into the Relationship of the Pharmaceutical Industry with the National Health Service*, Cmnd 3410 (London: HMSO, 1967).

18 Cooper, *Rationing Health Care*.
19 *Report of the Committee of Enquiry into the Cost of the National Health Service*, Cmd 9663 (London: HMSO, 1956), p. 50.
20 J. A. Meyer, *Health Care Cost Increases* (Washington, DC: American Enterprise Institute, 1979).
21 Office of Health Economies, *Trends in European Health Spending*, Briefing no. 14 (London: OHE, 1981).
22 *Report of the Committee of Enquiry into the Cost of the National Health Service*, para. 367.
23 A. Seldon, *Charge* (London: Temple Smith, 1977).
24 *Report of the Royal Commission on the National Health Service*.
25 Office of Health Economics, *Doctors, Nurses and Midwives in the NHS*, Briefing no.18 (London: OHE, 1981).
26 See *Inequalities in Health*, Cmnd 6502 (London: HMSO, 1980).
27 Cullis and West, *The Economics of Health*, p. 235.
28 ibid., p. 237.
29 R. Simpson, *Access to Primary Care*, Research Paper No. 6 for the Royal Commission on the National Health Service (London: HMSO: 1979).
30 D. Owen, *In Sickness or in Health: The Politics of Medicine* (London: Quartet, 1976).
31 T. McKeown, *The Role of Medicine: Dream, Mirage or Nemesis?* (London: Nuffield Provincial Hospitals Trust, 1976).
32 A. L. Cochrane, *Effectiveness and Efficiency*.
33 B. Abel-Smith and A. Maynard, *The Organization, Financing and Cost of Health Care in the European Community* (Brussels: EEC Commission, 1979).
34 M. Rein, *Social Science and Public Policy* (Harmondsworth: Penguin, 1976).
35 J. Le Grand, 'The distribtution of public expenditure: the case of health care', *Economica*, no. 45 (1978).
36 Andersen, Smedby and Anderson, *Medical Care in Sweden and the United States*.
37 R. W. Wilson and E. L. White, 'Changes in morbidity, disability and utilization differentials between the poor and the non-poor. Data from the Health Survey 1964 and 1973', Medical Care, 15, 8, in *Inequalities in Health*.
38 D. Wilson, *The Welfare State in Sweden* (London: Heinemann, 1979).
39 In *Inequalities in Health*.
40 Office of Health Economics, *Sickness Absence: A Review*, Briefing no. 16 (London: OHE, 1981).
41 International Social Security Administration, *Absenteeism and Social Security*, Studies and Research No. 16 (Geneva: ISSA, 1980).
42 ibid.; Office of Health Economics, *Sickness Absence: A Review*.
43 M. A. Doherty, 'National insurance and absence from work', *Economic Journal*, vol. 89 (March 1979).
44 Abel-Smith and Maynard, *The Organization, Financing and Cost of Health Care in the European Community*.

CHAPTER 7

The Personal Social Services

The personal social services have for many years been the fastest growing area of the welfare state in Britain, although they account for only about 1 per cent of GNP. This may appear to be high in view of the small number of people who use these services, but the greater part of it is accounted for by residential care, which is very costly. It had often been supposed that as the more widely used and better-known social services developed – cash transfers, health services, education, housing, manpower services – the role of the more personalised social services and of social work help with individual problems would gradually wither away. The reality has been very different. The numbers of elderly and of people with physical and mental handicaps, for example, have risen. Marital breakdown and single parenthood have become more common; alcoholism, drug abuse and baby battering are on the increase. The personal social services have expanded substantially, partly to fill gaps left by other services in order to provide for such contingencies, partly to guide people round the increasingly complex maze of welfare services, and also to give the personal counselling and support which is not available from any other source. This situation is by no means unique to the United Kingdom. However, it will not be possible in this chapter to attempt international comparisons of the kind made elsewhere. 'The domain identified with the personal social services is diffuse, broad, in transition and of uncertain boundaries. The country data are incomplete and inconsistent. The social function of programs may vary by countries.'[1] For these reasons it will be necessary to confine our attention to England and Wales.

It may be appropriate to preface this chapter with a short explanation of what is meant by the 'personal social services'. The common convention will be followed of using as the reference group the services which are the responsibility of the local authority social service departments in England and Wales (the administrative structure is somewhat different in Scotland and Northern Ireland). These services are concerned with meeting the personal needs of various groups such as those mentioned above, as well as with ensuring that they and any who seek the department's assistance are aware of, and are claiming, their rights to benefits provided by the social security, health, education and housing departments. In so far as services additional to these are required to meet special needs, it is the responsibility of the local social service departments to provide them, or to satisfy themselves that they are being provided, by voluntary or even profit-making organisations. The services needed may be *residential accommodation* for, say, the elderly who are too frail to care for themselves in their own homes, or children whose parents are unable, or perhaps unwilling, to look after them. In other cases *day care*, such as training centres for mentally handicapped adults, day centres and social clubs for the mentally ill, may be sufficient. In many cases services may be more appropriately provided in the client's own home – such *domiciliary services* as home helps or meals-on-wheels. It is also an important part of a social worker's function to give the personal support that his clients need in order to cope with the many situations of stress in which individuals and families find themselves. Working with individuals in this way is generally known as *casework*. In other situations it is more appropriate to work with groups of people with similar problems, such as single parents, teenagers with delinquency problems, alcoholics, groups that may learn from each other in discussing their mutual difficulties with the guidance of a trained worker. This is known as *group work*. In yet other cases social workers may work with sections of the community to help them, through tenants' associations and the like, to secure improvements in their housing and environmental circumstances and in their social amenities; this is *community work*. These three social work methods are collectively referred to as *fieldwork*. Much of the work undertaken by the social service departments is a matter of carrying out statutory duties laid on them by Acts of Parliament, such as the prevention of child abuse and neglect and the provision of home help services or of residential care for people unable to look after themselves in their own homes. In other cases (for example, with regard to the mentally disordered or the physically disabled) their responsibilities are more loosely defined. Following the report of the Seebohm Committee, which was set up in the mid-1960s to review the organisation of these services, legislation was passed in 1970 which brought together the various branches of the personal social services in new, combined departments in order to provide 'a community based and family orientated service, which will be available to all'.[2] Since reorganisation the rate of growth of the personal social services has accelerated, although other factors were already pushing up demand.

An important factor was the changing demographic composition of the population, as noted elsewhere (see p. 150). The elderly, and in particular the growing numbers of people over 75, make heavy demands on the personal social services, especially for residential care, the most costly form of service. Another factor has been the advances in medicine which keep alive more people born with handicaps of different kinds or disabled by accident or disease later in life. Moreover, more of the mentally ill can now live within the community with the aid of the new psychotropic drugs. In all these cases special services and the support of social workers may be required. Changing family patterns, the break-up of families as a result of divorce, separation or desertion entails increasing numbers of single parents who need assistance, and considerable numbers of children each year have to be found foster parents, adoptive parents or places in residential homes. Greater social and geographical mobility deprive many people of family support in times of stress, and fewer people turn to the Church for advice or assistance. At the same time, the demands of other professions, notably the medical, and of other government departments, such as education and housing and supplementary benefit, have been putting increasing pressure on the social service departments. More generally, public expectations of the personal social services have risen, and the increase in the supply of services has in turn helped to create demand.

The reorganisation of the social services also gave an impetus to developments in the social work profession itself. Prior to reorganisation, only a minority of the employees of the various children's and welfare departments had received any professional training in social work. The new departments required a higher degree of professional expertise and by the early 1980s 90 per cent of social work staff had a professional qualification. The position is, however, very different in residential and day-care establishments, where less than 5 per cent of the staff have any training at all, and that generally a nursing qualification.

DEMAND, SUPPLY AND THE RATIONING PROCESS

Two implicit assumptions have been made in our discussion so far: first, that those in need of personal services should have access to them; second, that government (local government, in this case) should provide the services. These assumptions need to be teased out. Two questions are at issue here: who pays, and who provides? The services required may be too costly for the individual client to pay for them at the time of use. This problem might be resolved, as has been proposed in the case of health care and education, by giving clients cash with which to buy these services for themselves; a suggestion has been made that applicants for personal social service or for social work help should be given 'vouchers' with which to pay for the services rather than relying on public provision.[3] A voucher system, of course, implies that a market operates in which services can be purchased for cash or exchanged for vouchers, or that such a market would come into being in response to subsidised demand. It is frequently claimed, however, that the demand for personal social services is such that privatisation is not possible. Such a view overlooks the extent to which there is already 'a mixed economy of welfare';[4] private provision is not as revolutionary an idea as it might appear at first sight, and clients may make payments even for publicly provided services. There are, too, a large number of private and voluntary homes for the elderly and some facilities for the mentally disordered, in which better-to-do families may prefer to purchase places rather than use local authority accommodation.

Local authorities may also use and pay for places in voluntary or private homes for persons for whom they have statutory responsibility, in order to supplement their own stock of residential accommodation; this partnership between public and private provision might well be extended. Again, many elderly people buy their domestic help privately instead of using the local authority home help service. Similarly, people with physical handicaps may choose to pay for adaptations to their homes to make them more suitable for their personal needs rather than apply for local authority assistance, which may in any case cover only part of the cost according to the applicant's financial means. More might prefer to do so if they were given vouchers to help them to purchase such services privately. There is no obvious reason for a public monopoly in the *supply* of such services, and a case can be made for allowing people more opportunities to exercise their personal preferences. Given the opportunity, some people might choose to supplement the service which their vouchers would purchase out of their own resources. Nevertheless, there are, admittedly, sectors of the personal social services where private provision would present more problems. There has been little tradition in the UK of private practice in the social work profession, as there has been in the US. Even if private provision were extended in other areas of the personal social services, this area might be left largely in the hands of the local authorities. Many of the functions of the social worker, where rationing of access to services or elements of control are concerned, are of a kind to lend support to this view. There are cases where the responsibility of the client is so diminished by age or mental disorder that the social service department has to make the decision about whether or not institutional care is required and, if so, of what kind. In other cases, such as the child in need of care or protection, parents, if given vouchers to buy residential care, might refuse to do so, believing it to be contrary to the child's best interests. Services which 'no one really wants if they are in a position to avoid having them'[5] and in which elements of compulsion or control are also involved are strong candidates for public provision.

To take another point: as part of the revolt against increasing bureaucratisation, much emphasis has been placed on local initiatives and voluntary endeavours. If more services were provided in this way, the problem of the 'free rider' would have to be faced. It is likely that there will always be people who will benefit from the activities sponsored by more philanthropic members of the community, without contributing time, money or effort towards such activities. Even if they do not themselves benefit directly, they will have the satisfaction of seeing others benefit without contributing, and their desire to be generous will be satisfied at no cost to themselves. The group likely to benefit from such activities may be kept to a manageable size so that there are no free riders.[6] Many mutual aid organisations, such as those designed for the welfare of the victims of specific disabilities, operate much on these lines, although they may also attract support from well-wishers who are unlikely to benefit from their contributions. On the other hand, the existence of government provision may well discourage such voluntary giving on the part of those with no direct likelihood of benefiting, on the grounds that they have already contributed through the tax system.

In whatever way supply is organised, the question of matching demand to supply remains. Resources are scarce and likely to remain so, and if services are provided at zero or low price, demand is likely to be in excess of supply, especially in the case of the more sought-after services. Decisions then have to be made about how much of a service should be provided in total and how that volume of service should be apportioned between potential recipients. Some form of rationing has to be employed. This would be necessary even if a voucher system were to be introduced; detailed investigations would have to be made to establish the claimants' need for service, and this would obviously be very much more difficult and more time-consuming than in the case of, say, educational vouchers.

Judge distinguishes between what he calls 'financial rationing' and 'service rationing'. The first is concerned with the procedures by which decisions are made as to the proportion of the GNP to be allocated to the public sector and its distribution among the different public expenditure programmes. At the local level decisions are taken by the social service departments as to how they will distribute their allotted resources between different geographical areas and different areas of need for which they have responsibility. 'In contrast, *service rationing* refers to those procedures, implicit or explicit, by which clients obtain access to social policy goods and services.'[7] Basically, service rationing is similar to the process which we discussed in Chapter 6 – how needs and wants are turned into demands for a service. In the case of the social services the process may, however, be even less clear-cut than in the case of medical attention. It is difficult enough for the old person, for example, to recognise that he has a need for medical attention and to turn that need into effective demand by visiting his medical practitioner. It is more difficult for the lonely old person to recognise, or to admit, that he has a need for social contacts, and if he does recognise it, he may not have the information necessary to express that want in the form of an application for a place in a luncheon club or a day centre. Bradshaw has developed what he calls a 'taxonomy of need' to demonstrate this quandary and to illustrate the process by which wants or needs are turned into demands.[8] He distinguishes between 'felt needs', which the individual may or may not put forward in the form of 'expressed needs', and 'normative needs', those defined by a professional by reference to what *he* thinks the client needs, always assuming (a big assumption) that the potential client is in contact with a professional, in this case a doctor, a health visitor or a social worker. Normative needs in this sense, are obviously paternalistic.

The *supplier* of the service, as in the case of the health services, plays a potentially important gate-keeper function in deciding whether any particular potential client shall or shall not have access to a particular personal social service. In this way he decides, on the basis of broad criteria which may be laid down by the social service department in general guidelines, between competing demands for a scarce service. The assignment of a service to a particular client entails assessment of the likely effectiveness of the service in meeting that client's need and an implicit judgement that the costs of the service are worth incurring for the good that is likely to be achieved.[9]

There are three broad sets of rationing procedures which have been described by Parker.[10] The first set, the 'restrictive', centres on the use of explicit or implicit deterrence. Eligibility criteria may limit the number of potential recipients; charges may, in some cases, hold back demand for a service; delaying procedures may postpone demand, sometimes to the point where a service is no longer needed, or the claimant gets completely discouraged, leaves the area or even dies. Secondly, the dilutant strategy operates when the client receives less service than he wants, say two hours' home-help service a week instead of an hour a day. Thirdly, the service may be terminated sooner than the client would wish, as, for example, when a family is deemed sufficiently stable for the children to be returned from foster care or residential home, although it may not feel ready to resume the burden of child-rearing at that point in time. Not all rationing procedures, of course, are operated by professionals. Hall, in his book *The Point of Entry*,[10] describes the important role, helpful or otherwise, which the non-qualified receptionist may play in rationing access to the social worker or in giving advice on her own initiative, although she does not have the professional qualifications normally thought necessary. This places great authority in the hands of all those people, professionals and non-professionals alike, who may override a client's personal preferences as to the amount and type of service which he receives. The client might be more prepared to make the decisions for himself, and might prefer to do so, if there were a more extensive private market and if he had the financial resources, or was given a voucher, with which to purchase services.

The potential client may himself decide whether or not to incur the opportunity costs necessary to turn his want into a demand even if the services are publicly supplied. The social service department may be some distance away; an appointments system may debar immediate service except in situations of crisis; the office hours may be difficult for a working man or woman; and so on. More subtly, a sense of personal inferiority may deter application. In other cases the department may be associated with 'authority', and the potential client may be fearful of the possible consequences of involvement. Or, more simply, he or she may be ignorant of the service available or of how to apply for it, and the social services department may be wary of publicising its services in case it should be overwhelmed by an increase in demand, especially if there are no sources of supply, other than those provided by the department itself, to satisfy the client's requirements.

There are no unequivocal criteria for deciding eligibility for services like, say, meals-on-wheels or places in adult training centres for the mentally handicapped. If such services became more widely available, then less stringent criteria would be used in assessing the need for the service; in this way the level of supply helps to determine the level of demand. Factors apart from the level of need may affect supply itself. An area in which the Churches, other voluntary organisations or private enterprise have been active in building children's or old people's homes, for example, or where taxable capacity has enabled more local authority homes to be built is able to provide more children and elderly people with residential accommodation, and the social services department adopts more liberal criteria for admissions. In 1977, for example, one in eight of the elderly people provided with accommodation by the local authorities were in voluntary or private homes. What happened in some areas in the late 1970s was that capital investment in new residential homes was written off, and the homes were left unused because local authorities could not afford to staff and run them. In such cases demand for places will be matched to supply by the application of more stringent criteria for admission, and many potential demands may remain unmet.

Different forms of service provision are, of course, substitutable, and the trade-offs between using alternative forms of caring must be taken into account. It is, for example, widely considered that residential accommodation for the elderly should be a measure of last resort, both in the interests of the individual old person and on grounds of economy. It is in fact difficult to see how the social service departments could cope with the strain on financial and manpower resources as the numbers of very old people in the population increase unless strong measures are taken to economise on the use of residential care. Suitable housing and a much increased supply of domiciliary services, such as home helps and meals in the home, are one alternative; paid foster care is another, with which some departments are already experimenting.

The supply of local authority social services is already augmented on a nil- or low-cost basis by relatives, friends or neighbours or by voluntary organisations and volunteers, as we have seen already. The voluntary organisations may provide services as the agents of the local authority, often employing professionally qualified staff to do so. Dr Barnardo's Homes, for example, provide accommodation for some of the most difficult children in the care of local authorities – children with physical, mental, behavioural or emotional problems. In cases such as these the local authority pays a fee for service, which covers part, but rarely all, of the cost. The voluntary organisations are providing a bonus out of their own capital resources, funds and expertise, and the social service departments are receiving a low-cost service. In other cases the voluntary organisations use local authority grants, as well as their own funds, to provide services that might not otherwise be available at all – for example, for client groups such as alcoholics or drug addicts, for whom it may be more difficult for the social service department to make direct provision because of the necessity to pay heed to the attitudes and preferences of the local ratepayers on whom they are, in large measure, dependent for finance.

When voluntary labour is being used and not being paid, or not fully paid, problems of product control may pose difficulties. The local authorities may have doubts about the quality and reliability of the low-cost service they are receiving but are reluctant to express their doubts in the normal way by withholding their custom. They may also, irrationally, value the service according to the nil or low price they pay for it and be unwilling to provide the training and support which would maximise the contribution that the voluntary organisation and volunteers could make to client welfare. The giver of a zero-price service, for his part, may expect some less tangible return for service rendered if no money changes hands and may resent criticism or lack of support for his freely given service.

The growth of government responsibility in the welfare field has raised basic questions about the role of the voluntary sector. Beveridge himself had no doubts here: '[The state] should in every field of its growing activity use where it can, without destroying their freedom and their spirit, the voluntary agencies for social advance, born of social conscience and of philanthropy. This is one of the merits of a free society.'[11] On cost grounds alone, the use of the voluntary sector has much to commend it, in the view of some more recent commentators. For example, Klein is of the opinion that 'one of the most interesting developments in the field of social care has been the growth of the "grey sector": smudging the usual distinction between paid and voluntary work, there has been the development of paid volunteers, such as child minders and foster parents.'[12] The respective roles of government, the voluntary sector and the community itself is perhaps one of the most crucial issues in the field of the personal social services.[13] A greater volume of service might be obtained from the 'grey sector' if more public money were used to give supplementary support to activities of this kind. Greater investment in community initiatives and more encouragement for private activities, whether voluntary or for profit, in the social service field might also yield sizable returns. The boundaries between public and private provision need not be drawn as rigidly as is often supposed, provided that the ultimate responsibility for meeting needs is clearly defined.

FINANCING THE PERSONAL SOCIAL SERVICES

Table 7·1 shows the growth in expenditure on the personal social services over the decade 1969–79 in relation to the social services as a whole and to GNP. They were, in fact, the fastest growing area of social expenditure throughout the period. It needs to be borne in mind, however, that the personal social services started out from a very low base indeed, and, to get things in perspective, even by 1979 they represented less than 1 per cent of GNP, whereas the social services as a whole amounted to nearly a quarter.

Table 7.1 *Expenditure on local authority personal social services, in relation to total social services expenditure and to GNP at factor cost*

	1969	*1971*	*1973*	*1975*	*1977*	*1979*
As percentage of total social services	2·6	3·1	3·9	4·5	4·2	4·4
As percentage of GNP	0·5	0·6	0·8	1·1	1·0	1·0

Source: *National Income and Expenditure* (London: HMSO, 1980).

Complex issues arise in any discussion of the finances of the personal social services, which are even more troublesome than in the case of the cash transfers and health services. Social security and health are national services; the personal social services are a local responsibility. Where services are provided on a national basis national benefits will do more to suppress individual preferences than when there is regional autonomy because they cannot cater so well for diversity of local needs. In most countries, as in Britain, cash benefits are national programmes;

at no time was it contemplated that this responsibility should be devolved to the regional governments of Scotland or Wales if devolution had been accepted. Britain, in fact, goes further than most countries in having a nationalised health service, and although this takes different forms in Scotland and Northern Ireland, the basic fact remains that the local administrative boards are appointed bodies, not elected ones, so the room for the individual to exercise his personal influence through the ballot box is limited. It is only in the limited field of the personal social services that a little scope is possible for fiscal federalism.[14] People could, in principle, move around to get the fiscal package which suited them best. Thus, for example, the retired person might choose to make his retirement home where he thought he would obtain the most advantageous package of welfare benefits. This of course is more likely to happen in the USA, where local differences in welfare provision are substantial, although even in the UK, as we shall see below, for historical and other reasons there are considerable regional variations in the availability of different welfare facilities. Although welfare services are a local responsibility, there has been mounting tension in the last few years over the delicate balance between central government control and local autonomy, especially where central and local government are of different political persuasions. Local government is dependent on central government for some 60 per cent or more of its revenues, but it does have other sources of finance, especially from the rates, under its more direct control. Moreover, the central government grants are block grants, not specific grants, which would appear to give the local authorities considerable freedom over their deployment. Central government has, however, exerted considerable influence over the ways in which these grants are spent. Many of the welfare duties carried out by the local authorities are statutory responsibilities laid down in central government legislation, and the DHSS takes this process further by laying down in its periodic circulars guidelines as to how local government should discharge its duties or use its powers. A return to

Table 7.2 *Local authority personal social services, England, expenditure year ended 1976/7 (percentage)*

Field work	16·3
Residential care	48·1
Support services:	
Day care	11·8
Community care, etc.	18·6
Administration	4·8
Research and development	0·5
(Of which payments by recipients	10·8)

Source: Health and Personal Social Services for England 1978 (London: HMSO, 1980).

specific grants for specific services, which has been widely advocated, would allow even closer government control but would meet with considerable resistance.

We turn now to take a closer look at the different components of local social service expenditure. Table 7·2 shows, as would be expected, that residential care makes far and away the biggest demands on local authority social expenditure accounting for nearly half of the total. Residential care for the elderly is the largest item here. In this latter instance charges levied on the consumers, which are related to their means, contribute 45 per cent of the total cost. The greater part of these charges, however, is met out of state retirement or supplementary pensions, so in effect what we are seeing here is a transfer of monies between different levels of government. In the case of day care (such as centres for the elderly or handicapped) and community care (like the home help and domiciliary meal services), the charges, which in some cases the local authority is required to levy, in fact contribute only very small amounts to the total cost. The costliness of a residential place may in some cases have unfortunate consequences for the patient or client if the hospital and local authority, dependent on different levels of government for their finances, attempt to shift the responsibility for the individual concerned, generally an old person, from hospital to residential home or vice versa (a move that is sometimes known as 'body-swapping'!). Most people in residential care, whether old persons or children, are there as a result of statutory duties imposed on the local authority by legislation. Statutory duties obviously have to be given precedence, and this fact in large part accounts for the high rate of expenditure on residential care for the elderly and for children. Residential and other services for the mentally ill and handicapped and for people with physical handicaps, as we have observed above, have suffered from the lack of statutory obligations on the local authorities, especially in times of low or zero growth in expenditure.

In considering expenditure, due regard must be had to possible trade-offs between different forms of service which are substitutable. Residential care is costly both because of the capital costs involved and because of the heavy burden imposed on current revenues by a highly labour-intensive service; here greater use might be made of domiciliary services and of services like paid fostering, as has already been suggested. Day care involves much lower 'hotel' charges and domiciliary services none at all, at least for the local authority. The greater part of such costs in these cases is borne by the recipient and his family and, by the nature of the case, is likely to be lower. Increased expenditure on adaptations to the homes of the physically handicapped or elderly, aids to mobility or home helps is likely in most cases to make it possible for more people to remain in their own homes.

Account should, however, be taken (as Wager, for example, suggests)[15] of the overhead costs incurred by the recipient of the service in maintaining his own home, or the opportunity cost to the relative who may have to give up paid employment to look after him. Nevertheless, in the majority of instances, as far as the local authority is concerned, domiciliary care is likely to be the most cost-effective form of provision. Unfortunately, the support and community care services are, by their nature, easier to cut back when economies are needed, and the home help services, the costliest of these provisions, has been particularly susceptible to cuts.

Increasing attention has been given to pricing policy and to the use of charges in the social services since the mid-1970s, partly in response to the need for economies in public expenditure. The relevant legislation generally gives the local authority the duty or the power to raise charges for personal social services, subject to the approval of the Secretary of State, provided they are 'reasonable' or related to cost or take into account the means of the recipient. The conditions vary from service to service, however, and there are, moreover, wide variations in the charges made by different authorities for the same service, in the means tests used to determine eligibility and the manner in which they are administered. Charges may serve different purposes. Parker distinguishes five: to raise revenue, to reduce demand, to check abuse, to determine priorities, and a symbolic role.[16] In practice, charges for personal social services raise little in the way of *net* revenue. The greater part of the charges for accommodation in old people's residential homes takes the form of inter-governmental transfers. There is some evidence that charges for the home help service, for example, or for day-nursery places, may reduce demand, but whether this is desirable is another matter. Charges for the accommodation of children taken into care may be aimed at enforcing parental responsibility and checking abuse of the system, but, given the negligible sums recovered in this way, it is doubtful whether they serve even a symbolic purpose! It is perhaps a little surprising at first glance to find the arch-proponent of a free health service, Aneurin Bevan, positively supporting charges for residential accommodation for the elderly. 'There is no reason at all why the public character of these places should not be very much in the background, because the whole idea is that the welfare authorities should provide them and charge an economic rent for them, so that any old persons who wish to go may go there in exactly the same way as many well-to-do people have been accustomed to go into residential hotels.'[17] The symbolic significance of charging here is obvious; the relationship between the old person and the provider of the service is to be one of reciprocity rather than the charity of the old poor law.

Consumer charges may serve yet another purpose: 'they provide policy-makers with information about consumers' preferences through their decisions about service consumption.'[18] In this way they reintroduce a certain measure of consumer sovereignty into the chargeable social services. This raises again the question of whether individual preferences would be better served if, instead of public provision of services, vouchers were to be given with which services might be purchased on the private market.

PROBLEMS OF ASSESSMENT AND EVALUATION

It is tempting to use the increase in real expenditure on the personal social services as an indicator of their achievements – particularly when this started from such a low base. The potential clients of the services have, however, also increased (although they are still relatively few in number), because of demographic and other changes. What are the *outcomes*, as far as the clients are concerned, of this increase in expenditure and service provision? There are no indicators here, like infant and maternal mortality rates and life expectancy which tell us something at least about the outcomes of the medical services, even if other contributory factors, such as improvements in nutrition, housing and environment, have also to be taken into account. 'Outcome measurement probably represents one of the most difficult tasks of research into the effectiveness of social care.'[19] Appropriate policy objectives have yet to be defined; appropriate tools of measurement have not so far been devised; and the relative importance of the different objectives have to be worked out. 'Client state' is presumably the ultimate indicator, but in the absence of a market this raises the further question of who is to put a value on such indicators – the client or the professional.[20] There have been a number of studies by members of the different caring professions, by academics of various disciplines and by administrators in the field which attempt to assess the outcome of different services in terms of improvements in client state.[21] Such studies, however, are concerned with particular groups of social service clients or are limited by geographical area. Their objectives and methodologies do not permit of legitimate comparisons. The indicators of outcome are often imprecise – perhaps inevitably so. For more practical purposes, we will, then, have to confine ourselves to 'proximate' measures of personal social service activity, which means looking not at outcomes but at inputs, such as the number of places provided in adult training centres for the mentally handicapped, in day nurseries for pre-school children or in residential homes for the elderly, in relation to the potential clientele. We can refine the discussion a little by looking at inputs in three different ways: (1) the movement in provision over time;

(2) present provision in relation to possible targets; (3), in some ways even more significant, the distribution of resources on a territorial basis. The last of these, of course, largely determines the equality or otherwise of individual access to the personal social services. While no explicit statement of intent has been made, as in the case of the NHS there is presumably some implicit assumption that individuals with like needs should receive like treatment, irrespective of where they happen to live. To achieve this, however, should resources be distributed 'evenly' or 'fairly'?[22] As the extent of need varies between different areas, the answer should surely be that resources should be distributed by some measure of 'fairness'. Many authorities, however, distribute resources – like social workers, for example – on a pro-rata population basis, given the difficulty of devising need-related formulae. In respect of some resources, of course, the freedom to allocate resources more fairly has in large measure been pre-empted. Different areas, as we saw above, have benefited more than others from the zeal of local voluntary organisations in building, say, children's homes, or have had the tax capacity to build their own homes. With constraints on new capital expenditure, only marginal adjustments are possible in capital stock, and it may be out of the question, for the present, to bring the supply of different facilities into a more appropriate relationship with local needs. Different local authorities may in any case take different views of their responsibilities, and various commentators have found that Labour councils are, on the whole, more likely to push the expansion of their welfare services.[23] The disaggregated information is not in any case available to permit any firm conclusions to be drawn about territorial distribution on any basis more refined than a regional one.[24]

In employing these different yardsticks it may make for greater clarity if we apply them to different identifiable client groups individually. We must also bear in mind the substitutability of many of the services, although it is very doubtful whether it will be possible to reach conclusions about the degree to which the shortfall in one service is compensated for by the relatively more liberal provision of another service which may serve the same end. The targets used in our second yardstick are, unless otherwise stated, taken from the government consultative document *Priorities for Health and Personal Social Services in England*,[25] issued in 1976 to provide a basis for reconciling the conflicting aims of central government (to promote national priorities) and of local government (to retain maximum autonomy to make its own choices in the light of local needs). These guidelines were worked out by civil servants and professionals and reflect what they considered necessary to meet 'normative need'. There is no way of knowing how far the guidelines accord with the 'felt needs' of the potential beneficiaries of the services.

SERVICES FOR CHILDREN

The statutory responsibilities of the local authorities are clear: to prevent child abuse and neglect and the breakdown of family life, to 'take into care' and to find alternative accommodation for the children when this in fact occurs and, under different legislation, to register and to inspect people who mind children for other people for profit. The number of children taken into care each year, frequently for relatively short periods, has grown steadily over the past quarter of a century. It is government policy that these children should, in their own interests, be boarded out with foster parents wherever possible, and this is also a less costly option for the local authority than providing places in residential homes. In practice, however, there has been relatively little change over time in the proportions of children who are fostered, placed in residential homes or otherwise accommodated in lodgings, hostels and so on. About one in two fostering arrangements break down before the natural parents are able to take the child back, and at the same time more and more of the children coming into care have physical, emotional or mental handicaps which make them difficult to foster. Social service departments might, however, find more people willing to foster if they were prepared (as a few are, admittedly) to take a closer look at their policies for remunerating foster parents. In general, foster parents are paid only a boarding charge in order to prevent people fostering for the 'wrong' motives (i.e. for profit). The social service departments are thus obtaining a low-cost service. More people, especially perhaps married women wanting paid employment, might come forward as foster parents if a proper salary were paid, and even then this would be less costly than a place in a residential home. This is an area where the boundaries between the public and voluntary sectors are being smudged, and more might well be done along these lines. Central government policy, as expressed in the DHSS guidelines, was to aim at a modest expansion in residential home places but also, alongside this, to develop non-institutional methods of caring, such as specialised fostering facilities. It was estimated that 5,000 children living in residential homes could be boarded out with suitable foster parents at a substantial saving (it cost £50 per week, even in 1975, to maintain a child in a home).

The social service departments have more discretion when it comes to providing facilities for pre-school children, such as day nurseries and pre-school playgroups. Day-nursery provision was greatly increased during the war years to cope with the children of mothers on war work, but since then places have fallen back to a figure of some 30,000. It is government policy not to encourage the growth of local authority day nurseries, which are expensive to build and to operate, but to encourage the expansion of less formal and less expensive methods of child care, like child-minding and part-time nursery groups. There is evidence that some parents are deterred from using day-nursery places on account of the often inconvenient hours of opening and the substantial fees that have to be paid.[26] That parents do not at present have equal access to day-care facilities of any kind is obvious when we look at the regional variations in the total number of places, full and part-time, in day nurseries, registered nursery groups and in the homes of registered child minders. The range per 1000 children under 5 was from 125 to 195 in 1979; that is in some areas as few as one child in eight was receiving some form of day care, either full- or part-time, while in others one in five could expect to do so. Faced with a shortage of places, many parents resort to illegal child-minders, who are not registered with local social service departments and whose premises and standards of caring are not subject to inspection.

THE ELDERLY

The statutory responsibilities of the social service departments are to provide home helps, laundry services and residential accommodation; as regards other services, the local authorities have ample powers of which they could make 'much more extensive and imaginative use'.[27] As in the case of the health services, however, there is little investment potential in welfare expenditure on the elderly; nor are the elderly themselves always as knowledgeable or as persistent as they might be in turning their wants into demands for service. There has been some progress in provision, but the government targets are still far from being met, and access to service still depends to a large extent on where an elderly person happens to live.

The domiciliary and day-care services are in general low-cost alternatives to residential accommodation. Since the early 1960s various studies have claimed that there was a shortfall in the supply of home helps, the most important and popular of these services, and recommendations have been made that the level of service should be doubled or even trebled.[26] A shortfall is not easy to assess, but surveys carried out among potential recipients of the service provide ample evidence of unmet wants. The DHSS target set in the mid-1970s aimed at the expansion of the service to cover 150 per 1000 of the 65 and over age group. By 1977 the figure had reached 88 per 1000, a 40 per cent increase over the 1970 figure, but subsequently there have been cuts on economy grounds in this low-cost preventive service. Surveys also suggest that in many cases the level of service provided does not meet the recipients' demands even when charges are made. In other cases the evidence suggests that charges, which are means-tested and vary widely as between local authorities, may deter people from applying for service or may restrict the amount of service that they are willing to purchase.[28] As far as the meals service is concerned, the DHSS guidelines suggested a doubling of the service to provide some meals every week for 200 out of every 1000 old people. Some progress was being made in the number of people receiving the service and in the numbers of meals they were receiving per week, but again the service has suffered from cutbacks in public expenditure. The same is true of day-care facilities, another preventive service. About 12,000 people (i.e. about two in every 1000 people aged 65 and over) were attending such centres by 1974. The DHSS in 1976 recommended a target of about three to four places for every 1000 elderly persons, but this would involve substantial increases in both capital and revenue expenditure. Regional and local variations in provision inevitably mean that individual access to service is very uneven. The number of elderly households receiving the services of a home help in 1979, for example, ranged from 129 to 194 per thousand as between regions. These regional inequalities are confirmed by a survey undertaken by Age Concern,[29] of the use made of social services by the elderly. Further, the standard of provision was found to be higher in areas where there are considerable voluntary involvement than in areas where the local authority alone provided the service, which substantiates the point made above that more attention and more money might usefully be given to the voluntary sector.

Similar local variations are to be found in the case of residential accommodation. By 1976 the number of people aged 65 and over being cared for in local authority homes, or in voluntary homes on behalf of the local authority, had reached 18·5 per 1000. The DHSS guideline was twenty-five beds per 1000. Given that the average age on entering residential accommodation has risen to nearly 83,[30] and that increasing numbers of residents have mental or physical disabilities, it seems likely that there is a serious shortfall in places, a point which the waiting lists in many areas substantiate. It is therefore all the more important that the 'right' elderly people should be occupying residential places. Evidence gathered over a number of years shows that numbers of old people who are occupying expensive residential places could live independently, given suitable housing and adequate domiciliary services, and, conversely, that some frailer residents need hospital care. As early as 1971 Carstairs and Morrison, for example, concluded from their investigation of old people in residential homes in Scotland that on a conservative estimate 30 per cent of the residents did not need the supportive care of a residential home, while 20 per cent needed more intensive forms of care.[31] Further, it is unlikely that individuals have equal access to residential care, irrespective of where they happen to live, when the number of places per 1000 elderly people can range from 17·2 to 19·2 according to region (1977 figures).

SERVICES FOR PEOPLE WITH HANDICAPS

Services for the mentally ill and handicapped and the physically disabled have suffered both from the looseness of the relevant legislation and from the low priority which the local authorities have given to their needs. The overall aim is to enable as many handicapped people as possible to live in the community and to lead lives as nearly normal as their disabilities permit.

In the case of the mentally ill and handicapped, this largely means providing in the one case day centres and in the other adult training centres, where they can take part in a range of social activities and perhaps begin to acquire some new and useful skills, together with homes and hostels for those who are unable to live in their family homes or who would benefit from learning to live independently. In its discussion document *Better Services for the Mentally Handicapped*[32] the government, in an attempt to stimulate local authority action, produced planning figures for the expansion of services over the next twenty years. For people with mental handicaps some 73,500 places were to be provided in occupational and training centres and 36,800 places in residential homes, foster homes and lodgings. By 1977 there were some 38,000 places in adult training centres (about half-way towards the planning figure) and some 10,000 places in homes and hostels (well under a third of the number thought necessary), and since then the rate of growth has slowed down. The community services for the mentally ill have been accorded even less priority, and specific targets were not spelled out in the discussion paper *Better Services for the Mentally Ill*,[33] published in 1975.

There has been some increase in the numbers of people with physical handicaps who receive a home help service or have their homes adapted in various ways to meet their special needs, but in the absence of guidelines it is impossible to make any estimate of the amount of progress being made. Informed opinion, however, does not give a high rating to the overall performance of the local authorities.

THE SOCIAL WORK CONTRIBUTION

It is impossible to give any firm indication of the improvements in client state which have resulted from the growth in the size and professionalisation of the social work profession. The increase in social service facilities, to which access is generally controlled by social workers, implies that more people 'in need' have been in touch with a social worker, but we cannot measure, and it is difficult to evaluate, the service given by the social workers in the way of support and guidance. Few studies of its own role have been undertaken by the social work profession. One important piece of empirical work[34] concluded that the elderly clients who were the subject of the survey on the whole gained more, in terms of both services received and the quality of the relationship established, if they were assigned to a professional social worker rather than to a professionally unqualified welfare assistant. However, this was due in large part to the smaller caseloads carried by the professionally qualified workers, and the study concluded that the needs of the great majority of elderly people could be catered for just as well by welfare assistants or voluntary workers.

We have said nothing so far about the clients of the personal social services whose needs do not fall into one of the identifiable categories discussed above. These other clients have a very wide range of problems – marital difficulties, truanting, homelessness, difficulties in coping with low incomes, poor health, drink problems and so on. In many cases the social worker may act only as an intermediary between the client and a service provided by another agency, the supplementary benefit office, the health, education or housing department. In other cases the social worker may provide considerable inputs of counselling and support in order to help a client to make use of such services, or such counselling and support may constitute the service itself. It is frequently maintained, and with some justification, that social workers are in many instances bridging gaps left by other forms of social provision. How efficiently and how effectively they do this, and what the nature and extent of their additional support for the client are, it is very difficult to measure. The social work profession must bear some of the responsibility here. With some notable exceptions, social workers have been reluctant to use what national survey material is already available (for example, from the General Household Survey, the National Child Development study, the research carried out by Age Concern) to help them to assess the performance of services in their own areas or as the basis for operational research. A strong case can be made for the continuous monitoring of the work of social service departments – a kind of internal audit – and, equally important, for monitoring users' 'expectations, views on the help they [are] receiving, and their satisfaction with the service'.[35] Some commentators go further than this and suggest that what is needed is an inspectorate for the personal social services, and for health too, comparable with the inspectorate for schools.[36]

NOTES

1 A. J. Kahn and S. B. Kamerman, *Social Services in International Perspective*, Discussion Paper No. 180 (Washington, D.C.: US Department of Health, Education and Welfare, 1978), p. 28.

2 *Report of the Committee on Local Authority and Allied Personal Social Services*, Cmnd 3703 (London: HMSO, 1968), para. 2.
3 K. Judge and J. Matthews, *Charging for Social Care* (London: Allen & Unwin, 1980).
4 A. Webb and G. Wistow, 'The personal social services', in *Government Policy Initiatives 1979–80. Some Case Studies in Public Administration* (London: RIPA, 1981).
5 A. M. Rees, 'Access to the personal health and welfare services', *Social and Economic Administration*, vol. 6, no. 1 (1972).
6 M. Olsen, *The Logic of Collective Action* (Cambridge, Mass.: Harvard University Press, 1965).
7 K. Judge, *Rationing Social Services* (London: Heinemann, 1978).
8 J. Bradshaw, 'A taxonomy of social need', in G. McLachlan (ed.), *Problems and Progress in Medical Care* (London: Oxford University Press, 1972).
9 A. Williams and R. Anderson, *Efficiency in the Social Services* (Oxford: Blackwell and Martin Robertson, 1976).
10 A. S. Hall, *The Point of Entry* (London: Allen & Unwin, 1974).
11 *Report on Social Insurance and Allied Services*, Cmnd 6404 (London: HMSO, 1948), p. 318.
12 R. Klein, 'The welfare state: a self-inflicted crisis?', *Political Quarterly*, vol. 51 (1980), p. 34.
13 C. Carter, 'A new direction in social policy', in M. Brown and S. Baldwin (eds.) *The Yearbook of Social Policy in Britain* (London: Routledge & Kegan Paul, 1980).
14 W. E. Oates, *Fiscal Federalism* (New York: Harcourt Brace Jovanovich, 1977).
15 R. Wager, *Care of the Elderly* (London: IMTA, 1972).
16 R. A. Parker, 'Charging for the social services', *Journal of Social Policy*, vol. 5, no. 4 (1976).
17 Judge and Matthews, *Charging for Social Care*, p. 32.
18 ibid., p. 107.
19 D. J. Challis, 'The measurement of outcome in social care of the elderly', *Journal of Social Policy*, vol. 10, no. 2 (1981), p. 179.
20 Williams and Anderson, *Efficiency in the Social Services*.
21 For example, P. Sainsbury and J. Grad d'Alarçon, 'The cost of community care and the burden on the family of treating the mentally ill at home', in D. Lees and S. Shaw (eds.), *Impairment, Disability and Handicap* (London: Heinemann, 1974); Economist Intelligence Unit, *Care with Dignity: An Analysis of Costs of Care for the Disabled*, Action Research for the Crippled Child monograph (London: National Fund for Research into Crippling Diseases, 1973).
22 Judge, *Rationing Social Services*.
23 For example, B. Davies, *et al.*, *Variations in Services for the Aged* (London: G. Bell, 1971).
24 B. Davies *et al.*, *Variations in Children's Services among British Urban Authorities* (London: G. Bell, 1972).
25 *Priorities for Health and Social Services in England*, DHSS (London: HMSO, 1976).
26 Judge and Matthews, *Charging for Social Care*.
27 M. Wicks, *Old and Cold* (London: Heinemann, 1978), p. 169.
28 A. Hunt, *The Home Help Service in England and Wales* (London: HMSO, 1970); Judge, *Rationing Social Services*.
29 Age Concern, *Profiles of the Elderly*, No. 8: *Their Use of the Social Services* (London: Age Concern, 1981).
30 *Growing Older*, Cmnd 8173, DHSS (London: HMSO, 1981).
31 V. Carstairs and N. Morrison, *The Elderly in Residential Care* (Edinburgh: Scottish Home and Health Department, 1971).
32 *Better Services for the Mentally Handicapped*, Cmnd 4683, DHSS (London: HMSO, 1971).

33 *Better Services for the Mentally Ill*, Cmnd 6233, DHSS (London: HMSO, 1975).
34 E. M. Goldberg, *Helping the Aged: A Field Experiment in Social Work* (London: Allen & Unwin, 1971).
35 E. M. Goldberg, 'Monitoring in the social services', in E. M. Goldberg and N. Connelly (eds.), *Evaluative Research in Social Care* (London: Heinemann, 1981), p. 278.
36 R. Klein and P. Hall, *Caring for Quality in the Caring Services* (London: Centre for Studies in Social Policy, 1974).

CHAPTER 8

Assessment and Recommendations

METHODS OF ASSESSMENT

In a well-known passage T. H. Marshall observes: 'There are many possible ways of classifying the aims of social policy, but the most helpful for our present purposes is that which distinguishes three types, which we may call the elimination of poverty, the maximisation of welfare and the pursuit of equality.'[1] The second of these classifications would appear so ample in scope as to include the other two and much else besides. It is appropriate therefore to direct attention to poverty and equality and to allow, as the analysis proceeds, for any other objective of policy that may seem to be relevant. Although there is a considerable overlap between some of the measures that may be recommended in order to prevent poverty and some of those designed to reduce inequality, there *need* not be any close coincidence between the two. The extent to which any overlap occurs will depend upon a variety of factors, in particular the interpretation given to the term 'poverty' and the pattern of income distribution held to be desirable. Suppose it were the case that virtually everyone, apart from chronic invalids and similarly handicapped groups, could earn an income which, if properly expended over an adult lifetime, would be sufficient to sustain expenditure at levels at least equal to that corresponding to some specified poverty level. As we observed in Chapters 1 and 2, a social security scheme might nevertheless be thought desirable because, without the compulsion thus applied, some people might not in fact make provision for periods of sickness and unemployment and for old age on a scale sufficient to keep them out of poverty as determined by the official scale. Social policy in this context would indeed be designed to provide protection against poverty but, apart from the special cases of chronic invalids, and the like, there need be no redistribution. The scheme would be paternalistic but not redistributive, or barely so. The great majority would pay for the 'insurance cover' they received. We have also observed that Beveridge was strongly attracted by this model. His emphasis was on the ending of poverty through a scheme that would restrict the need for 'public charity' and would establish the principle of benefits as of right. It is true that his own proposals did not correspond at all closely with this model, and that his package was in fact quite clearly progressive in its net incidence; but the fact remains that, in principle, he placed secondary emphasis on redistribution. The point is not just one of historical interest, for it is important to observe that an anti-poverty programme may entail only a little redistribution or quite a lot, according to the method of its financing and the criteria by which payments are made. Thus with a given scale of expenditure a selective scheme based on means tests will be more redistributive than one which provides benefits as of right irrespective of 'need'.

The crucial importance of the meaning given to the word 'poverty' has already been stressed. Thus if in a prosperous economy the standard of living of the lower-income groups were rising substantially, both common sense and common usage would point to the conclusion that poverty was diminishing. From a strictly relativist point of view, this conclusion would not, however, be accepted unless the *share* of the lower-income groups was also increasing. A situation can be easily enough conceived in which it would be necessary to choose between a reduction of poverty in the one sense at the expense of an increase in poverty in the other sense. Fortunately, such a situation need not always arise; but enough has been said to indicate that some trade-off between Marshall's first and third objectives might at times be necessary. (This, indeed, is what Rawls's difference principle implies – see p. 29 above.)

MEASURING REDISTRIBUTION

When attention is directed away from normative propositions to empirical assessments of the redistributive effect of the total fiscal package or of some particular welfare package, problems of a different kind are encountered. It is possible to envisage an ideally illuminating statistical exercise along the following lines. The calculations would begin with the distribution of income between different households before any benefits had been received or taxes paid – that is to say, with the distribution that would obtain in a country where there was no public finance. A fiscal system would then be introduced, and the benefits received and the taxes paid would be attributed to households arranged in the frequency distribution by size of original income. The relative changes caused by the net fiscal operation would then be revealed. It need scarcely be said, however, that no straightforward and unambiguous calculation could be made along these lines! It is true that the periodic exercises undertaken by the Central Statistical Office (CSO) for Britain are indeed presented in the manner described (see Table 8·1), and a broadly similar approach has been followed elsewhere.[2] The steps are the same as those in the hypothetical exercise described above, but the crucial point is that the starting-point is different, for these exercises cannot reveal what 'original income' would have been in the absence of any fiscal intervention.[3] To take just one example: the provision of

Table 8.1 *Redistribution of income between households; unadjusted and adjusted to a per equivalent adult basis, 1979*

	Quintile groups of households ranked by original income					
	Bottom fifth	*Next fifth*	*Middle fifth*	*Next fifth*	*Top fifth*	*Average over all households*
Average per household (£ per year)						
Unadjusted						
Original income	140	2,280	4,900	7,060	11,700	5,220
Cash benefits	1,680	1,120	510	400	380	820
Gross income	1,820	3,400	5,420	7,460	12,080	6,040
Direct taxes	10	360	970	1,450	2,620	1,080
Disposable income	1,810	3,040	4,450	6,010	9,460	4,960
Indirect taxes	410	770	1,130	1,440	2,040	1,160
Benefits in kind	730	800	970	960	990	890
Final income	2,130	3,080	4,290	5,530	8,410	4,690
Direct taxes as a percentage of gross income	*1*	*11*	*18*	*19*	*22*	*18*
Indirect taxes as a percentage of disposable income	*20–23*	*25*	*25*	*24*	*22*	*23*
Benefits in kind as a percentage of final income	*34*	*26*	*23*	*17*	*12*	*19*
Adjusted to a per equivalent adult basis						
Original income	170	1,980	3,760	5,460	9,130	4,100
Cash benefits	2,080	1,050	420	320	190	810
Gross income	2,250	3,030	4,180	5,770	9,320	4,910
Direct taxes	10	300	730	1,140	2,110	860
Disposable income	2,240	2,740	3,450	4,630	7,210	4,050
Indirect taxes	500	690	870	1,090	1,590	950
Benefits in kind	880	820	710	570	450	670
Final income	2,610	2,870	3,290	4,110	6,080	3,790
Direct taxes as a percentage of gross income	—	*10*	*17*	*20*	*23*	*17*
Indirect taxes as a percentage of disposable income	*20–22*	*25*	*25*	*24*	*22*	*23*
Benefits in kind as a percentage of final income	*34*	*29*	*22*	*14*	*7*	*18*

Source: CSO, *Economic Trends*, No 327 (January 1981).

retirement benefits by the state will reduce, through higher taxation, the ability to save for old age and will also weaken the incentive to do so, original income will then be lower precisely because fiscal measures will create a divergence between original income and final income. The first row in Table 8·1, therefore, shows the distribution of original income in a society in which heavy taxation and expenditure have had important effects on original income itself, and this row is, as a consequence, an unsatisfactory starting-point for subsequent statistical calculations designed to assess what the fisc has accomplished or failed to accomplish. Of course, this complication would not be serious if public expenditure were only marginal, equivalent to, say, 5 per cent of GNP. When the figure is nearly 50 per cent it is a different matter.

It does not follow that estimates of this kind are unilluminating. It is true that no grand, comprehensive assessment can be made of the redistributive effects of public finance, but, given the main features of the fiscal structure, the effect of changes in benefits or taxes can be cautiously inferred, and, furthermore, the respective effects of some of the different components of public expenditure and revenue may be broadly discussed. Unfortunately, there are other difficulties and limitations that affect even this more limited use of the calculations.

The CSO's calculations do not extend to the whole of public expenditure. Public goods such as defence are omitted, and so are some other items, with the result that about half of public expenditure is left out, including public investment. As it happens, what is left in corresponds fairly well to the activities usually grouped together under the heading of the welfare state: social transfers, health services, personal social services, welfare foods, education and housing subsidies. This may appear convenient enough in the context of the present volume, but the treatment of revenue poses further difficulties. The welfare services do not, of course, constitute a self-contained fiscal package financed solely by earmarked taxes but are substantially paid for from general revenue. Most of the main taxes are brought into the CSO's calculations, but a variety of items of revenue are left out, with the result that only about three-fifths of revenue is covered. The lack of balance between the two sides of the accounts as presented – half of expenditure and three-fifths of revenue – may tend to warp the interpretation of the figures. A further familiar set of problems arises in assessing the incidence of the taxation. Various assumptions, reasonable but not beyond criticism, have of necessity been made, but this is scarcely a matter on which certainty can be expected. It is, therefore, by no means surprising that a number of critics have viewed the whole exercise with scepticism.[4] (It should be observed in passing that similar difficulties are encountered in attempting to assess the effect of the fisc on a summary index of inequality, such as the Gini coefficient.)

The frequency distribution of households may be in bands of original income, or of final income, and these variants are shown at different places in the CSO inquiry. Of these, that by original income is given in Table 8.1. A further complication arises because, although the same number of households is included in each quintile in the summary, these households differ in the average number of individuals they contain. Thus there are relatively fewer individuals in the low quintiles where pensioners are heavily represented, and relatively more in the higher quintiles, and this clearly has a bearing on the social significance of the distribution. To adjust simply for numbers would, however, be insufficient. Differences in the composition of households need also to be taken into account, and a rough adjustment may be made by using the weights employed by the Royal Commission on the Distribution of Income and Wealth. These were: a married couple as 1·00; a single person as 0·61; a child as 0·27. In the investigation for 1979, of which some of the results are summarised in Table 8.1, an allowance has now been made for these complications by introducing 'equivalences' along the lines recommended by the Royal Commission on the Distribution of Income and Wealth in its Sixth Report.[5] The effect of doing this can be seen by comparing the lower part of the table with the upper part. It will be observed that inequality on the corrected basis is somewhat less, as might have been expected. The interpretation of the table can be further assisted by providing some bench-marks – too rarely done in the presentation of frequency distributions of the distribution of income. An obvious one is average adult male earnings for all workers before tax in 1979, which came to £5,273. Thus the average worker's household is to be situated rather above the middle quintile if there is only one earner in the house. It is likely that there will be more than one, probably the equivalent of 1¼ male workers, and this would place the household in the seventh decile. Another bench-mark is afforded by supplementary benefit. For an unemployed man with a dependent wife this came to £1,970, a figure which included the average housing allowance.

The estimates of the allocation of cash benefits can be taken to be reasonably accurate, as can the deductions for direct taxes. These two adjustments give disposable income. The progressive structure of direct taxes is shown at the bottom of each part, where these taxes are expressed as percentages of gross income (i.e. original income plus transfers). The incidence of indirect taxes raises more difficult problems but, given the assumptions made, the payment of these taxes is roughly proportional to disposable income. When benefits in kind are allocated, still more difficult assumptions are required before the estimates of final income are obtained. The net effect is clearly a substantial reduction in inequality. Indeed, the bottom quintile derives nearly all its final income from the fiscal process. The outcome can be summarised for quintile groups by expressing final income as a percentage of original income (see Table 8.2).

The net fiscal package as shown by these calculations is progressive. No support is given to the widely held view that the upper quintiles do better than the middle or lower groups, nor is support given to the view that the median voter so influences policy as to gain at the expense of those below and those above.

Table 8.2 *Final income as percentage of original income*

	Bottom fifth	*Next fifth*	*Middle fifth*	*Next fifth*	*Top fifth*	*Average*
Unadjusted figures	1,521	135	87·6	78·3	71·9	90·0
Figures adjusted for equivalences	1,535	145	87·5	75·3	66·6	92·4

The allocation of benefits and taxes between the different quintiles is shown, on the adjusted basis, in Table 8.3. About half of the cash benefits go to the lowest one-fifth, or three-quarters to the lowest two-fifths. In the case of benefits in kind, the corresponding figures are over a quarter and roughly a half.

Table 8.3 *Quintile groups adjusted by equivalence ratios*

	Bottom fifth	*Next fifth*	*Middle fifth*	*Next fifth*	*Top fifth*	*Total for all quintiles*
Cash benefits	51·2	25·9	10·3	7·9	4·7	100·0
Benefits in kind	25·7	23·9	20·7	16·6	13·1	100·0
Direct taxes	0·2	7·0	17·0	26·6	49·1	100·0
Indirect taxes	10·5	14·6	18·3	23·0	33·5	100·0

It must be remembered that not all taxation and not all public expenditure have been allocated, and the proportion unallocated is not the same in the two cases. An attempt at a more comprehensive calculation has been made for 1971 by Ruggles and O'Higgins.[6] Their estimates do not differ greatly from the CSO estimates for that year with regard to the distribution of the burden of taxation, nor does the inclusion of certain additional items of expenditure which are deemed by them to be in principle allocable. The combined effect is slightly less favourable to the lower deciles and marginally more so to the higher. They then go on to allocate expenditure on public goods which is unallocable except by the adoption of arbitrary assumptions. One such assumption is that the benefits accrue on a per capita basis and this reduces the net equalising effect – inevitably, given this assumption. The consequences that follow from two other assumptions are also investigated: the assumptions that the benefit from public goods such as defence is proportional to income and that it is proportional to capital. But we find it hard to attach any significance to these further assumptions.

Their general conclusion is clear. As Ruggles and O'Higgins observe, both their own and the CSO calculations show 'a net benefit redistribution which is strongly redistributive in favour of the lower income groups: in both absolute and relative terms net benefits decline as income increases'.[7]

The calculations discussed above relate to the short period of a year and cannot be expected to reflect at all adequately the effects over the life-cycles of those in the various income groups. At this point it is necessary once more to cast a sceptical eye on the estimates for original income. The low incomes, as we have observed, are in the main the incomes of those now retired, and these largely reflect both personal preferences about the disposition of income over time and also the effect of institutional arrangements for pensions. These points can perhaps be clarified by means of simplified examples. (a) Suppose there were no official pensions of any kind and no occupational pensions. Suppose, too, that there was no sense of family obligation on the part of the old towards the young or the young towards the old. Everyone would then have to save for old age. It may be objected that most people would be too poor to do so, but this objection overlooks the fact that people would not be paying taxes when at work on the scale required to finance pensions for those then retired. That is to say, there could and would be more voluntary saving if there were no compulsory levies. Capital sums would be accumulated from which incomes would be received, and the entries in the first row in the table for original income would then be substantially increased. Nevertheless, the retired would still appear relatively poor even if they had been thrifty, because they would have deliberately planned to consume the *capital* sums they had saved, for they have no thought for heirs, and this capital consumption would be reflected in lower planned *incomes* for retirement. (b) The assumptions may now be changed to allow for universal private occupational pensions. These pensions would be included as 'original income' for the purposes of the CSO table. (c) Now change the assumptions again in order to allow realistically for pay-as-you-go official pensions. The retired would not – according to the usual convention – be given any credit under 'original income' for the contributions they had made to the state scheme in the past, and the whole of their state pensions would appear as social security transfers. Their original incomes would be much smaller than in cases (a) and (b), and the redistributive effect of the fiscal process would appear larger.

The effect of these institutional conventions can be further illustrated by taking a quite realistic example. In 1983, when the British graduated pension scheme comes up for review, the number contracted out may well fall. If this proves to be so and if the proportion contracted out remains low thereafter, the figures for original income in some future CSO tables will be smaller than would have been the case with a higher proportion contracted out. A still simpler assumption can also serve as an illustration. Suppose state pensions were to be treated in the statistics as income in the same sense as occupational pensions, on the ground that contributions had been paid in the past, and credits were therefore recorded in row 1. The redistributive effect of the fiscal package would then look appreciably smaller.

If the analysis of redistribution is to be carried further, it is necessary to distinguish between (a) transfers between generations and (b) transfers within generations. Under pay-as-you-go arrangements today's workers provide the benefits for today's pensioners and can expect to receive such benefits themselves in due course from tomorrow's workers. Thus each generation helps its predecessor during a particular phase in the lifecycle of the latter and will later be helped in its turn. If, then, a snapshot picture of distribution was taken, such as that shown in Table 8.1, these inter-generational transfers would appear as vertical redistribution, and so indeed they would be from this point of view. It may or may not be the case, however, that the fiscal process is changing the vertical distribution of income between members of the same generation. What would ideally be required would be sufficient statistical information to trace net changes in the receipts of people in a given age cohort. To illustrate: suppose that Smith and Jones, now retired, belong to the cohort born in 1910. Robertson and Robinson, born in 1940, are now helping to provide the former with their pensions and this transaction will appear as a social security transfer from those currently well off to those less well off. But to get a fuller picture we should also need information about changes in the position of Smith in relation to Jones and of Robertson in relation to Robinson, and such cohort investigations encounter great difficulties, although valuable experiments have been made.[8]

In view of all these many difficulties, it must be conceded that the redistributive effects of the total fiscal package, or of the welfare services that are part of that package, cannot be assessed with confidence. It must at the same time be recorded that this fact has not deterred the more relentless critics of the welfare state from making sweeping assertions. Thus one group of its opponents does not hesitate to denounce it as extravagantly egalitarian and, in the end, deeply harmful to everyone because it undermines the basis of prosperity. A very different group is prepared to maintain that the welfare state is not redistributive at all but is only a cunning device used by the middle class to exploit the workers. In rejecting these extreme views, it may be held that some redistribution in favour of the lower-income groups takes place, although its scale is hard to determine at all accurately.

A rather more confident verdict can be given about the success achieved in setting a minimum and thus preventing 'poverty' in some sense of that term. This has been done partly through vertical redistribution but also through the discipline imposed by compulsory schemes. It is true that even this claim seems to be contradicted by the widely held view that poverty has not been eliminated at all but has persisted and has even become more extensive. As was shown in Chapter 4, however, this contention is based on a special and rather confusing use of terms. It is undeniable that supplementary benefit provides a floor for the incomes of those not at work. Even if some do not get themselves quite on *that* floor because, for one reason or another, they do not take up all the benefits that they are entitled to claim, they will still be able to stand on the floor provided by national insurance benefits. This latter floor will be on average about 25 per cent lower but, even so, will be well above what was regarded as the acceptable poverty level some years ago. For those at work there are other safeguards which also constitute floors at different levels. This fact can be recognised and its importance acknowledged without there being any agreement about the height at which these various floors should be set.

CONCLUSIONS AND SUGGESTIONS

Economic recession, like the immediate prospect of being hanged, serves to concentrate the mind. In the hard years of the late 1970s and early 1980s, the many items that make up the vast total of public expenditure have been examined with a sharply critical eye, not only in Britain but also in other countries that have been trying to bring inflation under control. In carrying out an exercise of this kind, and in making whatever changes in public expenditure seem appropriate, it is admittedly necessary to guard against the danger of extrapolating current economic conditions indefinitely into the future. That was what Keynes did, with fine but incautious rhetoric, in the late 1930s, when he predicted prolonged secular stagnation which could be prevented only by draconian policies. When this prophecy was not fulfilled and the well sustained growth and high levels of employment of the postwar decades came to be accepted as normal, it was scarcely surprising that programmes for public expenditure should reflect the assumption that output would continue to expand indefinitely. These over-optimistic assumptions have been shattered by recession. It is true that the attempts to cut back public expenditure – attempts made by both Labour and Conservative Governments in Britain – can be criticised on the Keynesian ground that in order to end a recession as soon as possible public expenditure should be increased, not reduced. The opponents of this view can point out that the recession of the late 1970s and early 1980s has not been of the kind that Keynes envisaged; for the deflation of output and employment has been accompanied by the continuing inflation of costs and prices. But this familiar controversy about macroeconomic policy lies beyond our scope. Whatever views may be held on that issue, critical examination of public expenditure is to be welcomed, including expenditure on the welfare state. This is so for a number of reasons.

To quote from an official report on social policies submitted to the then Labour Government by the Central Policy Review Staff:

> Public expenditure has been growing faster than production as a whole, and expenditure on social programmes has been growing faster than the rest of public expenditure. This has to some extent spared governments the task of cutting out low priority programmes in the social field, or indeed of having to decide which programmes should be given low priority. It has led to unrealistic expectations about the scope for improvements and extensions. It has also reduced the incentive to increase the efficiency of existing policies and programmes.[9]

Clearly, social expenditure could not rise for ever at a faster rate than GNP. A check had to be administered, and the exigencies of policy during recession – given their non-Keynesian interpretation – have provided the impetus to carry out a reassessment which should have been carried out in any case. As Klein observed after the first oil crisis: 'economic growth has stopped, and with it the hope that rising public expenditure on community services and social benefits could be painlessly financed without any reassessment of priorities.'[10] Moreover, we cannot simply take it for granted that, when the recession is over, the secular rate of growth of GNP will be as great in Britain, or indeed in other countries, as it was during the prolonged postwar boom.

Thus it is only right that the various objectives of public expenditure should be critically scrutinised, their respective merits assessed and the different means of attaining them investigated – with cost clearly seen, in every case, not as a mere book-keeping entry but as the sacrifice of some other benefits, whether public or private, that must then be foregone. Of course, the scrutiny of public expenditure is nothing new. It goes on all the time. But the recession has given it a new edge and, by virtue of its severity, has made it feasible to assess with more objectivity some items of expenditure that were formerly regarded as sacred cows. From the point of view of public welfare, this is a gain. There could, however, be a needless loss if widespread cuts were imposed in an insufficiently selective way. At the peak of the war effort Cherwell sent a minute to Churchill with the title 'Death by a Thousand Cuts', in which he pointed out that some of the further sacrifices then about to be imposed on the civilian population would contribute little or nothing to the armed forces or to the munitions industries but would probably so reduce the health and efficiency of the civilian population as to be, on balance, harmful to the war effort. And Churchill agreed. If waste is an evil, masochism is not a virtue.

Having said this, we wish to add at once that although some mistakes are always likely to be made and some unnecessary sacrifices exacted, there is no ground whatever for dramatic pronouncements about the total collapse of the postwar consensus with regard to the welfare state. It is true that the differences between the British parties' views on social expenditure had widened in the early 1980s; but there is no question of any government in Britain attempting to dismantle the welfare state. We believe that this is also true of the Continental European countries and would be so, if it came to the crunch, in the USA as well. But changes can be expected which, if they stop far short of its dismantling, may nevertheless have important consequences for the welfare state, and these changes may be the subject of bitter and often exaggerated controversy.

THE HEALTH SERVICES AND THE PERSONAL SOCIAL SERVICES

Let us begin with the health service and the personal social services in Britain. None of the main political parties has shown any inclination to scrap either of these services; nor have we found any reason why so drastic a policy should be recommended. To say this is not, however, to exclude any scope for reform, and some suggestions can now be made without attempting to summarise all that was said in Chapters 6 and 7.

Although the National Health Service accounts for about 6 per cent of GNP in Britain, some other countries spend substantially larger proportions of larger GNPs on their health services, from both public and private sources combined. This comparison might be held to give *prima facie* support to the view that the NHS has been starved of funds, or it could be interpreted to mean that Britain has a rather economical health service – unless it could be shown that the quality of what is provided in Britain is inferior to what is provided in the countries that spend more. Obviously, nothing definite can be concluded at this level of generality beyond the fact that the NHS is not the extravagant operation that some of its more hostile critics hold it to be.

When expenditure in real terms is to be curtailed or its rate of growth restrained, the economies required can come from (a) the more efficient use of resources in the supply of any given service within the present system or (b) the drastic reorganisation of the system or even its replacement by something else. It need scarcely be said that this second alternative is the less pleasant one, although it may unfortunately be the case that economies may be easier to achieve in practice under this heading than under (a), where possible economies, though not illusory, may be elusive. It is appropriate to add at this point that the economy campaign of the early 1980s has called not for a cut in total expenditure but merely for a restricted rate of growth – one which should, as it happens, be roughly equivalent to the rate of growth of GNP in 1982–3. In a dynamic service, however, some branches will be thrusting ahead at a faster rate but will be able to do so only if there are actual cuts elsewhere.

Various investigations have been made of the scope for economies under (a), and it is to be hoped that the DHSS will be prepared to take directive action, if this should be necessary, to ensure the implementation of any contingent recommendations in the face of what may sometimes be conservative habits of mind. An example might be less reliance on full-time in-patient treatment. 'Hotel' costs are a large part of the hospital budget, and no useful purpose is served by keeping in hospital overnight or over the weekend any patients whose condition allows them to go home. The medical staff may feel that it is nice to know that the patients are in their hospital beds even at times when no medical attention is being given – just as a firm with poor cost accountancy may carry unnecessarily large stocks of materials. If there is scope for economising here, this could have been done long ago, but an economy campaign may be needed to make those responsible for spending public money more cost-conscious. Another example might be the greater use (already made in some areas) of general practitioners and ancillary staff to deal with ailments that would otherwise receive hospital treatment. The possibility of imposing restrictions on the prescribing of drugs, which accounts for nearly one-tenth of all expenditure on health, raises some thorny questions. In some other countries (e.g. Sweden) a firmer line is taken. Doctors might be required to keep to a restricted list of drugs, and penalties might be imposed on those who prescribed branded drugs when cheaper and equally satisfactory substitutes were available. Such restrictions could, admittedly, have harmful effects on research and development, and clumsy intervention might save money only at an undesirable cost in terms of retarded pharmaceutical progress. Once again, however, the need to economise should be a stimulus to fresh assessment and change.

It has been said from time to time that in the training of doctors attention should be given to costing techniques and to health economics.[11] The suggestion is a sound one, although a good deal of time would have to elapse before the effect of such a change could make itself significantly felt. There remains the problem of finding some way of providing an incentive to economise without incurring unintentional risks from which patients might suffer.

Are there grounds for supposing that a system of health insurance along the lines of the Continental model would be more cost-effective and would also allow the total provision of health services to correspond more closely with people's personal preferences? If such a model were to be adopted, presumably the state would require that contributions should be made, at a specified minimum rate up to some specified level of earnings, to a registered insurance organisation. The latter would then be responsible for meeting any medical bills incurred by its members. Under such a system, there would need to be some special provision for low-income groups, but its financing might, in total, be on a less progressive basis than is the general tax revenue in Britain from which the NHS derives most of its finance. This need not, however, be a serious objection to such an insurance scheme if corrective action were taken to make the rest of the fiscal package, with health now removed, more progressive. Another difference is that the supply of medical services would not then be derived, as it now is in Britain, from a near monopoly. Economies of scale might be lost, but managerial efficiency might be improved with smaller units of supply. The net effect on costs cannot readily be assessed.

Of course, in such a system governmental control would be more remote, and attempts to reduce expenditure by changing the rates of contributions would probably take more time to be effective. Or if the trend is considered, there is no reason to suppose that expenditure would be less under an insurance scheme than under the NHS. There might, on the contrary, be more expenditure, and more would *not* be undesirable if it reflected a willingness to spend more on health services. When these services are financed almost entirely from what can be allocated to them from the total amount of revenue that has been extracted from the taxpayer, some preferences may be inadequately met. Under an insurance scheme, health services over and above what could be financed by the minimum compulsory levy could be obtained by making larger contributions.

A good deal more information would be required before the respective merits of the two methods – the NHS type on the one hand and the Continental insurance-type schemes on the other – could be reasonably assessed. Even then, account would have to be taken of the cost and disturbance that so drastic a reorganisation would entail.

Rather than embark on so large a change on the basis of inconclusive evidence, it would be wiser to make it easier for medical insurance to expand alongside the NHS. Its growth in Britain has already been rapid, but its scale is limited by the fact that those who pay for it are also obliged to pay for the NHS through taxation. Some way of providing a rebate could be devised. As a first step, the premiums paid to health-insurance organisations might be made deductible from liability to income tax.

A different approach would be to extend the range of charges for the services provided by the NHS. Of course, some charges are already made, but because of their low levels, the restricted list of items to which they apply and the categories of patients exempted, they contributed only 3 per cent to the total cost of the NHS in 1980. Consideration might be given to the case for extending the scope of charging to include general practitioner consultations – as is the case in France, West Germany, Sweden and, indeed, most Continental European countries. Exemptions would again be necessary, but a useful contribution to NHS costs might be made. Moreover, unnecessary calls on doctors' time for minor or imaginary ailments might be discouraged. Hospital treatment is a different matter. This should remain free. There is, however, a case for extending the use of pay and amenity beds for those who want some extra comfort.

We are aware of the fact that we are now discussing a highly controversial issue. To have a completely free health service, with no distinctions on grounds of class or wealth, is a fine, egalitarian ideal which must be treated with respect. Some may hold that it admits of no compromise and that is the end of the matter. Others would advance the argument that when payment is introduced those with larger purses will be able to jump the queue and get medical attention quickly even when their needs are less urgent than those of poorer people. This is a more pragmatic point, although still linked to egalitarianism. In reply, another pragmatic point can be advanced. This is that even without payment the ease and speed of access to medical attention is affected by class and by place of residence.

We would strongly insist that a careful assessment should be made of the probable supply position before the case for widely extended private purchase could be endorsed. That situation would appear to have changed, however, with an impending surplus of doctors relative to demand, as limited by NHS finances with the present small private fringe. If it is the case that more medical services would be available (without a long time lag) if more were spent, then the objection to private medicine is undeniably weakened. To look at the matter from a different angle, more finance would be available to provide services for those who did not pay if those who were prepared to pay were encouraged to do so.

The *personal social services* benefit only a small proportion of the population, but they are people who are often much in need of aid. The demand for these services can be expected to grow, with unemployment likely to remain at a high level for some years and with a gradual rise in the number of very old people in the elderly population. Residential care for the elderly already accounts for nearly half of the total expenditure on the personal social services, and more cost-effective ways of meeting requirements must be devised if the departments are not to be overwhelmed by the demographic changes of the next two or three decades. The most appropriate response would be to provide services designed to help old people to remain in their own homes. What this would imply is a substantial expansion of such domiciliary services as home helps, meals-on-wheels and the like, together with much greater provision for small sheltered housing units. The domiciliary services have been easy victims in the hunt for economies in local government expenditure. Such cuts, however, only add to the need for residential care, which is far more costly in terms of the claims made on public funds. Other arrangements might also be developed, such as foster care for the frail elderly, with provision for the paying of reasonable salaries. In these ways not only might public money be saved, but also the personal preferences of old people who do not like the prospect of institutional living would be better respected.

Similar points can be made regarding care for children. Moreover, parents might in some cases be able to keep their families together with more guidance and support from the social service departments. Practical tasks such as budgeting on a low income can be the cause of much friction and even of family breakdown, which could be averted by appropriate guidance.

With the growing number of old and handicapped people, it would make sense to employ more fully the services of volunteers. In particular, it should be possible to tap the reserves of voluntary effort among the younger members of the retired population. Social service departments have not always welcomed the services of volunteers, perhaps understandably, but this attitude will need to change in the future.

To sum up: the personal social services fulfil an important function that is likely to increase in importance. But the emphasis given to different approaches needs to be modified in the light of changing circumstances. Unfortunately, the economy campaign so far does not appear to have evoked the most appropriate responses.

SOCIAL TRANSFERS

The cost of providing social transfers reflects changing economic circumstances more directly and more strongly than does expenditure on the health services and the personal social services. The main reason is the swelling volume of expenditure on unemployment benefits and the loss of revenue from social insurance contributions and taxation. The total fiscal cost of unemployment under both headings combined can be very high. In 1981–2 it may be equivalent to over 5 per cent of GNP in Britain. If unemployment could be reduced even by half, the easing of fiscal pressure would therefore be very substantial. As long as bad times persist, it is exceedingly difficult to reduce total expenditure on social transfers – on the question-begging assumption that to do so would be desirable. If the real value of retirement and widows' pensions is to be maintained, apart perhaps from some quite minor variations from one year to the next, this in itself will reduce drastically the scope for economies because pensions are quantitatively so important. Unemployment benefit may be allowed to fall a little in real terms, as has happened in Britain, but there is no conceivable cut in benefit per head that could offset the effect of the large increase in the number of heads. A rise in total transfer expenditure, in real terms, is what was to be expected, not a fall. This is, of course, one instance of the difficulty of reducing current public expenditure during a recession. It is true that public investment can be cut and was, in fact, cut quite severely in Britain after the crisis of the mid-1970s, first by a Labour and then by a Conservative Government. But total public expenditure, current and capital combined, resists compression. Indeed, a great flurry of activity appears to be needed in order to prevent an appreciable rise. Thus a somewhat paradoxical position has been reached: a recession of the modern type, with prices still rising as employment falls, may foster wider acceptance of the case for economies, but the recession itself, while it lasts, will also make their attainment very difficult. It ought to be a great deal easier to check the growth in public expenditure relative to GNP, or even to reduce that relationship, when GNP itself is growing.

When we attempt to peer into the future, beyond the period of the recession, the uncertainties are very great. However, there is one forecast at least that can be made with some confidence. This is that unemployment, even if it declines, will remain high enough to blight the prospects of the elderly middle-aged who are out of work. A high proportion of them will never succeed in finding employment again before retirement age, and this cold fact ought to be reflected in the financial assistance they are given. In Britain they will receive the short-term supplementary cash benefit, which is 30 per cent below the long-term rate. In the buoyant economy of earlier years such a difference in scale rates was not indefensible, for in those circumstances unemployment could be regarded as a misfortune of short duration for which private provision could be made, apart from the assistance received from the authorities. When unemployment is heavy and prolonged the situation is rather different, as has already been recognised (1981) by the provision of long-term benefit to elderly people who are still two years below the pension age at which it normally begins. In our view, there is a case for lowering the minimum age still more to 55, say, for those who have been unemployed for more than a year. In some other countries, although their schemes are different, a similar adjustment may now be required.

This proposal raises the wider question of flexibility with respect to retirement age. The case for flexibility has been accepted in Denmark. The age of retirement on full pension has been raised and lowered by turns. The case for adopting this practice elsewhere at least deserves consideration, on the assumption that it would be used sparingly. It must be anticipated that such changes might be thought inequitable as between one age group of elderly people and another and might encounter opposition. It would also seem to rip still more the already tattered banner of social insurance – which need not be regretted if social insurance is regarded as a confusing myth anyway. It is only fair to add that if the idea of a social insurance system were more consistently applied, we should have old-age, not retirement, pensions, with no restrictions on the incomes that pensioners might earn. If the pension age were at least adjustable with changing economic circumstances and if there were also better provision for part-retirement, the system could be made reasonably flexible.[12]

Various changes have been made since the mid-1970s in the procedure for the *indexation of benefits*, but the case for further changes will have to be considered in due course. To assume that the current arrangement could and should persist indefinitely would be to beg a question about the objectives of policy, for when economic recovery takes place and the real incomes of those at work begin to rise once more, the ratio of real social transfers to real earnings will start to decline because benefits are now indexed only for changes in prices. This will happen with regard to supplementary cash benefits as well as to the national insurance benefits, with the implication that Britain now has a *static* poverty level. If this static level were to be retained, the number of families 'in poverty' would gradually decline with the rise in real incomes from production. The question, then, is whether, and if so by what method, real benefits ought once more to be increased. That some increases are likely to be made with the passage of time can perhaps be taken for granted, but these could be on a discretionary basis instead of being determined by the application of some formula or formulae. The usual formula, not only in Britain but in many other countries, has been to link benefits to some index of average gross earnings. In Chapter 5 it was shown that this procedure can have unintentional and perhaps undesirable effects on distribution. It was recommended that if benefits are to be linked to earnings, the link should be to an index of earnings net of income tax.

There are, of course, various other possibilities, as can be seen by considering the ways in which the poverty level might be adjusted. Although the notion of a poverty level that was unchanged in real terms for indefinitely long periods might be generally rejected, there might be some support for the view that benefits should not rise fully in proportion to real net earnings – the quasi-static poverty level of chapter 5. Poverty, in other words, may be defined in relation to time and place but need not necessary be regarded as so very relative that the poverty level must be raised every year by the full proportion of any rise in earnings. The adopting of a more cautious formula of this kind could be accompanied by an undertaking that if growth gave place to depression, real benefits would be maintained even if real disposable earnings had fallen. Proponents of the strongly relativist approach should reflect that if poverty is indeed only relative, then the poverty level ought to fall when real earnings fall as well as rising when real earnings go up – an unwelcome but logical inference. No doubt many people would want a higher standard than the floor thus provided but would be left to make private provision – as Beveridge expected them to do. Sharp differences of opinion about a quasi-static poverty level are to be expected. Value judgements are obviously involved, and there is also a question of consistency. It is hard to see how such an arrangement could be consistently recommended on the ground that it keeps paternalism within bounds if at the same time there was an elaborate scheme for the provision of graduated official pensions.

It is always unwise to sign post-dated cheques payable in an uncertain future. This, unfortunately, is what was done in Britain when the graduated pension scheme was adopted in 1975. Twenty years are to elapse before benefits are to be paid, but no fund is being accumulated. In the meantime current contributions are being spent on current outlays. Commitments are growing, but no provision is being made to meet them. It was, of course, recognised from the outset that contributions would have to rise at a later stage, but it is one thing to recognise such a fact and quite another to provide for it. To make matters worse, the cost of the scheme was underestimated.[13] It is now a matter of urgency and importance that some of the scheme's provisions be changed before future pensioners feel that they have earned rights they cannot be denied.

The prospect for the elderly in the opening years of the new century is favourable – provided the economy is able to bear the cost of the schemes now in force, which will become increasingly onerous as these schemes reach maturity. Net incomes from work should be replaced to the extent of at least 70 per cent for a wide range of income groups when both official and occupational benefits are taken into account. As less money is required to support a given standard of living after retirement, pre-retirement standards of living will often be fully maintained. This may seem an outcome much to be desired; but it is not at all apparent that the state, for its part, should make provision on this scale by imposing heavy taxes on working families, often with children to support, or should require this to be done through occupational schemes.

It is no more than realistic to assume that benefits conditional upon means-testing will be important – indeed, they will be of increasing importance for a time as a consequence of long-term unemployment. The opposition to means tests has been carried too far in some political and academic circles, and extravagant denunciation tends to perpetuate the very feeling of stigma that is so much deplored. A more constructive approach would be to see how selective assistance could be provided more efficiently. Selective assistance with housing is what matters most, but this fact is not peculiar to Britain. We feel it to be worth repeating once more that in Sweden about half the pensioners receive means-tested assistance with housing (a higher proportion than in Britain), but there appear to be no complaints about stigmatisation or about inadequate take-up. Nor are those who receive such assistance described as 'poor'. Britain may have something to learn from Sweden in this respect; so may the USA.

Some suggestions for improving selective assistance were made in Chapter 4, especially with regard to housing. What remains to be discussed, however, is a selective device different from supplementary benefit. That is a negative income tax.

NEGATIVE INCOME TAX

Various proposals of great ingenuity have been advanced over the years for the institution of a negative income tax or, alternatively, a social dividend.[14] For simplicity, we shall confine attention to a negative income tax and, for the same reason, will attempt to present only the essential features of such a scheme.

All incomes would be assessed for tax. A break-even point would be determined for a tax unit of any given size, depending upon the number of dependants in the family. If an assessed income exceeded the level at the relevant break-even point, there would be a liability for tax. If it fell below that level, then the tax liability would be negative. That is to say, the family would receive a cash payment from the tax authorities instead of being obliged to make one to them. This negative tax might (a) be such as to raise the family's income fully to the break-even point or (b), as is proposed in some variants of the proposal, would provide some specified fraction of the difference between the family's income and the break-even point. (It will be seen that the family income supplement is such an arrangement, for half of the difference between actual income and the bench-mark is met in this case). The case for (b) is that it would afford some incentive for self-help.

Let us now direct attention to (a). We shall assume that the break-even point corresponds to the poverty level appropriate to the size of family and that any shortfall in its income would be fully made up. We shall also assume, for the moment, that the problem of dealing with housing costs has been solved, so that appropriate poverty levels can readily be determined without the confusion that arises when the actual housing costs of every family are met, as at present in the UK.

What advantages might follow from the adoption of a negative income tax? At times these advantages have been considered very great. The welfare state, as at present organised, entails the allocation of very large sums of money as taxation, of which a substantial part is returned to those who have paid the taxes. In short, the gross transfers in cash and kind are, it may be held, much larger than the net. Not only does this imply what many critics regard as an excessive degree of paternalism, but it also adds to the burden of taxation, and people resent heavy taxation. As a consequence, the amount of public money available for other purposes is to this extent restricted. Furthermore, when taxation is heavy there is a natural tendency to press for increases in earnings in order to sustain real disposable incomes. Thus inflationary pressure is increased. If, then, a negative income tax could succeed in raising the ratio of net transfers to gross transfers, that, it is claimed, would be a significant advantage.

The force of the argument set out above depends partly upon the range of benefits to be replaced by a negative income tax, for this has obvious implications for its quantitative importance. If all benefits, in kind as well as in cash, were superseded, then the ratio of net to gross transfers would rise appreciably. The scope for achieving a net economy – especially if benefits in kind were to remain, so that the effect of the change would be restricted to cash transfers – should not be exaggerated. Admittedly, it may be tempting to assume that in an affluent society the number of families incapable of looking after their own needs must be small and, if economic growth continues, will become smaller still. There is, then, only a residual problem, with which a negative income tax, suitably designed, could cope easily enough. In part the validity of this reasoning rests on the assumption that the poverty level should be static for an indefinite period. In part the extent of poverty – by the SB standard of measurement – may not be fully appreciated at any point in time. According to Beckerman's calculations,[15] 83 per cent of the total expenditure on cash benefits in 1975 went to families which, without benefits of any kind, would have had incomes below the poverty level. Any calculation of this kind rests on particular assumptions, but the general conclusion is clear enough: the spill-over of benefits to persons above the poverty line is probably less than a fifth.

One reason why so many people are recorded as being in poverty before the receipt of any social security benefits is that the availability of these benefits weakens the incentive to provide for one's own needs and, at the same time, the compulsory levies reduce the ability to do so. There is another important reason. This is the pay-as-you-go basis of the social security schemes. Contributions have been made in the past and taxes paid, but no assets have been accumulated in a fund of which contributors could claim to possess a share. All they have is a claim to future benefits under Samuelson's famous but metaphorical 'social contract'.[16] In the past they have financed the transfers to previous beneficiaries, and the 'social contract' now entitles them to receive benefits when their turn comes. But the claims do not count as original income, as they would if expressed as annuities to which contributors could now lay claim. Suppose, then, that all pension rights were to be superseded by selective claims to assistance under a negative income tax. Those who had lost their rights to pensions and had received instead selective assistance from the tax authorities might reasonably resent this transition, which would make them dependent upon what some would regard as public charity. Others would be deprived altogether of any state benefits even after many years of contributions. If there had been no social security system in existence and we were starting from scratch, the scope for a negative income tax would be wider. But we are where we are.

The replacement of all benefits by a negative income tax would mean the complete abandonment of social insurance, with its earmarked contributions. As we have observed more than once, this is not really an insurance scheme, and the beneficiaries do not really pay for their safeguarding against risks. This, however, is not the most important point. The real question is whether earmarked contributions for specific benefits are desirable. Social insurance should not be supported on the false ground that it is like private insurance; nor should it be denounced on the ground that it is different. To follow either of these opposing courses is to attach too much importance to a title. Let us admit, then, that in the past many people (as well as Beveridge) have seen merit in an arrangement by which people contribute, and know themselves to be contributing, a significant part of the cost of the benefits they will receive, for by doing so their self-respect is less impaired. They are not wholly dependent upon what might otherwise be regarded as public charity. It may, of course, be the case that this old argument has now lost its force. As social insurance contributions and income tax are both deducted under the pay-as-you-earn system, the distinction between the two has undeniably been blurred. It may not however, have been wholly erased. We must also avoid the danger of being too parochial. There can be no doubt that in many countries there would be strong opposition to the replacement of pension rights by a negative income tax. The pension schemes of these countries, though hedged about with official regulations, are believed to have some degree of autonomy – all the more so because they are usually financed entirely from contributions made by employers and employees. The abandonment of these pension rights would certainly cause widespread concern, for future incomes would then be felt to depend to a dangerous extent upon annual budgetary decisions. These fears might be exaggerated, but they would certainly exist.

In any case, these foreign pension schemes could not be superseded in this way for the very good reason that they have been designed not so much to provide protection against poverty as to replace past income on a graduated basis. We have not been able to find much merit in graduated official pension schemes; but it is a fact that these schemes exist, and it would be foolish to suppose that they are likely to be abandoned. Britain has also acquired her own official graduated scheme – which may well have been a serious error in social policy. It is much to be hoped that some of the more extravagant features of this scheme will be removed, but again it would be unrealistic to hope that it will now be completely scrapped.

To exclude pensions as unsuitable for absorption into a negative income tax is equivalent to excluding roughly half of total expenditure on cash transfers, contributory and non-contributory combined. Of the others, which might be regarded as suitable? Although unemployment pay, like pensions, is part of social insurance, there would probably be much less reason to oppose the change in the case of a short-term benefit of this kind. Obviously child benefit and family income supplement might be replaced – as was contemplated in the proposals for a tax-credit scheme put forward, but not implemented, in 1972.[17] What would be of particular interest, however, would be to explore the possibility of substituting a negative income tax for supplementary benefit. Admittedly, in 1972 it was officially stated that it would not be possible 'to merge the administration of supplementary benefit with the income tax machine, since it is not part of the normal administration of income tax to take into account rent and rates and other special needs, nor to respond immediately to changes in these factors'.[18] There is no good reason, however, to regard this statement as definitive. What is not 'normal administration' in one period might become so in another. The question is whether this would in practice be feasible and not too costly. It is also relevant to observe that a tax-credit scheme – the provision of a tax credit of a given amount to families of a given size – is different from a negative income tax. The fact remains that the transfer of the functions currently performed by SB to another scheme would be an extremely difficult administrative operation. But it is to be anticipated that these functions will in any case be greatly changed. If the responsibility for means-tested housing assistance were to be transferred to the local authorities, with the means tests on a standardised basis, that would greatly reduce the burden carried by the SB offices. Means-tested assistance with domestic heating and with small items – such as special needs, for furniture and clothing – could become the responsibility of appropriate local government offices. We need not become involved in detail. The essential point is that the tax authorities would be responsible for the provision of scale-rate cash benefits only. Even so, could they respond quickly to changing family circumstances, on the assumption that some SB staff had been taken over to help with the job? Perhaps the right response is to ask whether there is reason why the response should be any slower than that of the SB offices. After all, new claimants would be able to go at once to the tax offices in order to stake their claims, just as they do today at the SB offices. The real question, perhaps, is not whether the tax offices would be slower; it is whether these offices might, in appropriate cases, be *better* able to take the initiative and to provide benefits even when no claim had been made. In short, take-up might improve if the authorities were responsible for seeing that those entitled to do so got their benefits. To this end they would need to have up-to-date information about incomes. A fully computerised tax system – not yet established in England and Wales – would clearly be required.

Much has been said about the stigma associated with means-tested benefits. No such feeling should be associated with receiving money from the tax authorities – rather, a delightful sense of novelty and achievement.

There are other advantages. With a negative income tax the benefits – or negative taxes – received would rise and fall smoothly in inverse proportion to income. This is not what happens now with certain specified benefits which are available up to a certain level and then cease abruptly (e.g. school meals for children). If enough of these other schemes, with their irregularities, were replaced by cash benefits through the tax system, the poverty trap could be closed to some extent. There would be a further gain, in that the integration of the tax and benefit systems would be ensured. Obviously (by definition), there would be complete integration if all benefits were supplied in the form of negative taxes. Even, however, if some cash benefits outside the negative income tax scheme were to be retained – in particular, pensions – a closer integration would be brought about. In particular, it would no longer be possible to fix tax allowances without regard to minimum levels of benefit, for the logic of bringing them together could no longer be ignored if there were a negative income tax. It is true that even without one, this last reform could be achieved, but there would not be the same direct compulsion to do so.

The complete abandonment of social insurance has been recommended not only by advocates of a comprehensive negative income tax, for it has been held that even without the latter, the finance required for social benefits could be better obtained from a progressive income tax than from contributions. It is undeniable that the employers' contribution is a bad tax. It is bad partly because it creates the illusion that, to this extent, the cost of social security is being met from profits and, as a consequence, there may be stronger pressure for enhanced benefits than would be the case if it were generally understood that the incidence of this tax will often be shifted by charging higher prices. It is true that an attempt to raise prices may encounter the obstacles posed by a strict monetary policy or a fixed exchange rate, but employment and industrial investment would then be likely to suffer. It can only be to a modest extent that the levy will be met directly from distributed profits. Furthermore, a high employers' contribution adds to the cost of using labour as a factor of production and that is a particularly perverse effect when unemployment is high. The current method of financing is therefore open to serious criticism, but the replacement of social security contributions by an addition to the income tax also encounters the serious objection that the marginal tax rate would be very high and might well undermine incentives. There are, however, other possibilities – in particular, an addition to value added tax which could be explicitly earmarked for social security if this were thought desirable.

For our part, we suggest only a limited use of a negative insurance tax to replace supplementary benefit and short-term insurance benefits – and this only on the assumption that the administrative problems could be solved. Pensions would still have to be financed partly out of contributions from employees if graduated state pensions were to be maintained, and this would still be appropriate even if the pension were flat-rate. Full financing by a graduated employees' contribution, as in the Netherlands, might be the best solution, for this would indicate clearly the fact that the social wage must be paid for and would permit a measure of vertical redistribution if this were held to be desirable. For these long-term benefits a combination of a graduated employees' contribution levied only on income above the exemption limit (see p. 97 above), together with an earmarked constituent of VAT in place of the employers' contribution, might be second-best. At all events, the case for some earmarking might be given proper weight. Indeed, this case is now implicitly conceded by those who recommend that compulsory health insurance should replace the financing of the health service from general taxation – although we have reservations about this proposal on other grounds.

The reforms considered above would be far-reaching in their effects and would imply significant changes both in the financing of cash benefits and in the means used for their disbursement. Even if such radical proposals were not to be accepted, there are a number of other reforms that could be adopted. It may be worth while to recapitulate in conclusion some of the points made in earlier paragraphs. With regard to the health services, these include various ways of achieving the greater cost-effectiveness that is generally regarded as desirable. There might also be a somewhat greater resort to charging (e.g. for amenity beds). We rejected the idea that the NHS should be scrapped and replaced by compulsory health insurance but suggested that the expansion of voluntary health insurance alongside the state system might be encouraged by allowing the insurance premiums to be deducted from tax liabilities. In the case of the personal social services attention was drawn to the need for preserving, and indeed expanding, certain services which would reduce the need for residential care. In this way not only would there be a financial saving, but also personal preferences would be better satisfied. Indeed, some such action is essential, for the expansion of residential care on a scale adequate to meet the needs of an ageing population would impose an intolerable strain on both money and manpower. With regard to cash transfers, the case for modifying the graduated pension was stressed. It is true that the full burden will not be felt for some time, but if changes are to be made, this should be done as soon as possible before rights are deemed to have been acquired. Attention was also drawn to the fact that the choice of a proper basis for the indexation of benefits will have to be made once more when economic recovery begins and real income starts to rise once more. We suggested that if a formula is to be used, it should be one that links benefits to average earnings net of income tax. We have assumed that means-tested assistance will continue to be important for an indefinite period and have therefore stressed the importance of improving the efficiency with which it is administered and of combating the sense of stigma that is said to accompany its receipt. Assistance with housing is a critically important item. The changes proposed by the government in 1981 will be a first step in the right direction but only a first step. The scale on which assistance in cash is provided should also be reviewed. In particular, we have recommended that the long-term unemployed who have reached the age of 55 or over should now receive benefit on the more generous long-term scale rate.

Whatever the form of financing, there can be no escape from unpleasant choices at a time when economic growth has stopped and, even when it resumes, may be at a slower rate than in the past. In any case, even if growth had been sustained, welfare expenditure could not have continued to grow indefinitely at a rate faster than that of GNP. In these circumstances, it is crucially important to consider again the basic objectives of the welfare state. If protection against poverty is the primary objective, as we believe to be the case, a discriminating approach is necessary, and in adopting that approach full account must be taken of the fact that unemployment on a substantial scale is likely to persist for years ahead, even on the most favourable assumptions. For an extended period after the war unemployment had ceased to be one of the main causes of poverty, but the situation has now deteriorated once more. It is true that inflationary pressure must be brought firmly under control, and it may also be true that the rapid growth of welfare expenditure has contributed to that pressure. In particular, it would be unwise to suppose that a rise in the social wage – that is to say, in welfare benefits – will be readily accepted for long as a substitute for increases in real take-home pay. But it must also be recognised that the hardship imposed by a combination of stagnant output and rising prices falls heavily and unfairly on some people, while others get off lightly. It is no doubt sadly inevitable that the incidence of this hardship will be inequitable, but an attempt should be made at least to temper this unfairness in the future in so far as this is possible within the limits set by general economic policy.

NOTES

1 T. H. Marshall, *Social Policy in the Twentieth Century*, 4th edn. (London: Hutchinson, 1977).

2 For example, for the USA, P. Ruggles and M. O'Higgins, 'The distribution of public expenditure and taxes among households in the United States', *Review of Income and Wealth*, vol. 2 (1981); for Sweden, T. Franzen, K. Lövgren and I. Rosenberg, 'Redistributional effects of taxes and public expenditure in Sweden', *Swedish Journal of Economics*, vol. 77 (March 1975).

3 A. R. Prest, 'The Budget and interpersonal distribution', *Public Finance*, vol. 28 (1968).

4 A. T. Peacock and P. Shannon, 'The welfare state and the redistribution of income', *Westminster Bank Review* (August 1968); Prest, 'The Budget and interpersonal distribution'; M. O'Higgins, 'Income distribution and social policy: an assessment after the Royal Commission on the Distribution of Income and Wealth', in M. Brown and S. Baldwin (eds.), *The Yearbook of Social Policy in Britain 1979* (London: Routledge & Kegan Paul, 1980).

5 Royal Commission on the Distribution of Income and Wealth, Report No. 6: *Lower Incomes* HMSO, 1978).

6 Ruggles and O'Higgins, 'The distribution of public expenditure'.

7 ibid., p. 305.

8 P. E. Hart, 'The dynamics of earnings 1963–73,' *Economic Journal* (September 1976); J. Creedy, *State Pensions in Britain* (London: National Institute of Social and Economic Research, 1982).

9 Central Policy Review Staff, *A Joint Framework of Social Policies* (London: HMSO, 1975), p. 1.

BIBLIOGRAPHY

Aaron, H., 'Demographic effects on the equity of social security benefits', in M. Feldstein and R. Inman (eds), *The Economics of the Public Services* (London: Macmillan, 1971).

Abel-Smith, B., *Value for Money in Health Services* (London: Heinemann, 1976).

Abel-Smith, B., 'Merrison's medicine for the health services', *New Society* (July 1979).

Abel-Smith, B., 'The welfare state: breaking the post-war consensus', *Political Quarterly*, vol. 51 (1980).

Abel-Smith, B. and Maynard, A., *The Organization, Financing and Cost of Health Care in the European Community* (Brussels: EEC Commission, 1979).

Abel-Smith, B., and Townsend, P., *The Poor and the Poorest* (London: Bell, 1965).

Abrams, M., *Beyond Three-Score and Ten* (London: Age Concern, 1978).

Ackerman, B. A., *Social Justice in the Liberal State* (New Haven, Conn.: Yale University Press, 1980).

Age Concern, *Profiles of the Elderly, No. 8: Their Use of the Social Services* (London: Age Concern, 1981).

Andersen, R., Smedby, B., and Anderson, O., *Medical Care in Sweden and the United States* (Chicago: University of Chicago Press, 1970).

Arrow, K. J., *Social Choice and Individual Values* (New York: Wiley, 1951).

Arrow, K. J., 'Uncertainty and the welfare economics of medical care', *American Economic Review*, vol. 53 (1963).

Atkinson, A. B., *Poverty in Britain and the Reform of Social Security* (Cambridge: Cambridge University Press, 1969).

Atkinson, A. B., *The Economics of Inequality* (London: Oxford University Press, 1975).

Atkinson, A. B., *The Distribution of Income and Wealth in Britain* (London: Allen & Unwin, 1976).

Atkinson, A. B., and Flemming, J. S., 'Unemployment, social security and disincentives', *Midland Bank Review* (Autumn 1978).

Atkinson, A. B.; Maynard, A., and Trinder, C. G., 'National assistance and low incomes', *Social Policy and Administration*, vol. 15, no. 1 (1981).

Atkinson, J. A., 'The developing relationship between the state pension scheme and occupational pensions', *Social and Economic Administration* vol. 11, no. 3 (1977).

Austin, M., and Posnett, J., 'The charity sector in England and Wales – characteristics and public accountability', *National Westminster Bank Quarterly*, no. 281 (August 1979).

Beattie, R. A., 'France' and 'Belgium', in T. Wilson (ed.), *Pensions, Inflation and Growth* (London: Heinemann, 1974).

Beckerman, W., 'The impact of income maintenance payments on poverty in Britain', *Economic Journal* (June 1979).

Berthoud, R., *et al.*, *Poverty and the Development of Anti-Poverty in the UK* (London: Heinemann, 1981).

Beveridge, W., *Voluntary Action* (London: Allen & Unwin, 1948).

Booth, T. A. (ed.), *Planning for Welfare* (Oxford: Blackwell and Martin Robertson, 1979).

Bradshaw, J., 'A taxonomy of social need', in G. McLachlan (ed.), *Problems and Progress in Medical Care* (London: Oxford University Press, 1972).

Breton, A., *The Economic Theory of Representative Government* (Chicago: Aldine, 1974).

Brittain, J. A., *The Payroll Tax and Social Security* (Washington, DC: Brookings Institution, 1972).

Brown, C. V., *Public Sector Economics* (Oxford: Martin Robertson, 1978).

Brown, C. V., *Taxation and the Incentive to Work* (Oxford: Oxford University Press, 1980).

Browning, E. K., 'Why the social insurance budget is too large in a democracy', *Economic Inquiry*, vol. 13, (Sept. 1975). Also subsequent exchange of views with K. V. Green,

Economic Inquiry, vol. 15 (July 1977), and with B. Bridges, *Economic Inquiry*, vol. 16 (Jan. 1978).

Bruce, M., *The Coming of the Welfare State* (London: Batsford, 1961).

Buchanan, J. M., *Inconsistencies in the National Health Service*, Occasional Paper No. 7 (London: Institute of Economic Affairs, 1966).

Buchanan, J. M., 'Social insurance in a growing economy', *National Tax Journal* (1968).

Buchanan, J. M., *The Limits of Liberty* (Chicago: University of Chicago Press, 1975).

Buchanan, J. M., 'Federalism and fiscal equity', *American Economic Review*, vol. 47 (1957).

Buchanan, J. M., and Tulloch, G., *The Calculus of Consent* (Ann Arbor: University of Michigan Press, 1962).

Carrier, J., 'The Merrison Report on the national health service', in M. Brown and S. Baldwin (eds), *The Yearbook of Social Policy in Britain* (London: Routledge & Kegan Paul, 1980).

Carstairs, V., and Morrison, N., *The Elderly in Residential Care* (Edinburgh: Scottish Home and Health Department, 1971).

Carter, C., 'The priorities of public expenditure', *Policy Studies*, vol. 1, no. 2 (1980).

Carter, C., 'A new direction in social policy', in M. Brown and S. Baldwin (eds), *The Yearbook of Social Policy in Britain* (London: Routledge & Kegan Paul, 1980).

Carter, C., and Wilson, T., *Discussing the Welfare State*, Discussion Paper No. 1 (London: Policy Studies Institute, 1980).

Challis, D. J., 'The measurement of outcome in social care of the elderly', *Journal of Social Policy*, vol. 10, no. 2 (1981).

Cochrane, A. L., *Effectiveness and Efficiency* (London: Nuffield Provincial Hospitals Trust, 1971).

Colberg, M. R., *The Social Security Retirement Test: Right or Wrong?* American Enterprise Institute (Washington, DC: 1978).

Collard, D., *Altruism and Economy* (Oxford: Martin Robertson, 1978).

Cooper, M. H. (ed.), *Social Policy: A Survey of Recent Developments* (Oxford: Blackwell, 1974).

Cooper, M. H., *Rationing Health Care* (London: Croom Helm, 1975).

Creedy, J., *State Pensions in Britain* (London: National Institute of Economic and Social Research, 1982).

Creedy, J., *Taxation and National Insurance Contributions*, Working Paper No. 30 (University of Durham: Dept of Economics, 1980).

Creedy, J., 'The new government pension scheme: a simulation analysis', *Oxford Bulletin of Economics and Statistics* (February 1980).

Creedy, J. (ed.), *The Economics of Unemployment in Britain* (London: Butterworth, 1981).

Cullis, J. G., and West, P. A., *The Economics of Health* (Oxford: Martin Robertson, 1979).

Culyer, A. J., *Need and the NHS* (Oxford: Martin Robertson, 1976).

Culyer, A. J., *The Political Economy of Social Policy* (Oxford: Martin Robertson, 1980).

Culyer, A. J., 'Economics, social policy and social administration: the interplay between topics and disciplines', *Journal of Social Policy*, vol. 10, no. 3 (1981).

Culyer, A. J., Williams, A., and Lavers, R. J., 'Health indicators', in *Social Trends* (London: HMSO, 1971).

Cuvillier, R., 'The housewife: an unjustified financial burden on the community', *Journal of Social Policy*, vol. 8, no. 1 (1979).

Daniels, N., *Reading Rawls* (Oxford: Blackwell, 1975).

Danziger, S., Haveman, R., and Plotnick, R., 'How income transfer programmes affect work, savings and the income distribution: a critical review', *Journal of Economic Literature*, vol. 19, no. 3 (1981).

Davies, B., *Social Needs and Resources in Social Services* (London: Michael Joseph, 1968).

Davies, B., *Variations in Children's Services among British Urban Authorities* (London: Bell, 1972).

Davies, B., *Variations in Services for the Aged* (London: Bell, 1972).

Davis, K., and Schoen, C., *Health and the War of Poverty: A Ten Year Appraisal* (Washington, DC: Brookings Institution, 1975).

Derthick, M., *Policy-Making for Social Security* (Washington, DC: Brookings Institution, 1979).

Dinwiddy, R., and Reed, D., *The Effects of Certain Social and Demographic Changes on Income Distribution*, Background Paper No. 3, Royal Commission on the Distribution of Income and Wealth (London: HMSO, 1977).

Doherty, M. A., 'National insurance and absence from work', *Economic Journal*, vol. 89 (March 1979).

Donnison, D., 'A rationalisation of housing benefits', *Three Banks Review*, no. 131 (September 1981).

Dorfman, R., 'General equilibrium with public goods', in J. Margolis and H. Guitton (eds), *An Analysis of Public Production and Consumption and Their Relations to the Private Sectors* (New York: Macmillan, 1969).

Downs, A., *An Economic Theory of Democracy* (New York: Harper & Row, 1957).

Economist Intelligence Unit, *Care with Dignity: An Analysis of Costs of Care for the Disabled*, Action Research for the Crippled Child monograph (London: National Fund for Research into Crippling Diseases, 1973).

Fiegehen, G. C., Lansley, P. S., and Smith, A. D., *Poverty and Progress in Britain 1953–73*, National Institute of Economic and Social Research Occasional Paper No. 29 (Cambridge: Cambridge University Press, 1977).

Flowers, M., *Women and Social Security: An Institutional Dilemma* (Washington, DC: American Enterprise Institute, 1977).

Fogarty, M., *The Under-Governed and the Over-Governed* (London: Chapman, 1962).

Fogarty, M., *Pensions – Where Next?* (London: Centre for Studies in Social Policy, 1976).

Fogarty, M., 'The future of retirement pensions and retirement age in Britain', mimeo, Policy Studies Institute, 1980.

Foster, Peggy, 'The informal rationing of primary medical care', *Journal of Social Policy*, vol. 8, no. 4 (1979).

Franzén, T., Lövgren, K., and Rosenberg, I., 'Redistributional effects of taxes and public expenditure in Sweden', *Swedish Journal of Economics*, vol. 77 (March 1975).

Fresch, H. E., and Ginsburg, P. B., *Public Insurance in Private Medical Markets* (Washington, DC: American Enterprise Institute, 1978).

Friedman, M., *Capitalism and Freedom* (Chicago: University of Chicago Press, 1962).

Friedman, M., *Monetary Correction* (London: Institute of Economic Affairs, 1974).

Fuchs, V. R., 'The contribution of health services to the American economy', *Millbank Memorial Fund Quarterly*, vol. 44 (1966); reprinted in M. H. Cooper and A. J. Culyer (eds), *Health Economics* (Harmondsworth: Penguin, 1973).

George, V., *Social Security: Beveridge and After* (London: Routledge & Kegan Paul, 1968).

George, V., and Lawson, R. (eds), *Poverty and Inequality in Common Market Countries* (London: Routledge & Kegan Paul, 1980).

Gilbert, B., *The Evolution of National Insurance in Great Britain* (London: Michael Joseph, 1966).

Gilbert, B., *British Social Policy* (London: Batsford, 1970).

Glennerster, H., *Social Service Budgets: British and American Experience* (London: Allen & Unwin, 1975).

Gough, I., *The Political Economy of the Welfare State* (London: Macmillan, 1979).

Goldberg, E. M., *Helping the Aged: A Field Experiment in Social Work* (London: Allen & Unwin, 1971).

Goldberg, E. M., 'Monitoring in the social services', in E. M. Goldberg and N. Connelly (eds.), *Evaluative Research in Social Care* (London: Heinemann, 1981).

Goodman, J. C., *Social Security in the United Kingdom: Contracting out of the System* (Washington, DC: American Enterprise Institute).

Green, C., *Negative Taxes and the Poverty Problem* (Washington, DC: Brookings Institution, 1967).

Hagenbuch, W., *Social Economics* (Cambridge: Cambridge University Press, 1958).

Hall, A. S., *The Point of Entry* (London: Allen & Unwin, 1974).

Harris, A., *Social Welfare of the Aged* (London: HMSO, 1968).

Harris, A., *Handicapped and Impaired in Great Britain* (London: HMSO, 1971).

Harris, J., *William Beveridge: A Biography* (Oxford: Oxford University Press, 1977).

Harris, R., and Seldon, A., *Over-ruled on Welfare* (London: Institute of Economic Affairs, 1979).

Harsanyi, J. C., 'Cardinal welfare, individualistic ethics and interpersonal comparisons of utility', *Journal of Political Economy* (August 1955); reprinted in E. S. Phelps (ed.), *Economic Justice* (Harmondsworth: Penguin, 1973).

Hart, P. E., 'The dynamics of earnings 1963–73', *Economic Journal* (September 1976).

Heclo, H., *Modern Social Politics in Britain and Sweden* (New Haven, Conn.: Yale University Press, 1974).

Heidenheimer, A. J., Heclo, H., and Adams, C., *Comparative Social Policy* (London: Macmillan, 1975).

Hemming, R., and Kay, J. A., 'Occupational pension schemes: Problems and Reform' (mimeo) (London: Institute for Fiscal Studies, 1981).

Hemming, R., and Kay, J. A., *The Costs of the State Earnings-Related Pension Scheme*, Working Paper No. 21 (London: Institute for Fiscal Studies, 1981).

Henle, P., 'Recent trends in retirement benefits related to earnings', *Monthly Labour Review*, vol. 95 (June 1972).

Hill, M., *Understanding Social Policy* (Oxford: Blackwell and Martin Robertson, 1980).

Hochman, H., and Rogers, J. D., 'Pareto Optimal Redistribution', *American Economic Review*, vol. 59 (1969).

Horlick, M., 'Mandating private pensions: experience in four European countries', *Social Security Bulletin*, vol. 42, no. 3 (1979).

Hunt, A., *The Home Help Service in England and Wales* (London: HMSO, 1970).

Hunt, A., *The Elderly at Home* (London: OPCS/HMSO, 1978).

Institute of Economic Affairs, *The Long Debate on Poverty* (London: IEA, 1973).

Institute of Economic Affairs, *The Economics of Charity* (London: IEA, 1973).

Institute for Fiscal Studies, *Proceedings of the Conference on Proposals for a Tax Credit System* (London: IFS, 1973).

International Labour Office, *Convention 102*, Concerning minimum standards of social security (Geneva: ILO, 1952).

International Social Security Administration, *Absenteeism and Social Security*, Studies and Research No. 16 (Geneva: ISSA, 1980).

Israel, S., and Teeling-Smith, G., 'The submerged iceberg of sickness in society', *Social and Economic Administration*, vol. 1, no. 1 (1967).

Judge, K., *Rationing Social Services* (London: Heinemann, 1978).

Judge, K., 'Beveridge: past, present and future', in C. Sandford, C. Pond and R. Walker (eds), *Taxation and Social Policy* (London: Heinemann, 1980).

Judge, K., 'State Pensions and the Growth of Social Welfare Expenditure', *Journal of Social Policy*, vol. 10 (October 1981).

Judge, K., and Matthews, J., *Charging for Social Care* (London: Allen & Unwin, 1980).

Kahn, A. J., and Kamerman, S. B., *Social Services in International Perspective* (Washington, DC: US Department of Health, Education and Welfare, 1978).

Kaim-Caudle, P. R., *Comparative Social Policy and Social Security* (London: Martin Robertson, 1973).

King, M. A., and Atkinson, A. B., 'Housing policy taxation and reform', *Midland Bank Review* (Spring 1980).

Klein, R. (ed.), *Inflation and Priorities* (London: Centre for Studies in Social Policy, 1975).

Klein, R., 'The welfare state: a self-inflicted crisis?', *Political Quarterly*, vol. 51 (1980).

Klein, R., 'Health services', in P. M. Jackson (ed.), *Government Policy Initiatives 1979–80: Some Case Studies in Public Administration* (London: Royal Institute of Public Administration, 1981).

Klein, R., and Hall, P., *Caring for Quality in the Caring Services* (London: Centre for Studies in Social Policy, 1974).

Knapp, M., 'Planning for balance of care of the elderly: a comment', *Scottish Journal of Political Economy*, vol. 27, no. 3 (1980).

Kramer, R. M., 'Voluntary agencies in the welfare state', *Journal of Social Policy*, vol. 8, no. 4 (1979).

Kuusi, P., *Social Policy for the 1960s* (Helsinki: Finnish Social Policy Association, 1964).

Lansley, S., 'What hope for the poor?', *Lloyds Bank Review*, no. 132 (April 1979).

Lawson, R., and Stevens, C., 'Housing allowances in West Germany and France', *Journal of Social Policy*, vol. 3, no. 3 (1974).

Layard, R., Piachaud, D., and Stewart, M., *The Causes of Poverty*, Background Paper for the Sixth Report of the Royal Commission on the Distribution of Income and Wealth (London: HMSO, 1978).

Lees, D. S., *Health through Choice* (London: Institute of Economic Affairs, 1965).

Le Grand, J., 'The distribution of public expenditure: the case of health care', *Economica*, no. 45 (1978).

Lenin, I., *The State and Revolution* (London: Central Books, 1972).

Lerner, A., *The Economics of Control* (Lo. don: Macmillan, 1944).

Levitan, S. A., *Programs in Aid of the Poor for the 1980s* (Baltimore and London: Johns Hopkins University Press, 1980).

Lindsay, C. M., and Buchanan, J. M., *The Organization and Financing of Medical Care in the United States* (London: British Medical Association, 1969).

Lynes, T., 'Industrial injuries scheme at the cross-roads', *New Society*, 13 November 1980.

Lynes, T., *The Penguin Guide to Supplementary Benefits*, 4th edn (London: Penguin, 1981).

McClements, L. D., *The Economics of Social Security* (London: Heinemann, 1978).

McKean, R. N., 'Economics of trust altruism and corporate responsibility', in Edmund S. Phelps (ed.), *Altruism, Morality and Economic Theory* (New York: Russell Sage Foundation, 1975).

McKeown, T., *The Role of Medicine: Dream, Mirage or Nemesis?* (London: Nuffield Provincial Hospitals Trust, 1976).

Marshall, G. P., *Social Equals and Economic Perspectives* (London: Penguin, 1980).

Marshall, T. H., 'Value problems and welfare-capitalism', *Journal of Social Policy*, vol. 1, no. 1 (1972).

Marshall, T. H., *Social Policy in the Twentieth Century*, 4th edn (London: Hutchinson, 1977).

Maynard, A., 'The medical profession and the efficiency and equity of health services', *Social and Economic Administration*, vol. 12, no. 1 (1978).

Maynard, A., and Ludbrook, A., 'What's wrong with the National Health Service?', *Lloyd's Bank Review*, no. 138 (1980).

Meade, J. E., *The Structure and Reform of Direct Taxation*, Report of a committee under the chairmanship of J. E. Meade (London: Allen & Unwin, 1978).

Menzies, A. M., 'The Federal Republic of Germany and the Netherlands', in T. Wilson (ed.), *Pensions, Inflation and Growth* (London: Heinemann, 1974).

Meyer, J. A., *Health Care Cost Increases* (Washington, DC: American Enterprise Institute, 1979).

Moggridge, D. (ed.), *Collected Writings of John Maynard Keynes*, vol. 27: *Activities 1940–46* (London and Cambridge: Macmillan and Cambridge University Press, 1980).

Mooney, G. N., 'Planning for balance of care of the elderly', *Scottish Journal of Political Economy*, vol. 25, no. 2 (1978).

Mueller, D. C., *Public Choice* (Cambridge: Cambridge University Press, 1979).

Muir Gray, J., 'The deficiencies of the Royal Commission: a practitioner's viewpoint', in M. Brown and S. Baldwin (eds), *The Yearbook of Social Policy in Britain 1979* (London: Routledge & Kegan Paul, 1980).

Munnell, A. H., *The Future of Social Security* (Washington, DC: Brookings Institution, 1977).

Musgrave, R. M., *The Theory of Public Finance* (New York: McGraw-Hill, 1959).

Musgrave, R. M., and Peacock, A. T., *Classics in the Theory of Public Finance* (London: Macmillan, 1967).

National Association of Pension Funds, *Survey of Occupational Pension Schemes 1980* (London: NAPF, 1981).

Nicholson, J. L., 'The redistribution of income', in A. B. Atkinson (ed.), *The Personal Distribution of Income* (London: Allen & Unwin, 1976).

Oates, W. E., *Fiscal Federalism* (New York: Harcourt Brace Jovanovich, 1972).

Office of Health Economics, *Trends in European Health Spending*, Briefing No. 14 (London: OHE, 1981).

Office of Health Economics, *Sickness Absence: A Review*, Briefing No. 16 (London: OHE, 1981).

Office of Health Economics, *Doctors, Nurses and Midwives in the NHS*, Briefing No. 18 (London: OHE, 1981).

O'Higgins, M., 'Income distribution and social policy: an assessment after the Royal Commission on the Distribution of Income and Wealth', in M. Brown and S. Baldwin (eds), *The Yearbook of Social Policy in Britain 1979* (London: Routledge & Kegan Paul, 1980).

O'Higgins, M., and Ruggles, P., 'The distribution of public expenditure and taxes among households in the United Kingdom', *Income and Wealth* (September 1981).

Okner, B. A., *The Social Security Payroll Tax: Some Alternatives for Reform*, General Series Reprint 306 (Washington, DC: Brookings Institution, 1975).

Olsen, M., *The Logic of Collective Action* (Cambridge, Mass.: Harvard University Press, 1965).

Orshansky, M., 'Counting the poor: another look at the poverty profile', *Social Security Bulletin*, vol. 28, no. 1 (1965).

Owen, D., *In Sickness or in Health: The Politics of Medicine* (London: Quartet, 1976).

Parker, R. A., 'Social Administration and scarcity', in E. Butterworth and R. Holman (eds), *Social Welfare in Modern Britain* (London: Fontana, 1975).

Parker, R. A., 'Charging for the social services', *Journal of Social Policy*, vol. 5, no. 4 (1976).

Peacock, A. T., *The Economics of National Insurance* (Edinburgh: Hodge, 1952).

Peacock, A. T., and Rowley, C. K., *Welfare Economics: A Liberal Restatement* (London: Martin Robertson, 1975).

Peacock, A. T., and Shannon, P., 'The welfare state and the redistribution of income', *Westminster Bank Review* (August 1968).

Peacock, A. T., and Wiseman, J., *The Growth of Public Expenditure in the United Kingdom* (Princeton, NJ, and London: National Bureau of Economic Research and Oxford University Press, 1961).

Pechman, J. A., Aaron, H. J., and Taussig, M. K., *Social Security: Perspectives for Reform* (Washington, DC: Brookings Institution, 1968).

Perlman, M. (ed.), *The Economics of Health and Medical Care* (London: Macmillan, 1974).

Phelps, E. S. (ed.), *Economic Justice* (Harmondsworth: Penguin, 1973).

Piachaud, D., 'Peter Townsend and the Holy Grail', *New Society* (10 September 1981).

Pigou, A. C., *Economics of Welfare* (London: Macmillan, 1920).

Pilch, M., and Carroll, B., *State Pension Ages: Flexibility – the Key to Equality* (London: Nobel Lowndes, 1976).

Pinker, R., *Social Policy and Social Theory* (London: Heinemann, 1971).

Pinker, R., *The Idea of Welfare* (London: Heinemann, 1979).

Plattner, M. F., 'The welfare state v. the redistributive state', *Public Interest*, no. 55 (1979).

Pole, J. D., 'The economics of mass radiography', in M. Hauser (ed.), *The Economics of Health Care* (London: Allen & Unwin, 1972).

Political and Economic Planning, *Family Needs and the Social Services* (London: Allen & Unwin, 1961).

Pond, C., 'Tax expenditure and fiscal welfare', in C. Sandford, C. Pond and R. Walker (eds), *Taxation and Social Policy* (London: Heinemann, 1980).

Prest, A. R., 'The Budget and interpersonal distribution', *Public Finance*, vol. 28 (1968).

Prest, A. R., *Social Benefits and Tax Rates* (London: Institiute of Economic Affairs, 1970).

Prest, A. R., 'The negative income tax: concepts and problems', *British Tax Review* (November–December 1970).

Rawls, J., *A Theory of Justice* (Oxford: Oxford University Press, 1972).

Rees, A. M., 'Access to the personal health and welfare services', *Social and Economic Administration*, vol. 6, no. 1 (1972).

Rein, M., 'Social class and the health service', *New Society*, 20 November 1969.

Rein, M., *Social Science and Public Policy* (Harmondsworth: Penguin, 1976).

Rhys-Williams, B., and Kaldor, N., *Minutes of Evidence to Select Committee on Tax Credit* (London: HMSO, 1973).

Rhys-Williams, Lady, *Something to Look Forward to* (London: Macdonald, 1943).

Rhys-Williams, Lady, *Taxation and Incentives* (London: Oxford University Press, 1953).

Robb, B., *Sans Everything* (London: Nelson, 1967).

Robbins, L. C., *The Nature and Significance of Economic Science* (London: Macmillan, 1932).

Robbins, L. C., 'Economics and Political Economy', *American Economic Review*, Papers and Proceedings (May 1981).

Robson, W. A., *Welfare State and Welfare Society* (London: Allen & Unwin, 1976).

Rowntree, B. S., *Poverty: A Study of Town Life* (London: Macmillan, 1899; 2nd edn 1902).

Rowntree, B. S., *Poverty and Progress*, 1st edn (London: Longman Green, 1941).

Rowntree, B. S., and Lavers, G. B., *Poverty and the Welfare State* (London: Longman Green, 1951).

Ruggles, P., and O'Higgins, M., 'The distribution of public expenditure and taxes among households in the United States', *Review of Income and Wealth*, vol. 2 (1981).

Runciman, W., *Relative Deprivation and Social Justice* (London: Routledge & Kegan Paul, 1966; Harmondsworth: Penguin, 1972).

Sainsbury, P., and Grad d'Alarçon, J., 'The cost of community care and the burden on the family of treating the mentally ill at home', in D. Lees and S. Shaw (eds), *Impairment, Disability and Handicap* (London: Heinemann, 1974).

Samuelson, P. A., 'An exact consumption-loan model of interest with or without the social contrivance of money', *Journal of Political Economy* (December 1958).

Sandford, C., *Social Economics* (London: Heinemann, 1977).

Sandford, C., 'Taxation and social policy: an overview', in C. Sandford, C. Pond and R. Walker (eds), *Taxation and Social Policy* (London: Heinemann, 1980).

Schultze, C. L., *The Public Use of Private Interest* (Washington, DC: Brookings Institution, 1977).

Schulz, J. H., *The Economics of Aging* (Belmont, Ca.: Wadsworth, 1980).

Schweinitz, K. de, *England's Road to Social Security*, Perpetua edition (New York: Barnes, 1961).

Seldon, A., *Charge* (London: Temple Smith, 1977).

Seldon, A., *Whither the Welfare State?* (London: Institute of Economic Affairs, 1981).

Sen, A., *Collective Choice and Social Welfare* (San Francisco and Edinburgh: Holden Day and Oliver & Boyd, 1970).

Sen, A., *On Economic Inequality* (Oxford: Oxford University Press, 1973).

Shanas, E., Townsend, P., and Wedderburn, D., *Living Conditions of the Aged in Three Industrial Societies* (London: Routledge & Kegan Paul, 1968).

Simpson, R., *Access to Primary Care*, Research Paper No. 6 for the Royal Commission on the National Health Service (London: HMSO, 1979).

Sleeman, J. F., *Resources for the Welfare State* (London: Longman, 1979).

Smith, Adam, *The Wealth of Nations*, ed. R. H. Campbell, A. S. Skinner and W. B. Todd (Oxford: Oxford University Press, 1976).

Steiner, P. O., 'Public expenditure budgeting', in A. S. Blinder *et al.* (eds), *The Economics of Public Finance* (Washington, DC: Brookings Institution, 1974).

Tinker, A., *The Elderly in Modern Society* (London: Longman, 1981).

Titmuss, R. M., *The Gift Relationship: From Human Blood to Social Policy* (London: Allen & Unwin, 1970).

Titmuss, R. M., *Commitment to Welfare*, ed., B. Abel-Smith, 2nd edn (London: Allen & Unwin, 1976).

Titmuss, R. M., *Essays on 'The Welfare State'*, ed. B. Abel-Smith, 3rd edn (London: Allen & Unwin, 1976).

Tobin, J., 'On limiting the domain of inequality', *Journal of Law and Economics*, vol. 13 (1970).

Tobin, J., Pechman, J. A., and Mieszkowski, P. M., *Is a Negative Income Tax Practical?* (Washington, DC: Brookings Institution, 1967).

Townsend, P., *Poverty in the United Kingdom* (London: Allen Lane, 1979).

Townsend, P., and Wedderburn, D., *The Aged in the Welfare State* (London: Bell, 1945).

Tulloch, G., *The Vote Motive* (London: Institute of Economic Affairs, 1976).

Vickrey, W. S., 'An exchange of questions between economics and philosophy', in A. D. Ward (ed.), *The Goals of Economic Life* (London: Harper, 1953); reprinted in Edmund S. Phelps (ed.), *Economic Justice* (Harmondsworth: Penguin, 1973).

Wager, R., *Care of the Elderly* (London: IMTA, 1972).

Walker, A., 'The social creation of poverty and dependency in old age', *Journal of Social Policy*, vol. 9 no. 1 (1980).

Walley, J., *Social Security: Another British Failure* (London: Knight, 1972).

Weale, A., *Equality and Social Policy* (London: Routledge & Kegan Paul, 1978).

Weale, A., 'Paternalism and social policy', *Journal of Social Policy*, vol. 7, no. 2 (1978).

Webb, A., and Wistow, G., 'The personal social services', in *Government Policy Initiatives 1979–80: Some Case Studies in Public Administration* (London: RIPA, 1981).

Weisbrod, A., 'Collective-consumption services of individual-consumption goods', *Quarterly Journal of Economics*, vol. 78 (August 1964), pp. 471–7.

Wicks, M., *Old and Cold* (London: Heinemann, 1978).

Wicksell, K., 'A new principle of just taxation' (1896), reprinted in R. A. Musgrave and A. T. Peacock (eds), *Classics in the Theory of Public Finance* (London: Macmillan, 1967).

Wickstead, P., *The Commonsense of Political Economy*, ed. L. C. Robbins (London: Routledge, 1933).

Wilensky, H., *The Welfare State and Equality* (Berkeley: University of California Press, 1975).

Williams, A., and Anderson, R., *Efficiency in the Social Services* (Oxford: Blackwell and Martin Robertson, 1976).

Willis, J. R. M., and Hardwick, P. J. W., *Tax Expenditure in the United Kingdom* (London: Institute of Fiscal Studies, 1978).

Wilson, D., *The Welfare State in Sweden* (London: Heinemann, 1979).

Wilson, R. W., and White, E. L., 'Changes in morbidity, disability and utilization differentials between the poor and the non-poor. Data from the Health Survey 1964 and 1973', Medical Care, 15, 8, in *Inequalities in Health* (Black Report) (London: HMSO, 1971).

Wilson, T. (ed.), *Pensions, Inflation and Growth* (London: Heinemann, 1974).

Wilson, T., 'The market and the state', in T. Wilson and A. Skinner (eds), *The Market and the State: Essays in Honour of Adam Smith* (Oxford: Oxford University Press, 1976).
Wilson, T., 'Welfare economics and the welfare state', *Swedish Journal of Political Science*, no. 5 (1980).
Wilson, T., 'The finance of the welfare state', in A. T. Peacock and F. Forte (eds), *The Political Economy of Taxation* (Oxford: Blackwell, 1981).
Wiseman, J., 'The choice of optimal social expenditures', *Public Choice and Public Finance*, no. 307 (1980).

OFFICIAL PUBLICATIONS

BRITAIN

A Happier Old Age, DHSS (London: HMSO, 1978).
A Joint Framework of Social Policies, Report of the Central Policy Review Staff (London: HMSO, 1975).
Assistance with Housing Costs, DOE (London: HMSO, 1981).
Better Pensions, Cmnd 5713 (London: HMSO, 1974).
Better Services for the Mentally Handicapped, Cmnd 4683, DHSS (London: HMSO, 1971).
Better Services for the Mentally Ill, Cmnd 6233, DHSS (London: HMSO, 1975).
Circumstances of Families, Ministry of Pensions and National Insurance (London: HMSO, 1967).
'Effects of taxes and benefits on household income', Central Statistical Office, *Economic Trends* (January 1980).
Employment Policy, Cmd 6527 (London: HMSO, 1944).
Enquiry into the Value of Pensions, Cmnd 8147 (London: HMSO, 1981).
Financial and Other Circumstances of Retirement Pensioners, Ministry of Pensions and National Insurance (London: HMSO, 1966).
General Household Survey (London: HMSO, 1978).
Government's Expenditure Plans 1981/2 to 1983/4, Cmnd 8175 (London: HMSO, 1981).
Growing Older, Cmnd 8173, DHSS, (London: HMSO, 1981).
Health and Personal Social Service Statistics for England 1978, DHSS (London: HMSO, 1980).
Health Services Costing Returns: Year Ended 31st March 1979, DHSS (London: HMSO, 1981).
Improved Protection for the Occupational Pension Rights and Expectations of Early Leavers, a Report of the Occupational Pensions Board (London: HMSO, 1981).
Income during Initial Sickness, Cmnd 7864, DHSS (London: HMSO, 1980).
Inequalities in Health (the Black Report), Cmnd 6502, DHSS (London: HMSO, 1980).
National Income and Expenditure (London: HMSO, published annually).
Occupational Pension Schemes 1975, Fifth Survey by the Government Actuary (London: HMSO, 1978).
Occupational Pension Schemes 1979, Sixth Survey by the Government Actuary (London: HMSO, 1981).
Population Projections 1974–2014, Office of Population Censuses and Surveys (London: HMSO, 1976).
Prevention and Health: Everybody's Business (London: HMSO, 1976).
Priorities for Health and Personal Social Services in England, DHSS (London: HMSO, 1976).
Proposals for a Tax-Credit System, Cmnd 5116 (London: HMSO, 1972).
Public Expenditure on the Social Services, Third Report from the Social Services Committee, House of Commons (London: HMSO, 1981).

Reform of the Industrial Injuries Scheme, Cmnd 8402, DHSS (London: HMSO, 1981).
Reform of Personal Direct Taxation, Cmnd 4653 (London: HMSO, 1971).
Regional Trends, Central Statistical Office (London: HMSO, 1981).
Report of the Committee of Enquiry into the Cost of the National Health Service (the Guillebaud Report), Cmd 9663 (London: HMSO, 1956).
Report of the Committee of Enquiry into the Relationship of the Pharmaceutical Industry with the National Health Service (the Sainsbury Report), Cmnd 3410 (London: HMSO, 1967).
Report of the Committee on Local Authority and Allied Personal Social Services (the Seebohm Report), Cmnd 3703 (London: HMSO, 1968).
Report on Social Insurance and Allied Services (the Beveridge Report), Cmnd 6404 (London: HMSO, 1942).
Report of the Royal Commission on the National Health Service (the Merrison Report), Cmnd 7615 (London: HMSO, 1979).
Royal Commission on the Distribution of Income and Wealth: Report No. 5, *Third Report on the Standing Reference*, Cmnd 5999 (London: HMSO, 1976); Report No. 6, *Lower Incomes*, Cmnd 7175 (London: HMSO, 1978); Report No. 8, *Fifth Report on the Standing Reference*, Cmnd 7679 (London: HMSO, 1979).
Sharing Resources for Health in England, Report of the Resource Allocation Working Party (London: HMSO, 1976).
Social Security Pensions Bill 1975, Report by the Government Actuary on the Financial Provisions of the Bill, Cmnd 5928 (London: HMSO, 1975).
Social Security Statistics 1980, DHSS (London: HMSO, 1980).
Social Trends, no. 11 (London: HMSO, 1981).
Supplementary Benefits Commission Reports, DHSS (London: HMSO, various years).
Take-Up of Supplementary Benefits. SBC Discussion Paper (London: HMSO, 1978).

THE EUROPEAN COMMUNITIES

Comparative Tables of the Social Security Systems in the Member Countries of the European Communities, 11th edn (Brussels: Commission of the European Communities, 1981).
European Social Budget 1980 (Brussels: Commission of the European Communities, 1979).
Perspective on Poverty in Europe (Brussels: Commission of the European Communities, 1977).

THE OECD

National Accounts of OECD Countries 1961–78 (Paris: OECD, 1980).
Public Expenditure on Income Maintenance Programmes (Paris: OECD, 1976).
Welfare State in Crisis (Paris: OECD, 1981).

GENERAL INDEX

Note: detailed references to welfare arrangements in countries other than the UK are given under each country heading and are not repeated elsewhere in the index.

NAME INDEX